Cross-border Perspectives and Interdisciplinary
Approaches of Life Quality

*Cross-border Perspectives*
*and Interdisciplinary Approaches of Life Quality*

Gina-Aurora NECULA, PhD
Carmelia Mariana DRAGOMIR BĂLĂNICĂ, PhD
Alexandra-Monica TOMA, PhD

Published in 2022 by CEEOLPRESS,
Frankfurt am Main, Germany



Typesetting: CEEOL GmbH, CEEOLPress
Layout: Alexander Neroslavsky


ISBN: 978-3-949607-20-2
E-ISBN: 978-3-949607-21-9

Gina-Aurora NECULA, PhD
Carmelia Mariana DRAGOMIR BĂLĂNICĂ, PhD
Alexandra-Monica TOMA, PhD

# Cross-border Perspectives and Interdisciplinary Approaches of Life Quality

2022

# TABLE OF CONTENTS


FOREWORD . . . . . . . . . . . . . . . . . . . . . . . . . . . . . . 1

Gina-Aurora NECULA,
Alexandra-Monica TOMA
BUILDING A NONVIOLENT IDENTITY
WHILE SURROUNDED BY ICONS OF VIOLENCE . . . . . . . . . . . . . . . 3

BĂLĂNICĂ DRAGOMIR Mariana Carmelia
ECOTOURISM, AS A STEP FORWARD TOWARDS
NEW STANDARDS IN ENVIRONMENT PROTECTION . . . . . . . . . . . . . 25

Delia OPREA
QUALITY OF LIFE: ACHIEVEMENTS AND EXPECTATIONS
IN SOCIAL MEDIA POLITICAL COMMUNICATION . . . . . . . . . . . . . 49

MANOLACHI Veaceslav,
MANOLACHI Victor
FACTORS DETERMINING THE COMPOSITION
OF MEANS AND METHODS OF STRENGTH TRAINING
OF ATHLETES SPECIALISING IN SPORTS WRESTLING . . . . . . . . . . 77

Dimitrie STOICA,
Maricica STOICA
FOOD WASTE AND ITS IMPACT ON THE FUTURE OF MANKIND . . . . 205

Georghe BRANIȘTE,
Dumitru PRODAN,
Viorel DORGAN
EXERCISES FOR IMPROVING THE LIFE QUALITY
OF PEOPLE WITH DISABILITIES . . . . . . . . . . . . . . . . . . . 225

Georgiana CIOBOTARU
INTERCULTURAL COMMUNICATION COMPETENCE
AND ITS IMPLICATIONS ON THE INTEGRATION
OF FOREIGN STUDENTS . . . . . . . . . . . . . . . . . . . . . . . 243

Alexandra-Monica TOMA
THE PRAGMATICS OF FACEBOOK INTERACTIONS
IN ROMANIA AND THE REPUBLIC OF MOLDOVA . . . . . . . . . . . 269

Podaru Geanina Marcela
MATERIALS FOR A BETTER LIFE - TRENDS AND PERSPECTIVES . . . 289

Ramona Mariana Călinică
GDP AND INFLATION - MACROECONOMIC INDICATORS
THAT MAY REFLECT AN IMPROVED ECONOMIC WELL-BEING . . . . . 317

DRĂNICERU Mihai
INTERNATIONAL LEGAL STANDARDS
FOR THE PROTECTION OF GOVERNMENT OFFICIALS
DURING THE PERFORMANCE OF THEIR DUTIES . . . . . . . . . . . . . 333

Alina-Mihaela CEOROMILA
PROGRESS AND SUITABILITY
OF LIFE QUALITY INDICATORS IN IMAGISTIC ANALYSIS . . . . . . . . 355

Andrei NASTAS
THE CRIMINAL POLICY IN THE REPUBLIC OF MOLDOVA
IN THE ATTEMPT TO INCREASE THE QUALITY OF LIFE . . . . . . . . . 373

LUPAȘCU Daniela Eugenia
LEARNING FOREIGN LANGUAGES AS A SOCIAL PRACTICE . . . . . . . 403

ENACHE Ciprian-Mugurel
COMPARATIVE ANALYSIS AND
THE EVOLUTION OF COMMUNICATION SERVICES . . . . . . . . . . . . 415

Alina Ionela PREDA
WELL-BEING FOR MIGRANTS: LINGUISTIC AND
CULTURAL ASPECTS TO IMPROVE EMOTIONAL INTELLIGENCE . . . . . 435

# FOREWORD

There is no universal standard to define the quality of life, no unique and one-size-fits-all way to determine what brings individual well-being and satisfaction. However thorough and ambitious research might be in determining the upper and lower limits of the concept, its multidimensional nature escapes clear-cut definitions, as it encompasses objective and subjective factors from a wide range of disciplines. In a nutshell, quality of life research focuses on the opportunities and challenges related to meeting people's needs in order for them to achieve well-being.

The most recent studies on QOL approach two different perspectives: subjective well-being, which refers to the self-perceived levels of satisfaction and personal fulfilment, and objective measurements of QOL, which aim to analyse it in relation to social, economic, and medical parameters.

The uniqueness and originality of the present volume lie in the fact that it combines subjective and objective approaches, using various instruments in order to determine the factors that influence QOL.

Being a concept that has registered revaluations and reclassifications over time, we believe that the present volume is all the more valuable as it gathers in its pages contributions from researchers not only from various fields (i.e., sociocultural, linguistic, economic, legal, sportive, environmental), but also from neighbouring countries, one of them as EU member, Romania, which refers to standardized parameters at the European level, and the other, the Republic of Moldova, being a recent applicant for EU membership. Consequently, besides the goal of tackling what defines well-being for Romanians and Moldovans, the research shares a comparative approach set against a complex and volatile geopolitical context. The countries share a common language, history, and values, but they have come to grow apart in terms of national identity, opportunities, and setbacks. Thus, this study also explores what unites or divides them and the complex connections between these two nations.

The challenges the researchers faced resided in the scarcity of previous contrastive studies and in the difficulty to bring together so many perspectives in order to create a coherent and eloquent picture of the life Romanians and Moldovans live and of the measures to be taken to meet their needs and enhance welfare. The volume contains chapters that investigate, using both subjective tools and objective measurements, various aspects of QOL, covering linguistics, education, communication, law, sports, engineering, ecology, economy, etc. Albeit very diverse, these perspectives come to create a mosaic image of this part of Europe, to identify problems and imbalances, to investigate the root cause of low welfare, and, most importantly, to propose solutions and means to implement them.

It is the belief of the authors that any research of QOL should venture into such a multifaceted approach, as welfare depends on so many factors from all fields of knowledge, and the connection between human needs and their perceived fulfilment is affected by very subtle elements, like sociocultural context, education, temperament, etc. However, this is only the beginning of the road, as the authors of this study intend to further their research by including a larger amount of data to be processed, interpreted, and translated into viable actions for the future.

# BUILDING A NONVIOLENT IDENTITY WHILE SURROUNDED BY ICONS OF VIOLENCE

**Gina-Aurora NECULA,** Cross-Border Faculty,
"Dunărea de Jos" University of Galati, Gina.Necula@ugal.ro

**Alexandra-Monica TOMA,** Cross-Border Faculty,
"Dunărea de Jos" University of Galati Monica.Toma@ugal.ro

## ABSTRACT

This paper mostly analyses the way violence is re-branded through public monuments belonging to a controlled manipulative narrative and how language is aimed to conceal reality, covering past trauma and pain and turning them into glamorous concepts like victory and glory. Art and language subtly translate societal violence and restructure reality.

In many Moldovan cities, monument tanks or communist statues are an important part of the urban scenery. Their significance is deeply rooted in the rhetoric of identity, and they are perceived as symbols of heroism and patriotism, seemingly coexisting with the lights and shadows of the still troubled Moldovan identity.

Following field research and a questionnaire conducted in Taraclia and Comrat, this paper shows that these monuments are forms of structural/cultural violence that connect and feed direct violence. The analysis revealed the extensive use of underhand euphemisms to refer to war and violence, with the purpose of mystifying and misrepresenting the war icons on public display and the use of physical force towards children and women. Glorified physical aggression makes people believe violence can be used to achieve discipline, to show bravery, and firmness of hand.

These results are associated with the way Moldovans describe themselves as hard-working, hospitable, and kind. By using sociolinguistics, the paper intends to show that, against the background of Russian propaganda about victory, glory, and heroism, a narrative mirrored by tank monuments and communist statues, and given a history of domestic violence concealed by euphemisms, the Moldovan social construct of national identity is trying hard to incorporate non-violent values. Torn between various tools of propaganda, consisting of many cultures and being a pinnacle of multilingualism, the heterogeneous Moldovan people are confusedly building their fragmented identity on the ashes of a tormented history.

**Key words**: *structural violence, cultural violence, direct violence, euphemism, propaganda*

## INTRODUCTION

However disconcerting and distressing it might be, violence is an essential part of our existence. It can take many shapes, and it is eloquently mirrored by culture and language. Related to either physical force, the use of power, or both, resulting in physical harm and/or psychological trauma, this manifest or latent trait of human nature strongly influences how we perceive life and express ourselves. Violence is usually born where there is a "difference between the potential and the actual, between what could have been and what is." (Galtung 1969: 168).

Following a first-hand experience in South-Eastern Europe, this paper started off as an attempt to understand a rather confusing contradiction observed during recurring visits to the Republic of Moldova, namely the contrast between the mellow-hearted Moldovan personality and the cult for war symbols. It is our experience that most Moldovans are caught between the aspiration towards Occidental values and a strong Soviet Union influence, having suffered the trauma of being cut from their Romanian roots. Consequently, being torn apart by the tidal tendencies of several cultures, the heterogeneous Moldovan people strive to reconcile the contradictions of language (even if the state language is Romanian, there is wide use of Russian, Bulgarian, and Gagauz languages), the Romanian heritage, and the remnants of the Russian mentality.

The key assumption is that the statues reminiscent of communist leaders, the tanks, cannons, or machine guns on public display, which are commonplace in the Republic of Moldova, are deeply rooted in the rhetoric of identity. Moreover, Moldovans' testimonies illustrate the positive perception of such symbols. There is a far-going contradiction between the poetics of violence and the way Moldovans perceive themselves as a fairly peaceful, hard-working, and hospitable people. To tackle such assumptions, the paper presents the interpretation of a quantitative and qualitative study conducted in the Republic of Moldova, which combines field research with a questionnaire.

## STRUCTURAL VIOLENCE AND CULTURAL VIOLENCE

In order to explain how violence can be expressed through language, art, and other means of expression, we shall start by explaining two key concepts: structural violence and cultural violence, both coined by Johan Galtung. Structural violence (a process), as opposed to personal (behavioural) violence (an event), refers to forms of violence that may indirectly harm people as a result of an unequal distribution of power and resources and is embedded in societal structures. "A key aspect of structural violence is that it is often subtle, invisible, and accepted as a matter of course" (Lee 2019: 124), which makes it difficult to discern and measure.

However, given that both direct/behavioural and structural violence involve an "avoidable insult to basic human needs", Galtung builds a taxonomy of basic needs: survival needs, well-being needs, identity needs, meaning needs and freedom needs (Galtung, 1990: 292). The most relevant ones for this paper are the need connected to identity, to the feeling of alienation and segmentation, which might appear as a result of being desocialised away from a culture and resocialised into another (for instance, through language).

Structural violence can be coded through symbols that are used to make aggression acceptable, heroic, and even desirable. This has been referred to as cultural vio-lence, which implies "those aspects of culture, the symbolic sphere of our existence – exemplified by religion and ideology, language and art, empirical science, and formal science (logic, mathematics) – that can be used to justify or legitimize direct or structural violence. Stars, crosses, and crescents; flags, anthems, and military parades; the ubiquitous portrait of the Leader; inflammatory speeches and posters – all those come to mind." (Galtung, 1990: 291) The causal flow starts off from cultural violence and reaches direct violence.

## THE ICONS OF WAR

First, we shall briefly revise the monuments under analysis and a few historical facts that would help explain their significance. Until the declaration of independence, the Republic of Moldova was one of the 15 republics of the former URSS and was filled with Soviet monuments. Statues of Lenin used to tower every district centre and town hall of bigger villages, while monuments portraying Soviet soldiers were a common sight. In front of the government building from Chișinău, there was Vladimir Lenin's statue, and the parliament was filled with images of Marx and Engels (Preașcă, 2019).

At present, most of such reminiscences of the past have disappeared. However, in the Republic of Moldova, 17 statutes of the Bolshevik leader Vladimir Lenin and two of Karl Marx's are still in place. Interestingly enough, even though in 1991, the Moldovan Parliament adopted a law that decided to liquidate such communist symbols, five Soviet monuments were however included in the Register of Monuments from the Republic of Moldova, as resulted from the Ministry of Culture's official web page. These include statues of Serghei Lazo and Grigore Kotovski, a depiction of the *liberation* of Chișinău city by the Soviet army, the monument of the fighters for Soviet Power and the statue of the young heroes who sacrificed themselves for freedom.

Another widely discussed topic in the Moldovan press involves the Soviet tanks displayed in several localities of the country. Besides the communist statues mentioned above, the Republic of Moldova has several tanks that serve as war monuments, mostly commemorating the Second World War, located in: Comrat, Coșnița, Tiraspol, Cornești, Pohrebia, Cahul, Leușeni, Bălți, Dubăsari etc. (*În Republica Moldova sunt șapte tancuri monument*, 2016, Rață, 2015, Stan, 2015). The history behind such monuments suggests these were weapons actually used in the Second World War, somehow preserved or found and refurbished to meet the requirements for public display.

The tank from Cornești, Ungheni district, attracted public attention in 2016 when the Ministry of Defence decided it should be torn down, as it was a symbol of war horrors. The socialists, opposing this decision, guarded it night and day to keep it from being dismantled. Eventually, the tank stayed in place. In 2018, it was painted in the colours of the Romanian flag, to the dissatisfaction of several members of the Socialist Party of Ungheni. They repainted the tank and the platform in green (Preașcă,

2019). In 2019, the same tank made the news because Vadim Krasnoselski, the leader of the separatist administration of Tiraspol, declared he wanted to propose that the authorities from Chișinău hand over the tank to Tiraspol. The reason was the poor condition of the decommissioned weapon, that, if handed over, would be refurbished and displayed as a tribute to the Soviet army's victory. Ungheni press reported at the time that the tank had no historical value, as it was not a relic of the Second World War. (Grâu, 2019)

The tank from Leușeni, located 10 km away from the Romanian border, was taken out of the Prut River in 1967 and installed on a platform for everybody to see. A Moldovan newspaper also reports that it was painted in the colours of the Romanian flag, on top of which the map of extended Romania (united with the Republic of Moldova) was impressed, as a way to express the association with the Romanian ancestry. This happened on the 23 of August, exactly 79 years after the Ribbentrop-Molotov pact was signed, through which Bessarabia and Bucovina were taken out of Romania and annexed to the Soviet Union (Tancul de la Leușeni..., 2018). This is an eloquent illustration of the clash between two opposing powers and influences.

Another war symbol, the monument from Coșnița, is reported to be one of the tanks engaged in the fights from May 1944. It fell in the Nistru River, and it was later refurbished and ennobled with the status of a monument. With a very suggestive name, the Freedom Tank from Comrat, a T-34, symbolises the weapons that defended

Comrat against the Germans on 22 august 1944 and is considered to be a symbol of victory, as explained by the Moldovans who live there (*Pe teritoriul Moldovei sunt 8 tancuri...*, 2019).

In Transnistria, the centre of Tiraspol is marked by the Memorial of Glory, located in Suvorov Square, to commemorate the veterans and heroes of World War II, the Soviet-Afghan War and the Transnistrian war. Among the monuments, there is a decommissioned tank suggestively placed next to an orthodox chapel. In the vicinity, a statue of Lenin oversees the square. People of Tiraspol take photos of the monument and integrate it in their seemingly peaceful life. The symbolism of such an association of elements reflects the pillars of propaganda: violence as embodied by a war weapon and personified through the emblematic figure of Lenin.

One of the Moldovan tanks stands out because of the history behind it. In Taraclia, one of the little cities located in Gagauzia, next to the building of the "Grigore Țamblac" University, a decommissioned tank lifted on a platform, repainted, and covered in lake, honours the Moldovans who fought in the Afghanistan war. The fact that, against expectations, this is a rather recent monument, unrelated to the Second World War, suggests that its erection comes to mirror a tradition of having war heroes cherished through the display of weapons, thus perpetuating violent symbolism.

The weapons briefly presented above "are reminders of the Soviet past and most of them are directed towards West", as explained through an online article (*În Repub-*

*lica Moldova sunt șapte tancuri-monument,* 2016), as a silent warning to occidental values. When asked, some inhabitants often refer to the Second World War as the *Great War for the defence of the country or the Great Patriotic War,* thus verbalising the assimilation of a Soviet myth and their feeling of pride in this heroic accomplishment.

We believe that these monuments are one of the most subtle methods of influencing public opinion, thus proving Helmus et al.'s assumption that *"the Kremlin's narrative spin extends far beyond its network of media outlets and social media trolls"* (Helmus, 2018: 8). To quote Boulegue et al., "Russian vectors of influence encompass a variety of forms and actors: identity politics invoking the Russian world narrative and Soviet nostalgia; politicized promotion of the concept of 'compatriots' (involving national minorities and ethnic Russians); language use; appeals to supporters of unification with Romania and anti-Romanian movements alike; instrumentalization of separatism and the frozen conflict in Transnistria, and overall anti-Western sentiment." (Boulegue, 2018: 29).

Moreover, the tank monuments presented above are signs of structural violence because they relate to the idea of identity and refer to a powerful narrative about glory. We believe that using weapons as monuments is more detrimental to the collective psyche than statues of communist figures because inanimate tools of destruction are put on a pedestal and presented as symbols to be honoured. Such icons of violence displayed for everybody may result in a lack of empathy and the objectification of the enemy.

Moreover, they make people accustomed to seeing, on an everyday basis, symbols that glorify violence.

## FINDINGS OF THE FIELD RESEARCH

Before presenting the research results, it is of utmost importance to note that multiculturalism in the Republic of Moldova is unfathomable and only paralleled by its linguistic diversity. The 2014 census reports that the ethnic structure of the population is: 73.7% of the population – Moldovans, Ukrainians, and Russians – 10.5%, Gagauzs – 4.5 % of the population, Romanians – 6.9%, Bulgarians – 1.8%. However, there are regions where Romanian language, although the official language of the state, is seldom used (Comrat – the heart of Gagauzia, for example), while Russian and Gagauz are more frequent. Most Moldovans speak at least two languages (Romanian and Russian). It is actually quite striking to see that a rather small country is inhabited by so many cultures and that on a hundred kilometres range, there are deep changes in the language used in everyday life and the ethnicity of the people one encounters.

To assess the influence of publicly displayed symbols of war on Moldovan people, the field research has been completed through a questionnaire with 40 respondents, aged 22 – 40, from Taraclia and Comrat. The latter was conducted in Romanian, which is a second language for most respondents, so it is possible that some linguistic subtleties were lost on the participants. The five items were phrased so that they would connect the perception of monument tanks and communist statues (cultural violence) to the attitude towards direct violence against children and women, as well as to the respondents' description of their national identity.

When asked what publicly displayed tanks and weapons refer to, 45% of the respondents answered by evoking the historical event: the Second World War. However, another 40% used depictions like „the great victory" and „heroism" instead of flatly naming the event they commemorate. Only two answers bitterly mentioned Russian propaganda. The second item asked respondents to freely associate the monuments with words. Similarly, 40% said "victory", while more than 60% of the answers used other words with positive connotations. While the first items referred to cultural violence, the third and the fourth questions referred to direct aggression towards children and women. The answers showed that, while almost 70% considered violence towards children could be justified, the percentage was reversed in what women are concerned. The respondents gave various explanations to justify violence, which we will analyse later. The fifth and last item in the survey asked respondents to define their national identity in three words, thus attempting to facilitate a connection between the perception of war icons, the attitude towards direct violence and the main traits of Moldovan people, as defined by themselves.

## INTERPRETATION OF DATA

The questionnaire shed light on the way war symbols are perceived and the extent to which structural violence can pour into direct violence. The structure of the enquiry aims to show the connection between these two types of aggressiveness to conclude whether there is a causality between them. Publicly displayed symbols are used to perpetuate and nurture historical fiction that consists of an archetypal tale of heroism, sacrifice, bravery, and national pride. In order to hide aggression and the petty, painful details of war, the dreadful aspects of communism, language is used as a shield to obliterate the obnoxious images, thus sanitising memory and communication.

What stands out when analysing the results of the survey is the extensive use of euphemisms to refer to both cultural and personal violence, but with different connotations and causes.

Euphemisms are created between semantics and pragmatics. Orwellian in nature, euphemisms are double-talk, "sweet-sounding, or at least inoffensive, alternatives for expressions that speakers or writers prefer not to use in executing a particular communicative intention on a given occasion". (Burridge, 2012: 66). Hugh Rawson speaks about two types of euphemisms: positive ones that *"[...] inflate and magnify, making the euphemized items seem altogether grander and more important than they really are and negative ones that deflate and diminish"* (Rawson, 1983: 1). The latter are used with defensive purpose, mostly when making reference to taboo-marked concepts. Both positive and negative euphemisms can be used consciously or unconsciously, this second category consisting of "[...] mainly of words that were developed as euphemisms, but so long ago that hardly anyone remembers the original motivation" (Rawson 1983: 3). In this paper, we are interested in the category of positive euphemisms that are used unconsciously and that can also be associated with the category that Kate Burridge identifies as underhand euphemisms – aimed to mystify and to misrepresent:

> "There is a sense in which all euphemism is dishonest. No euphemism says it how it is – in a given context, something tabooed can be acceptably spoken of using a euphemism but not using a direct term. However, the euphemistic vocabulary of language varieties such as military, political and medical jargons adds additional dimensions of guile and secrecy to the disguise. Here euphemism is used, not so much to conceal offense but to deliberately disguise a topic and to deceive." (Burridge, 2012:68).

Mystification of historical facts is at the core of the euphemisms used to answer the first two questions, thus proving Orwell's insightful comment that every war is represented not as a war but as "an act of self-defence against a homicidal maniac". For approximately 45% of the respondents, Second World War is no longer a violent event that scarred a generation and led to futile bloodshed but the "great victory", the "great patriotic war", a display of "heroism". These are words fed by the Russian ethos aimed to describe the Russian army's victory against Nazi Germany. Initially intended to enliven the spirits of the population, so that it would defend the homeland, the Great Patriotic War remained a closed-circuit term (post-Soviet countries) of political significance that symbolizes Soviet heritage, and that is still an integral part of the collective psyche.

However, some respondents perceive tanks and communist statues just as remainders of the Second World War, without putting a positive twist on it, and some perceive them as elements of Russian propaganda. If connected with the demographics, we notice that the ones speaking of victory are not fluent Romanian language speakers and fall within the minority groups, while respondents identifying such monuments as Russian propaganda have good control of Romanian language and are Moldovans as ethnicity, usually with close relations to Romania.

The second question of the questionnaire is an extension of the first, associating tank monuments and communist statues with concepts like "victory", "heroism", "pride", "respect/sacrifice", "war", most with a positive connotation, even if the direct reference is an inanimate combat object. Such words make violence legitimate, put a glorious spin on it, and objectify the enemy. The story behind is full of double-talk and refers to the sacralised victory over Nazism, a messianic myth of saving the world from pure evil, concealing the dark sides of the war and the true reasons behind subsequent military interventions.

It is interesting to point out that, when asking the questions referring to violence towards children and women, the interviewer had to clarify the term violence each time for the respondents to understand. The first reaction was, in most cases, to shy away from the word *violence*; following that, after adding nuance to it, they would accompany their answer with some explanation.

The use of euphemisms was extensive in response to these questions. In this case, euphemisms are not linked to the Great Patriotic War narrative but relate to a cultural background where violence is not called by its right name and where it can be employed to get submission from more vulnerable categories. "Discipline", "firm hand", and "correction" are all euphemisms used to explain why aggression towards children might be legitimate and refer to authoritarian and aggressive parenting. Violence against women is associated with justifications like "It is a form of love!", "Women have to be shown the right way" or "women need to know boundaries". Surprisingly, some women also describe domestic violence as a way to show affection.

The fact that 70% of the respondents do not believe violence towards women is justified while the same percentage admit aggression towards children is puzzling. We believe that it might be explained by the fact that popular culture in the Republic of Moldova is more permissive to disciplining one's children through physical punishment, as this is deemed to be a valid parenting model. Also, children might be considered to be, in the family hierarchical model, a category at the bottom of subordination, and there is a higher level of dependence. However, these conclusions need further analysis.

In terms of how Moldovans define themselves as a people, we have to refer to the concept of nation, which can be defined as "a named human community that occupies its historic homeland, has a shared history, a common mass public culture, myths of common ancestry, shared symbols, traditions and customs, and demonstrates self-awareness as a nation" (Tartakovsky, 2010, 1850). National identity derives from the perception of the nation and is a social construct showing the sense of belonging following interpersonal and group interactions.

Interviewed Moldovans mostly use the word "hard-working" to define themselves. A possible motivation for such a perception would find its roots in the long years of communist oppression and the feeling of being wronged by history, left at the whims of powerful political forces, while obeying the rules others set. Most respondents said the words with a sigh. However, Moldovans also believe they are "hospitable", "kind", and "joyful", a description which builds an image that does not consciously incorporate violence but quite the opposite values. Less frequent but still evocative, the perception of the Moldovans as "stupid" or "gullible" might relate to their being the playground of many types of propaganda. We would also like to stress that the qualities of the Moldovan people, as mentioned by them, can all be associated with a passive and even submissive attitude, probably resulting from their troubled and uncertain past, communist oppression, and showing the tidal tendencies that have always marked this area found at the border of opposing influences.

The answers reveal the still powerful strength of the Russian narrative related to the Great Patriotic War, the positive perception many Moldovans have of the symbols of war, which are still part of the scenery, and also the attempt to conceal violence through euphemisms. Using physical force to subdue children and women seems justified in some cases, but the words used to describe this aim to embellish the ugly truth of violence against the background of a culture still working on archaic principles, considering discipline as a fair reason for using various forms of abuse.

It is interesting that respondents that described the tanks as remnants of war, without using a description like victory and heroism, were also the ones who disapproved of violence towards children and women and described the Moldovan identity as being a combination of hospitability, kindness and stupidity.

## CONCLUSION

To conclude, war monuments like tanks and communist statues are still a common sight in the Republic of Moldova and are a display of structural and cultural violence. Such icons of war that evoke a history of aggression and retaliation are rebranded, through the influence of Russian manipulation, as symbols of national pride and are considered by some to be part of the Moldovan national identity. The depiction of the Second World War as the "great victory" or the use of euphemisms such as "heroism", "pride" are clear indicators of a propagandistic narrative deeply rooted in people's minds, referring to the messianic salvation by the Russian army. However, there are some that call it propaganda, showing they are aware of the strategy. These are usually of Moldovan ethnicity and also refer to the horrors of the communist regime.

Direct violence is considered justified by most respondents in what children are concerned (even though they change the word violence with other words), percentage reversed when the question refers to women. Euphemisms related to the idea of personal aggression are employed: "discipline", "correction", "firm hand". Violence is even described as a form of showing love by both men and women. Language is used to understate and mystify a violent reality. We believe that the model of misrepresenting violence displayed by the tanks and the statues of Lenin and other communist heroes influenced Moldovan culture, creating a pattern of concealing reality through art and language that subsequently applies to other types of violence. Glorified physical aggression translates into believing that violence can be used to achieve discipline, to show bravery and firmness of hand.

However, there is a struggle between such societal models and the kind-hearted and hospitable nature of Moldovan people, who used to work hard to achieve their goals while being in the mists of the power play between east and west. There is a collective trauma of being separated from both Romania and Russia and an internal tidal fight to reconcile all the different cultures and languages under a unified structure. It is our belief, after completing the field research and discussing with many more Moldovans than the one who undertook the questionnaire, that the Moldovan people is trying to build a unique identity amidst crisis and uncertainty, and the icons of violence that surround them only make it more difficult for them to part from the idea that violent behaviour, however packed in myths, will always be alienating.

# REFERENCES

Boulegue, Mathieu, Lutsevych, Orysia, Marin, Anais (2018). *Civil Society under Russia's Threat: Building Resilience in Ukraine, Belarus and Moldova*, The Royal Institute of International Affairs, https://www.chathamhouse.org/sites/default/files/publications/research/2018-11-08-civil-society-russia-threat-ukraine-belarus-moldova-boulegue-lutsevych-marin.pdf (Last accessed: 7/08/20).

Burridge, Kate (2012). "Euphemisms and Language Change: The Sixth and Seventh Ages", in *Jurnal in English Lexicology*, http://journals.openedition.org/lexis/355

Galtung, Johan (1969). "Violence, Peace, and Peace Research" in *Journal of Peace Research*, Vol. 6, No. 3, pp. 167–191.

Galtung, Johan (1990). "Cultural Violence", in *Journal of Peace Research*, Vol. 27, No. 3., pp. 291-305, https://www.jstor.org/stable/423472?seq=1 (Last accessed: 3/08/20).

Helmus, Todd C., Bodine-Baron, Elizabeth, Radin, Andrew, Magnuson, Madeline, Mendelsohn, Joshua, Marcellino, William, Bega, Andriy, Winkelman, Zev (2018). *Russian Social Media Influence: Understanding Russian Propaganda in Eastern Europe*, Santa Monica: Rand Corporation,

Lee, Bandy X. (2019). *Violence: An Interdisciplinary Approach to Causes, Consequences, and Cures*, New York, NY: Wiley-Blackwell.

Rawson, Hugh (1983). *A dictionary of euphemisms and other doubletalk. Being a compilation of linguistic fig leaves and verbal flourishes for artful users of the English language*, London & Sydney: Macdonald & Co Ltd.

Tartakovsky, E. (2011). "National Identity", in *Levesque R.J.R. (eds) Encyclopedia of Adolescence*, New York: Springer.

**Romanian language on-line resources:**

Biroul Național de Statistică al Republicii Moldova, https://statistica.gov.md/pageview.php?l=ro&idc=479 (Last accessed: 7/08/20).

Grâu, Lina (30.09.2019). „Vadim Krasnoselski cere Chişinăului tancul instalat ca monument în raionul Ungheni, lângă Prut" [Vadim Krasnoselski Asks Chisinau to be Given the Tank Installed as Monument in Ungheni District, near Prut River], în *Radio Europa Liberă Moldova*, https://moldova.europalibera.org/a/30137786.html

Ministerul Culturii. *Portalul Guvernamental al Datelor Deschise*, Registrul Monumentelor Republicii Moldova ocrotite de stat [Register of State Protected Monuments], https://date.gov.md/ckan/ro/dataset/5180-registrul-monumentelor-republicii-moldova (Last accessed: 3/08/20).

Preaşcă, Diana (2019). "Pietrele şi politica. Ce facem cu ele?" [Rocks and Politics. What to Do with Them?], in *ReportajeMoldova.org*, https://reportaje.moldova.org/pietrele-si-politica-ce-facem-cu-ele/ (Last accessed: 3/08/20).

Primele ştiri (2016). "În Republica Moldova sunt şapte tancuri-monument" [There are Seven Monument Tanks in the Republic of Moldova], https://primelestiri.md/in-republica-moldova-sunt-sapte-tancuri-monument---45145.html (Last accessed: 3/08/20).

Rață, Mariana (10.10.2015). "R. Moldova, sub TANCURI" [The Republic of Moldova, under TANKS], în *Ziarul Național*, https://www.ziarulnational.md/r-moldova-sub-tancuri/

Stan, Liviu G. (10.10.2015). "Tancurile sovietice din Republica Moldova, o gaură neagră financiară" [Soviet Tanks of the Republic of Moldova, a Financial Black Hole], în Infoprut, http://infoprut.ro/41456-tancurile-sovietice-din-rep-moldova-o-gaura-neagra-financiara.html

Televiziunea centrală (09.05.2019). "Pe teritoriul Moldovei sunt 8 tancuri monumente de pe vremea Marelui Război. În ce localități mai pot fi găsite" [On Moldovan land, there are 8 Monument Tanks Left after the Great War. Where are they located], https://tvc.md/pe-teritoriul-moldovei-sunt-8-tancuri-monumente-de-pe-vremea-marelui-razboi-in-ce-localitati-mai-pot-fi-gasite-video (Last accessed: 7/08/20).

Ziarul Național (23.08.2018). "Tancul de la Leușeni, cu țeava îndreptată spre Prut, VOPSIT în culorile tricolorului: Harta României întregite pe monumentul sovietic" [The Tank from Leuseni, directed towards Prut River, PAINTED in the Tricolored Flag: United Romania's Map on the Soviet Monument], https://www.ziarulnational.md/tancul-so-vietic-de-la-leuseni-cu-teava-indreptata-spre-prut-vop-sit-in-culorile-tricolorului-si-cu-harta-romaniei-intregite/ (Last accessed: 7/08/20).

# ECOTOURISM, AS A STEP FORWARD TOWARDS NEW STANDARDS IN ENVIRONMENT PROTECTION

**BĂLĂNICĂ DRAGOMIR Mariana Carmelia**
Cross-Border Faculty, "Dunărea de Jos" University of Galati,
carmelia.dragomir@ugal.ro

## INTRODUCTION

This paper reflects the progress made by Romania and the Republic of Moldavia in environmental management and ecotourism, highlighting the regulatory framework, the implementation of green economy practices, environmental monitoring, public participation, education for sustainable development, and other relevant issues related to the protection of atmospheric air, biodiversity and protected natural areas, water resources management, waste, and chemicals management.

The United Nations Environment Program (UNEP) defines green economy as an economy that leads to increased human well-being and social justice while significantly reducing environmental risks and environmental deficiencies (UNEP, 2012). Thus, the concept recognizes the inseparability of the three pillars of sustainable development – social, economic, and environmental development.

Ecotourism is an environment service that refers to the socially responsible provision of hotels and other tourist facilities with a low environmental impact to tourists seeking a tourism experience. Such services can be generally classified as "tourism services" and, although not on the list of essential environmental services, they pertain to the liberalisation of environmental services, which can be widely interpreted (UNEP, 2021). Tourism services, such as exports, are especially important for many developing countries, generating considerable revenues; ecotourism is a small but growing niche segment of this industry. A key issue in this regard is whether the environmental benefits of allowing foreign tour operators to provide such services outweigh the shortcomings. Tourism is well-known for developing foreign-owned enclaves that provide few low-skill jobs and sending profits abroad. Ecotourism, to the extent to which it can be separated from the more general concept of tourism, may differ in that it seeks to lead to local benefits, but the final decision on costs and the benefits of liberalisation should be made on a country-by-country basis.

The relationship between ecology and politics has its own dynamics: from the need to reconcile environmental requirements with political interests to the elaboration of the foundation of environmental policy and its inclusion as a key factor in shaping general plans for socio-economic development. Setting forth the basic elements of sustainable development and green economy by reaching political consensus is a modern approach to environmental problems. The main priority of environmental policy is increasing the use of natural resources, which mainly implies a system of priority targets in all areas, including economy, law, management system, education, and culture (Ministry of Environment, 2016, p 303).

The solution to modernising the economy in Romania and the Republic of Moldova should also take into account the natural wealth of the country and its global ecosystem, which open up great opportunities for the development of the international and domestic market for ecosystem services and environmental investments. Considering this, it is necessary to ensure regional cooperation, based on the assessment of natural services, in order to increase the value of natural wealth and to turn it into a commodity, including providing a wide range of ecosystem services, which should rely on gaining access to the international market as a means to compensate for the efforts to preserve and increase natural wealth. This would allow Romania and the Republic of Moldova to become strong energy players, as well as environmental donors, which implies capitalization, the countries thus benefiting from their ecosystems.

It is important to use the country's great potential for developing economic nature management in areas like renewable energy, ecological agriculture, ecotourism, sustainable forest management. The development of the "environmentally friendly" goods and services market is still awaiting implementation.

## 2. ECOTOURISM

The term "ecological tourism", as a trend in domestic tourism, is a rather recent concept coined in 1980 by the Mexican economist Hector Ceballos-Laskurein. He defined ecotourism as a combination between travelling and protecting nature while getting with flora and fauna. Approaching local species of flora and fauna with respect and showing appreciation for nature are key attitudes for ecological tourism (Ceballos-Lascurain, 1996).

Currently, there have been controversies regarding the concept of ecological tourism. Authors of different countries define the term differently. Until now, several definitions of ecotourism have been proposed, among the most relevant being the following:

– any form of tourism based on the attractiveness of the natural environmental of a particular country (from scuba diving to travelling through the savannah).

– tourism that involves environmental education and acquiring information about environmental protection and knowledge about all the elements that are based on ecologically sustainable principles.

– trips to unique corners of world with the goal to study rare plants, animals, and various types of ecosystems.

– travels that can contribute to the conservation of positive synergies between tourism, biodiversity and local communities. Such trips do not violate the integrity of ecosystems and are focused on grasping the essence of natural, cultural and ethnographic phenomena from a particular region. At the same time, ecotourism creates economic conditions, and makes nature conservation beneficial to local residents (Ministry of Environment, 2016, p 241).

An internationally agreed definition is: ecotourism is a form of tourism aiming to observe and become aware of the value of nature, and local traditions, which must meet the following conditions:

a) contribute to the conservation and protection of nature;

b) use local human resources;

c) imply an educational component, promoting respect for nature and awareness of the tourists-local communities dynamics;

d) have a minimal negative impact on the natural and socio-cultural environment.

Mainly, ecotourism activities may include (National Centre for Sustainable Development Foundation, 2012, page 6):

– various adventure activities (e.g. rafting, canoeing, equestrian tourism on pre-arranged routes, cross-country skiing, bicycle excursions on arranged routes, etc.);

– guided excursions / hikes;

– nature observation tours (flora, fauna);

– trips to experience nature conservation activities;

– trips to local communities (visiting cultural sites and traditional farms, attending traditional cultural events, consuming traditional food, purchasing traditional products).

***Agrotourism*** is tourism that takes place at the countryside, where tourists lead a rural lifestyle during their holidays, being accommodated in backyards, farms, and hamlets. The term ***rural tourism*** is often used in connection with such recreational activities. There is no generally accepted definition of rural tourism.

***Ethno-ecological tourism*** is aimed at studying specific ethnic groups, their life in their natural habitat, and the interaction with the natural environment. It mostly refers to small nationalities living in greater harmony with their natural environment.

***Historical and regional tourism*** addresses the history of the interactions between people and the natural environment. The synonymous terms *sustainable tourism* and *green tourism* are widely used, referring to forms of tourism where technology has a minimal impact on the environment.

***The principles of ecotourism*** are based on the mankind's desire of to achieve sustainable development of territories, to preserve biological and sociocultural diversity. The main principles of ecotourism are:

– visits to well-preserved natural areas;

– non-depleting, sustainable use of natural resources, conservation of natural, social and cultural diversity;

– compliance with certain (sometimes strict) rules of conduct;

– unlike conventional types of tourism, less and responsible use of natural resources;

– environmental education for tourists, their participation in local cultural and nature management activities;

— careful planning of ecological tours, an integrated approach to their development and implementation;

– integration of ecotourism into regional development plans;

– participation of the local population in the development of tourism, and offering financial and other benefits for locals;

– environmental training for the staff working in the field of ecotourism.

***The development of ecotourism*** mainly targets four aspects:

– ***economical***, by increasing the degree of capitalization of resources, especially of the least known ones, to reduce the pressure on the most exploited;

– ***ecological***, by ensuring the rational use of all resources, reducing and eliminating waste, recycling it, ensuring the conservation and protection of the environment, reducing the process of stealing agricultural and forestry land from the agricultural and forestry circuit;

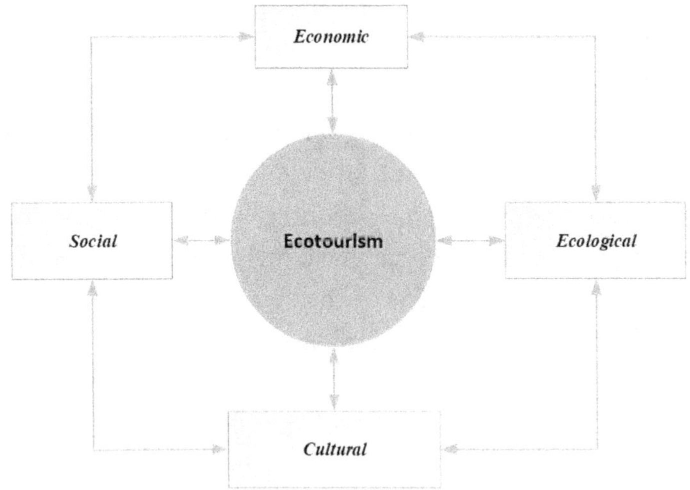


**Figure 1:** Ecotourism development plans

– ***social***, by increasing the number of jobs, maintaining traditional trades, attracting the population to practice different forms of tourism;

– *cultural*, by capitalizing on the special elements of civilization, art and culture, which express a certain cultural identity and develop the spirit of tolerance.

Ecotourism can ensure a broader spectrum of traditional economic activities, without marginalizing or replacing them. Ecotouristic activities offer specific opportunities, the local population and the tourism industry being motivated to use the natural resources in a sustainable way and to appreciate the value of natural and cultural objectives.

## 2.1. ECOTOURISM IN ROMANIA
## 2.1.1. ECOTOURISM RESOURCES IN ROMANIA

Romania has a very varied natural capital. Due to the physical-geographical conditions, which include mountains, plains, major hydrographic networks, wetlands and one of the most beautiful delta systems (the Danube Delta), Romania is the only country on the continent that detains 5 of the 9 biogeographical regions of the European Union (continental – 53% of the country's surface, alpine – 23%, steppe – 17%, Pannonian – 6%, and Pontic – 1%). Romania has a high biological diversity, both at the level of ecosystems and at the level of species (INCDT, 2007).

Natural and semi-natural ecosystems account for about 47% of the country's surface. 783 habitat types were identified and characterized (13 coastal habitats, 143 area-specific habitats wetlands, 196 habitats specific to pastures and meadows, 206 forest habitats, 90 habitats specific to dunes and rocky areas and 135 habitats specific to agricultural land). The general result is the diversity of flora and fauna. Due to its geographical position, flora and fauna have Asian influences from the north, Mediterranean – from the south and continental European components – from the northwest.

At national level, 283 species of animals and plants of European interest have been identified, of which 57 species of mammals, 16 species of amphibians, 19 species of reptiles, 60 species of fish, 69 species of invertebrates and 62 species of plant species.

There are significant populations of large carnivores: wolves (2,500 – 4,600 specimens), brown bears (5,500 – 7,000 specimens), and lynx (1,200 – 2,200 specimens). They constitute about half of the existing herds in Europe (except Russia), and are a symbol of Romanian wildlife and natural habitats.

The country is home to more than half of the Carpathian Mountains, one of the most important European ecoregions, as well as to the Danube Delta, the most important wetland in Europe, with over 3,000 pairs of pelicans, representing over 80% of the European population. Also, Romania is one of the few European countries that still has virgin forests (about 77% of the total remaining in the Carpathian region). Along with the natural setting, it also benefits from an ethnographic and folkloric potential of great originality and authenticity (Ministry of Agriculture and Rural Development, 2015).

This spiritual dowry, represented by traditional architectural values and techniques, traditional crafts, folklore and ancestral customs, popular holidays, etc., to which numerous historical and art monuments, archaeological remains, and museums are added, enhances and completes the ecotourism potential of the country.

## 2.1.2. PROTECTED NATURAL AREAS IN ROMANIA

According to the Government Emergency Ordinance no. 57/2007 on the regime of protected natural areas, conservation of natural habitats, wild flora and fauna, with further amendments, completed by Law no. 49/2011, protected natural areas are "terrestrial and / or aquatic areas where there are species of wild plants and animals, biogeographic, landscape, geological, paleonthological, speleological or other types of elements and formations, with special ecological, scientific or cultural protection, which has a special protection and conservation regime, established according to the legal provisions ".

In order to ensure the special measures of protection and conservation in situ of natural heritage assets, a differentiated regime of protection, conservation and use was established, according to the following categories of protected natural areas:

a) national interest: scientific reserves (IUCN category I), national parks (IUCN category II), natural monuments (IUCN category III), nature reserves (IUCN category IV), nature parks (IUCN category V);

b) international interest: natural sites of the universal natural heritage, geoparks, wetlands of international importance, biosphere reserves;

34

c) Community interest or "Natura 2000" sites: sites of Community importance, special conservation areas, special avifauna protection areas;

d) county or local interest: established only on the public/private domain of the administrative-territorial units, as the case may be.

In Romania, there are 30 major protected natural areas of national interest, namely: Danube Delta Biosphere Reserve (576,421.1 ha), 13 national parks (with a total area of 317,419.2 ha) and 16 natural parks (with a total area of 770,026.5 ha).

**Figure 2:** Natural protected areas in Romania

Besides these protected natural areas, Romania also has 916 scientific reserves, nature monuments, and nature reserves. Many of these protected natural areas are included in national parks, nature parks and the Danube

Delta Biosphere Reserve. Under these conditions, it is estimated that the protected natural areas in Romania (except for Natura 2000 sites) cover over 7% of the country's land area.

A large part of the national territory is covered by the Community network of Natura 2000 protected areas, as follows:

- 171 SPA sites (Special Avifauna Protection Areas), with a total area of 3,875,297.6 ha., representing approximately 16.26% of the Romanian territory – established by G. D. no. 971/2011 for the amendment of G. D. no. 1284/2007 on the declaration of avifauna special protection areas as an integral part of the European ecological network Natura 2000 in Romania, with further amendments and completions, and by G. D. no. 663/2016, on setting up the protected natural area regime and declaring of avifauna special protection areas as an integral part of the European ecological network Natura 2000 in Romania.

- 435 SCI sites (Sites of Community Importance), with a total area of 4,650,970.0 ha., representing approximately 19.51% of the Romanian territory - established by the Minister's of Environment and Forests Order no. 2387 of 2011 amending the Minister's of Environment and Sustainable Development Order no. 1964/2007 on setting up the protected natural area regime for sites of community importance, as an integral part of the European ecological network Natura 2000 in Romania and by Order no. 46/2016 on setting up the protected natural area regime and declaring the sites of community importance as an integrated part of the European ecological network Natura 2000 in Romania.

Cumulatively, the sites included in the European Natura 2000 Network cover approximately 23% of the national territory (some SCIs and SPAs overlap). Protected natural areas of international interest are of special importance, among which we mention the following:
  - the three Biosphere Reserves (Danube Delta, Retezat, and Pietrosul Rodnei),
  - the only natural site of the universal natural heritage existing in Romania (Danube Delta Biosphere Reserve),
  - the only geopark in Romania included in the European Geoparks Network and in the UNESCO Global Geoparks Network (Țara Hațeg Dinosaurs Geopark),
  - a number of 19 Ramsar sites – wetlands of international importance.

## 2.1.3. ECOTOURISM AND TECHNICAL INFRASTRUCTURE

The tourist reception structures with accommodation functions represent the most important component of the specific technical and material base, as they respond to one of the fundamental tourists need, namely rest, overnight stay. The dimensions and the spatial distribution of the accommodation means determine the characteristics of all other components of the technical and material base of tourism and, implicitly, the magnitude of the tourist flows. Over time, various types of tourist reception structures have been built with accommodation functions inside the protected natural areas, as well as near them, and their number and type vary considerably. There are parks that do not have a sufficient number of accommodation units (for example Măcinului Mountains National Park, Balta Mică a Brăilei Natural Park, Grădiştea Muncelului Cioclovina Natural Park, Comana Natural Park). However, in most cases, this is compensated by the tourist reception structures with accommodation functions built in the localities from the immediate vicinity of protected natural areas (e.g. Brăila for Balta Mică Natural Park in Brăila, Arad for Lunca Mureşului Natural Park, Galați for Lunca Joasă a Prutului Inferior Natural Park, Călimăneşti for Cozia National Park, etc.).

Another highly important form of accommodation for natural areas, which could be integrated into ecotourism programs, is hunting lodges (137 nationwide). The visiting and information infrastructure has an key role in promoting the management objectives of the protected natural areas and in making the general public aware of the measures to be taken in order to preserve natural species/habitats, in the context of sustainable management of natural resources.

## 3. ECOTOURISM IN THE REPUBLIC OF MOLDOVA
## 3.1. THE NATURAL HERITAGE OF THE REPUBLIC OF MOLDOVA

The Republic of Moldova has a rich set of objectives and natural complexes of touristic importance, which allows the development of ecotourism as a sustainable form of tourism. It is worth mentioning that the country is home to natural ecosystems with a potential to develop ecotourism in protected areas and other natural areas and optimal natural conditions for outdoor tourism activities: hiking, observing flora and fauna, sports and cultural activities (Aşevschi V., Fondos T., Bencheci M., 2014, pages 143-146).

Protected areas, and especially national parks, nature reserves, biosphere reserves, monuments of landscape architecture are gaining real value in tourism. At the same time, there are other elements of specificity for the Republic of Moldova, complementary to tourism, such as:

1. clean air, less polluted, compared to many other destinations in the region;

2. tasty vegetables and fruits (with the possibility of testing the level of chemical treatment in laboratories at regional level);

3. tasty traditional cuisine;

4. production of diverse and high-quality wines;

5. varied and rich popular culture;

6. rich cultural potential, including various cultural events, etc.

This potential needs to be harnessed, developed and promoted. The most appropriate mechanism is setting up partnerships where each partner diligently assumes his responsibilities, including cooperation with the relevant central public administration authorities and the local public administration authorities in the vicinity of these resources (Gribincea C., 2021, pages 229-239).

**Table 1.** Distribution of the state protected natural areas located within the limits of the forest fund managed by the state forestry authorities by category and size

| No. | Name of protected area categories | Number of objects | Occupied area, ha |
|---|---|---|---|
| 1. | **State nature reserves** | 5 | 19,378 |
| 2. | **Monuments of nature** | 32 | 785,2 |
| | a) geological and paleontological | 20 | 660,3 |
| | b) botany | 12 | 124,9 |
| 3. | **Natural reservations** | 60 | 7,791 |
| | a) forestry | 51 | 5,001 |
| | b) medicinal plants | 8 | 2,740 |
| | c) mixed | 1 | 50 |
| 4. | **Landscape reservations** | 40 | 32,804.4 |
| 5. | **Resource reservations** | 4 | 478 |
| **TOTAL:** | | **141** | **61,236.6** |

Source: http://www.moldsilva.gov.md/pageview.<br>php?l=ro&idc=214&t=/Viata-padurii/Ariile-protejate

Ecotourism in the Republic of Moldova has evolved in tandem with the development of tourism heritage management. According to the Tourism Strategy 2020, the Republic of Moldova is a small country with various objectives of tourist interest, located at short distances from the main cities – hotel centres. There are over 15,000 anthropogenic tourist attractions and over 300 important natural areas in Moldova. Several thousands of prehistoric resorts have been attested, about 400 settlements from different historical epochs, about 50 ancient fortified fortresses, about 500 early medieval settlements, numerous medieval earthen fortresses, 6 medieval stone fortresses (in various stages of preservation), over 1000 protected architectural monuments, about 50 Orthodox monasteries. This patrimony is rather uniformly dispersed on the national territory, and its value has the potential to attract tourists. Unfortunately, the degradation state of heritage site makes them less attractive.

## 3.2. NATURAL PROTECTED AREA IN REPUBLIC OF MOLDOVA

The national natural potential is one of the main elements which attracts and directs the flow of tourists and other visitors to destinations in the Republic of Moldova. Law no. 1538-XIII of 25.02.1998 on the fund of state natural protected areas establishes a complex system of natural areas under state protection: 12 categories of protected natural areas (over 66.5 thousand ha), which include 178 different types of reservations, 130 natural monuments and 433 secular trees. 8 types of protected areas correspond to the IUCN classification, and four categories are of national interest (botanical garden, dendrological garden, landscape architectural monument, zoos).

The Republic of Moldova, a small country from Southeastern Europe, has a significant touristic potential in terms variety of natural monuments of historical, cultural, and aesthetic value, which is a prerequisite for the successful development of tourism (Florea S.,2005).

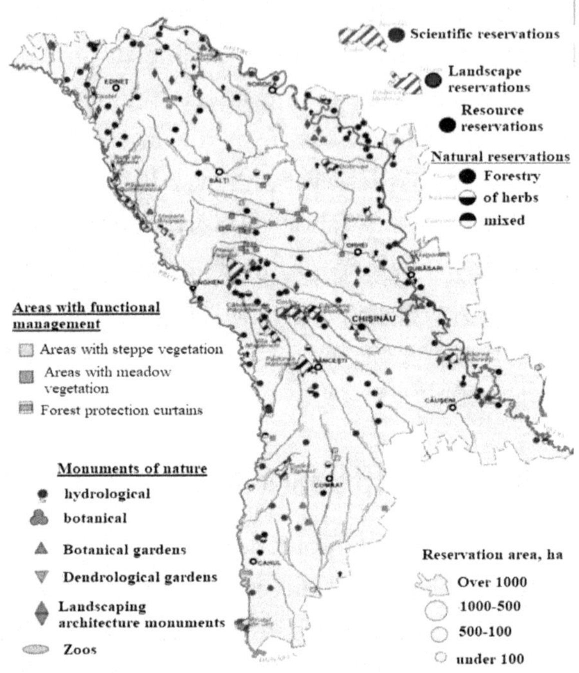


**Figure 3:** Natural protected area in Republic of Moldavia
Source: http://moldsilva.gov.md/

The natural heritage of the Republic of Moldova includes a variety of natural areas, including: 12 categories of protected natural areas (total area: 195,154.1 ha), which include 1 national park, 3 wetlands of international importance, 178 various types of reservations, 130 natural monuments and 446 secular trees. Eight types of protected areas correspond to the classification of the International Union for Conservation of Nature, and four categories are of national interest (botanical garden, dendrological garden, landscape architectural monument, zoo). The majority of protected natural areas are located in the perimeter of rural localities, which creates premises for the development of tourism in rural areas (Hămuraru M., Buzdugan A., 2019, pages 7-14).

A considerable part of the attractions existing in the vicinity of protected natural areas can become a part of ecotourism routes. Among the most representative natural areas with potential for the development of green tourism are: the scientific reservation "Codrii" (5,172 ha), the scientific reservation "Plaiul Fagului" (5,642 ha), the scientific reservation "Pădurea Domnească "(6,032 ha), the scientific reserve" Prutul de Jos "(1,609 ha), the landscape reserve" Trebujeni "(500 ha), the landscape reserve" Suta de movile "(1,072 ha), the landscape reserve" Codrii Tigheci " (2,519 ha), the "Hârbovăț Forest" landscape reservation (2218 ha), "Misilindra" forest nature reserve (1.7 ha), "Grădina Turcească" landscape reserve (224 ha), "Căpriana-Scoreni" landscape reserve (1,762 ha), etc (Tourism Development Department, 2003).

All scientific reserves have their own administration, which is directly subordinated to the national environment authority. There are 63 nature reserves (8,009 ha or 4.10% of the total protected areas) in the Republic of Moldova. They consist of areas rich in certain species of flora and fauna, which require protection given their scientific and aesthetic value. Over 97% of the nature reserves and 96% of the landscape reserves are managed by the Moldsilva State Agency.

The 5 scientific reservations include: Codru-Strășeni district, Lozova village; Iagorlîc-Dubăsari district, Goian village; Prutul de Jos – Vulcănești district, the village Slobozia Mare; Plaiul Fagului – Ungheni district, Rădenii village Old; Pădurea Domnească Glodeni and Fălești districts. Orhei National Park has an area of 33792.09 hectares, being the only national objective included in this category. Some of the landscape reservations are: Hîrbovăț forest, Between villages Hîrbovăț and Bulboaca, detour Hîrbovăț forestry; the geological and paleontological complex in the Lopatnic river basin – along Lopatnic River; the floodplain near Antonești – west of the village of Antonești; Cimișlia ravines- south of the town of Cimișlia; Hîncești forest – between the villages of Lăpușna and Mereșeni, the Logănești forest district; Căpriana-Scoreni – between the villages of Lozova, Vorniceni, Pănășești, Trușeni, Cojușna, Căpriana forest district; etc. There are 3 wetlands of international importance in the Republic of Moldova: *Lacurile Prutului de Jos* (nr.1029 in the Ramsar List) 19 152,5 ha, location: Cahul district; *Nistrul de Jos* (nr.1316 in the Ramsar List) 60 000 ha, location: Căușeni and Ștefan Vodă districts, Territorial unit on the left bank of the Dniester; *Unguri-Holoșnița* (nr.1500 in the Ramsar List) 15 553 ha, location: Ocnița, Dondușeni and Soroca districts (Government of the Republic of Moldova, 2020).

Referring to accommodation possibilities near the protected natural areas, the Tourism Agency from the Republic of Moldova uses data from the National Bureau of Statistics regarding the visits to collective tourist reception structures with accommodation functions depending on the origin of tourists (total, including non-residents). However, there is no statistical information available about protected areas.

# CONCLUSION

Given the necessity to find solutions to environmental issues, which would ensure harmony between people and nature, sustainable development is becoming a priority for the activity of civil society. As societies evolve and the standard of living increases, environmentally friendly approaches become stringent, ensuring social wellbeing and prosperity, and of a growing interest to citizens. The country's priorities in innovation policy, energy efficiency, and economic modernization, in accordance with modern requirements, naturally determine the attainment of sustainable development.

One of the solutions for reaching such objectives is a creating and developing environmental education program for different categories of visitors in the protected natural areas, as well as in the travel agencies offering recreation, excursions, etc. in these protected areas. It is also necessary to mitigate the considerable difficulties for nature reserves and parks that arise when working with the local population living in close proximity to a particular nature reserve or national park. Such solutions are set against the need to balance the socio-economic contradiction between the desire for exploit natural resources for economic benefits (forest cutting, grazing livestock, etc.) and the restrictions that must be observed to protect the nature in the areas.

# References


United Nations Environment Programme (UNEP), Annual Report 2021 https://www.unep.org/resources/annual-report-2021

UNEP. (2012). Global Environment Outlook 5 – Environment environment for the future we want https://www.unep.org/resources/global-environment-outlook-5

Ceballos-Lascurain, Hector. (1996). Tourism, Ecotourism, and Protected Areas. The World Conservation Union(IUCN) and The International Ecotourism Society. Gland, Switzerland. 315 pages.

Fundația Centrul Național pentru Dezvoltare Durabilă, *Natura 2000 în România*, București, (2012), pag 6.

Ministerul Agriculturii și Dezvoltării Rurale, *Programul Național de Dezvoltare Rurală 2014-2020*, Versiunea aprobată 26.05.2015

Ministerul Mediului, Agenția Națională pentru Protecția Mediului, Raport privind starea mediului în România în anul 2016, (2016) pag. 24.

http://www.anpm.ro/anpm_resources/migrated_content/uploads/16103_6%20CONS.%20NAT,%20Biodiversitate,%20Biosecuritate.pdf

Fundația Centrul Național pentru Dezvoltare Durabilă, *Natura 2000 în România*, București, (2012), pag 6.

Ministerul Mediului, Agenția Națională pentru Protecția Mediului, Raport privind starea mediului în România în anul 2016, (2016) pag. 303

INCDT, *Planul de Amenajarea a Teritoriului Național – Secțiunea VIII – Zone Turistice. Proiect de fundamentare – Analiza și diagnoza potențialului turistic la nivelul unităților administrativ-teritoriale*, București, (2007).

http://www.rosilva.ro/articole/cabane__p_1497.htm

Aşevschi V., Fondos T., Bencheci M., Ecoturismul – principala formă de manifestare a turismului durabil în Republica Moldova Noosfera. Revista ştiinţifică de educaţie, spiritualitate şi cultură ecologică, (2014), Pag. 143-146, Numărul 10 / 2014 / ISSN 1857-3517.

Gribincea C., Ecotourism and the structure of natural potential in the Republic of Moldova and Romania, (2021), https://ibn.idsi.md/sites/default/files/imag_file/229-239_4.pdf ,

Hămuraru M., Buzdugan A., (2019). The potential of the development of ecotourism in the Republic of Moldova through the prism of national tourist areas, June 2019 DOI: 10.7862/rz.2019.mmr.9, Modern Management Review, MMR, vol. XXIV, 26 (2/2019), p. 7-14.

Guvernul Republicii Moldova, Ministerul Educaţiei şi Cercetării, Strategia de dezvoltare a turismului „Turism 2020" (2020). https://mecc.gov.md/ro/content/strategia-de-dezvoltare-turismului-turism-2020

http://www.moldsilva.gov.md/pageview.php?l=ro&id-c=214&t=/Viata-padurii/Ariile-protejate

https://www.legis.md/cautare/getResults?doc_id=108578&lang=ro

Departamentul Dezvoltarea Turismului al RM. *Strategia de Dezvoltare Durabilă a turismului în Republica Moldova în anii 2003-2015*, (2003). Chişinău. 74 p.

Florea S., (2005). *Patrimoniul turistic al Republicii Moldova*, Tipografia centrală, Chişinău 352 p.

# Quality of Life: Achievements and Expectations in Social Media Political Communication

**Delia OPREA** Cross-Border Faculty,
"Dunărea de Jos" University of Galati delia.oprea@ugal.ro

## 1 SOCIAL MEDIA IN POLITICS

Social media allows people to interact freely with others and offers multiple discussion topics. Being used by billions of people around the world, social media is one of the defining technologies of our time. The time spent on social media and the massive presence of the population using it make social media a territory in which aspects of private real-life are exposed to the public eye, as all kinds of personal, professional, psychological, social, etc. issues are publicly portrayed in many types of discourse, framed into the modern obsession of networking. Social media networks also provide the opportunity to share opinions with a far wider audience. These opinions reveal expectations, fears, disappointments, personal ideas about the subject area, and sometimes even all types of reactions regarding a posted idea. Politicians are no exception, having begun to use social media communication extensively. The so-called web 2.0 platforms reduced the costs of spreading the information, went beyond national borders and eliminated the intermediates between politicians and voters (Bakardjieva, 2009; Bode, 2012; Serazio, 2014; Dimitrova, Shehata, Strömbäck & Nord, 2014).

In this particular way, communication was made more horizontal than vertical by enabling direct replies (Ellison et al., 2014; Matsa & Michell, 2014; Deters & Mehl, 2012; Burke, Kraut & Marlow, 2011). The propagation of information (all kinds of information) is now done in a very different way than before (faster and more directly) and gives all of us (politicians included) the daily opportunity to talk to each of the followers/voters "personally". Moreover, if we look at the share function of Facebook posts, we can easily imagine the possibilities of disseminating the information, sometimes in a non-controllable way.

In the matter of political communication on social networks, one of the most striking characteristics is their ability to spread information. Thus, information can consist of ideas, opinions, but also images, reactions (like, love, care, etc., share) shared when posting and/or commenting. The propagation speed and the audience are different from traditional communication, not only in the political field, but in all communication fields. In this way, politicians also make themselves and their official plans known quickly and easily. This is why most of the important politicians have started using social media in a professional direction. Of course, the price paid for such type of dissemination is another advantage of using social networks, which results in drawing the attention of a large number of citizens with a relatively low budget (Duggan, Ellison, Lampe, Lenhart & Madden, 2015; Ellison, Vergeer, Hermans & Sams, 2013).

This type of so-called transparent governance will be embraced by more and more leaders as it becomes easier for this category of professionals to interact with their public. Instead of wasting time and money on long travels in order to interact with citizens, politicians and government officials now use online tools to strengthen these connections. In one way, we can speak about a change in how politicians govern and how the public is governed. We see different waves of civic participation and engagement being transformed by social media. Nowadays, with social media, citizens can be part of, or at least have the impression of being part of the ideas, plans and initiatives in an easier way than ever before.

If, before social media, governments, along with the traditional media, were the gatekeepers of information, now the relationship has been turned on its head, says Taylor Owen of the University of British Columbia[1]: "This largely symbiotic relationship has been radically disrupted by the concurrent rise of digital technology and the social media ecosystem that it enabled. Nowhere is this challenge more acute than in the world of international affairs and conflict, where the rise of digitally native international actors has challenged the state's dominance."

Political news now seems more accessible through social media than through traditional ways. A new study

---

1   https://www.weforum.org/agenda/2016/04/6-ways-social-media-is-changing-the-world/, accessed on February 23, 2022.

from Pew Research[2] claims that about one in five U.S. adults gets their political news primarily through social media. This way, those who do get their political news primarily through social media tend to be less well-informed and more likely to be exposed to unproven claims than people who get their news from traditional sources, says the same study. Given this direction of political communication, social networks play an increasingly important role in campaigns and electoral periods – first in the ultimately unsuccessful candidacy of Howard Dean in 2003, then in the election of the first African-American president in 2008, to give only two important examples, and again in the Twitter-driven campaign of Donald Trump. *The New York Times*[3] reports that "The election of Donald J. Trump is perhaps the starkest illustration yet that across the planet, social networks are helping to fundamentally rewire human society." Because social media allows people to communicate more freely, they also provide increased opportunities for debates, supporting groups, power influential groups in various domains, like education, environment, non-governmental issues, human right, and, of course, politics.

---

2   Survey of U.S adults conducted Oct.29-Nov.11, 2019."Americans Who Mainly Get Their News on Social Media Are Less Engaged, Less Knowledgeable", https://www.pewresearch.org/journalism/2020/07/30/americans-who-mainly-get-their-news-on-social-media-are-less-engaged-less-knowledgeable/pj_2020-07-30_social-media-news_00-01/, accessed on January, 23, 2022.
3   https://www.nytimes.com/2016/11/17/technology/social-medias-globe-shaking-power.html, accessed on January, 19, 2022.

# 2. Quality of Life and the Standard of living. Theoretical perspectives

In order to trace the two dimensions of the quality of life proposed by this chapter, achievements and expectations, respectively, we will initially focus on the sociological perspective it entails. Quality of life is a general indicator that refers to the identification and measurement of certain social, psychological, and economic indices at a societal level.

Without trying to give too theoretical a definition of what quality of life means, we mention that, from a sociological point of view, this concept is different from the concept of standard of living. The main difference between standard of living and quality of life is that the measurement of the former is more objective while the latter is more subjective. Living standards (which give the standard of living), such as gross domestic product, poverty rate, and environmental quality, can be measured and defined by numbers while quality of life factors, such as equal protection under the law, freedom from discrimination and freedom of religion, access to quality health care, quality and availability of education, economic and political stability, are more difficult to measure and are particularly qualitative. Both indicators can help us get a general picture of life in a particular location at a given time.

Quality of life is, therefore, more subjective and less intangible. The United Nations' Universal Declaration of Human Rights, adopted in 1948, provides an excellent list of factors that can be taken into account in assessing the quality of life. It includes many things that citizens in the United States and other developed countries take for granted but which are not available in a significant number of countries around the world. Although this statement is over 70 years old, in many ways, it still represents an ideal to be achieved rather than a baseline state. Factors that can be used to measure the quality of life include the following: freedom from slavery and torture, equal protection of the law, freedom from discrimination, freedom of movement in the country of origin, the presumption of innocence, the right to have a family, the right to be treated equally regardless of sex, race, language, religion, political beliefs, nationality, the right to privacy, freedom of thought, freedom of religion, free choice of employment, the right to fair wages, the right to rest and leisure, the right to education, the right to human dignity, the right to life expectancy.

In order to assess some of these life quality aspects, we conducted a study aimed to qualitatively analyse more than 38,000 online comments of those who contributed (through reactions and posts) to the post made by the President of Romania, Klaus Iohannis, on October 5, 2021, on the most popular social network in Romania, namely Facebook, regarding the consultations he was obliged to make in order to establish a Prime Minister. The post, which we will reproduce below, has attracted more than 38,000 comments, 1,500 shares and 42,000 reactions, which revealed, among others, the current state of the quality of life in Romania. In this chapter, we aim to highlight, through the achievements versus expectations dichotomy, precisely this state of quality of life, so direct and real, sometimes uncensored, expressed through the replies, comments, ironies, characterisations offered by the followers of the President of Romania, Klaus Iohannis, on the social network Facebook.

## 3. CONTEXT: THE ROMANIAN POLITICAL CRISIS

The three-month political crisis in the autumn of 2021 overlapped with the most virulent wave of the Covid pandemic that hit Romania and the elections in the two political forces that formed the Cîțu government.

The political crisis began on September 1, 2021, after USR PLUS representatives boycotted the government meeting because they disagreed with the way the Anghel Saligny programme was adopted.

On the same day, Prime Minister Florin Cîțu dismissed USR Minister of Justice Stelian Ion after he refused to ratify the programme. The timing coincides with the outbreak of wave four of the Covid pandemic.

September 2, 2021 – The National Permanent Bureau of the National Liberal Party unanimously voted to continue supporting Florin Cîțu as head of government. The next day, USR announced the submission of a motion of censure against the government together with the Alliance for the Unity of Romanians (AUR) – entitled "The dismissal of the Cîțu government, Romania's only chance to live!"

On September 6, 2021, the governing coalition broke up. USR co-presidents Dan Barna and Dacian Ciolos announced that all ministers will leave the cabinet on September 7. The same day, Florin Cîțu dismissed all the secretaries of state, prefects and sub-prefects appointed by USR PLUS.

On September 8, 2021, Prime Minister Florin Cîțu complained to the Constitutional Court that Parliament violated constitutional provisions regarding the initiation, submission, and communication of motions to the government. The PSD voted, in the Joint Permanent Bureaux, "for" postponing the motion vote until the court had ruled.

October 5, 2021: Parliament convened and debated the motion tabled by PSD "STOP poverty, price-gouging and criminals! Down with the Cîțu Government!". 281 MPs voted in favour of the motion of censure, none against it. Florin Cîțu's government was overthrown.

October 20, 2021: Following the meeting that brought together the two chambers, the Senate and the Chamber of Deputies, the proposal for the investiture of Dacian Ciolos and his cabinet failed with 88 votes in favour, 184 against and 0 abstentions.

October 21, 2021: President Klaus Iohannis appointed retired General Nicolae Ciucă to form a new government. Klaus Iohannis has twice appointed General Nicolae Ciucă to form a new government. He succeeded only after making an alliance with PSD.

In November of the same year, lengthy and unnatural negotiations followed between PNL and PSD (the two main parties in Romania with opposing political views), but it was not until November 25, 2021 that the Ciucă government was sworn in by Parliament with 318 votes in favour.

This is the chronology of a political crisis considered useless by experts[4], because while PNL was arguing with USR, wave 4 of the pandemic was in full swing. It was considered one of the most difficult periods Romanians have ever gone through while helplessly witnessing the overlapping of two crises: while political leaders were arguing and negotiating positions, hospital morgues were full to brimming, and Romania ranked first in Europe and third in the world regarding deaths caused by Covid-19.

## 3. THE ROMANIAN PRESIDENTIAL COMMUNICATION ON SOCIAL MEDIA

In 2014, the current Romanian President, Klaus Iohannis, became the first politician in Europe to reach one million fans on Facebook, surpassing Merkel, Sarkozy, and Hollande (Sasu & Androniciuc, 2017: 462). Currently, Klaus Iohannis continues to be the most popular Romanian politician on Facebook, with over 1,890,000 fans, followed by former prime minister Victor Ponta (814,380 fan base).

The social media activity of the Romanian President, Klaus Iohannis, is not intensive at the moment (Facebook: 10 posts in December 2021, 4 posts in November 2021, 10 posts in October 2021, 9 posts in September 2021; Twitter: 12 Tweets in December, 7 Tweets in November 2021,

---

4   https://stirileprotv.ro/stiri/politic/2021-cronologia-unei-crize-politice-inutile-cand-pnl-se-certa-cu-usr-morgile-erau-pline.html, consultat pe 31 ianuarie 2022.

16 tweets in October 2021, 16 tweets in September 2021), but the number of reactions his posts stir is considerable, all the more that they seem uncensored, even though they abide by the rules of the social network.

Tuesday, on October 5, 2021, Klaus Iohannis, the President of Romania, announced that he would not call the political parties to talk earlier than the following week, even if the political crisis in Romania was in full force. Romania was, at the beginning of the winter season, without government, so without a decision factor, and the Romanian President was in no hurry to make a political decision in order to establish order in the country.

Fig. 1 Facebook post of Klaus Iohannis, from October 5, 2021

*«Trist, dar adevărat! Cuvântul care caracterizează cel mai bine România de azi este „criză". Suntem în plină pandemie, valul 4 ne-a lovit rău, suntem într-o criză a prețului la energie, o criză care este și europeană și globală și, în acest context, în Parlament a fost votată o moțiune de cenzură care mai adaugă o criză, cea a guvernării.*

*Situația a fost generată de politicieni cinici, unii purtând masca reformismului, alții clamând grija pentru români. USR a fost parte din coaliție, a plecat din guvern și a votat moțiunea împreună cu PSD și AUR. Astea sunt faptele, restul este discurs politic sau demagogie. Trebuie să găsim o soluție pentru că România trebuie guvernată și este momentul pentru decizii mature din partea politicienilor. Pentru a da timp partidelor să se întrunească în forurile interne și să vină cu o abordare matură, voi convoca consultări săptămâna viitoare ».*

*[Sad but true! The word that best characterises Romania today is "crisis".*

*We are in the midst of a pandemic, wave 4 has hit us hard, we are in an energy price crisis, a crisis that is both European and global and, in this context, a motion of censure has been voted in Parliament that adds another crisis, that of governance. The situation has been generated by cynical politicians, some wearing the mask of reformism, others claiming to care about Romanians. USR was part of the coalition, left the government and voted for the motion together with PSD and AUR. These are the facts, the rest is political discourse or demagogy. We must find a solution because Romania must be governed, and it is time for mature decisions from politicians. In order to give the parties time to meet in their internal forums and come up with a mature approach, I will convene consultations next week.]*

The Romanian Presidential post from October 5, 2021 had 14,000 smiles, 12,000 likes, 12,000 angry faces, 1,200 crying emojis, 378 shocked, 193 love, 115 hugs, 38,000 commentaries and 1,500 shares.

# 4. ROMANIAN QUALITY OF LIFE: ACHIEVEMENTS AND EXPECTATIONS THROUGH/IN SOCIAL MEDIA DISCOURSE

Politicians have changed the ways in which they interact with people, so new forms of political discourse have emerged as a result of dissemination through social media sites and applications. Nowadays, new modes of social and political participation are as important as the traditional offline modes of participation, becoming an important resort for political actions: informing by expressing political attitudes, views, mobilizing, and inviting to discussions and reactions.

Social media has brought about another significant change: there is now no filter on the way we speak. In the past, unless you spoke to people directly, you had no way to get your message across, regardless of your freedom of speech. Now we can use social media to get our uncensored messages out to thousands or even millions of people. Our growing use of social media is not just changing the way we communicate – it's changing the way we do business, the way we are governed, and the way we live in society.

The post made by the President of Romania on October 5, 2021 provoked a large number of reactions (42,000 reactions, 38,000 comments and 1,500 shares, as mentioned above) that bring to the forefront the impact that such a decision can have on the quality of life of Romanians. The achievement/expectation dichotomy becomes a real fault line, and the outrage against the President's decision to postpone the consultations, which would lead to the end of the crisis or would at least represent a step towards the end of the political crisis, the anger that the comments bring out is a very good barometer of the quality of life. Those who made comments are Romanians from home or abroad, who put their trust in the President (some even openly state this), even twice, thus expressing their expectations and the disappointments they experienced because of the situations that the same President caused or maintained.

Therefore, we have chosen to make, through a qualitative analysis of the comments extracted from the mentioned post, an inventory of the images that show what the Romanians wanted or want and what they received from the President, perhaps the most important political player with direct implications in achieving a socio-political balance.

In order to analyse what kind of attitudes towards the quality of life can be extracted or expected from social media discourse materialised as commentaries to a political presidential statement/post, we created a framework that can be applied to both dimensions in our approach. We have identified the main topics mostly presented in 38,000 commentaries: economic crisis, political crisis, educational crisis, sanitary crisis, and the pandemic, social issues like the labour market, the medical system, or political decisions. Of course, other adjacent themes were pointed out (infrastructure, justice, presidential preoccupations/passions in antithesis with the country's priorities), but most of the posts made by the Romanians who live in

Romania or abroad refer to the issues mentioned above. In regard to these four major issues, we have chosen to extract those *phrases* expressing characterisation, opinions or feelings, and actions (already made or expected). In this way, we came to a framework that permitted us to clearly see the problems identified by Romanians in relation to their quality of life. The framework pursued functions like a two-sided mirror, one regarding achievements and the other one regarding expectations related to the quality of life in Romania.

**Table 1** Life Quality and Social Media communication – a Framework

| Topic/issue related | X1 | X2 | X3 | X4 |
|---|---|---|---|---|
| Characterisations | | | | |
| Opinions /feelings | | | | |
| Actions | | | | |

In the next two subchapters, we extract a sample of online discourse (and we kept the Romanian version, too) in order to have a proper dimension of the directions in which online communication in politics goes when referring to life quality.

## ACHIEVEMENTS

Social media has encouraged people to use computers and mobile phones in order to express and share their concerns on social/political/personal/economic/educational issues without actually having to engage actively in real life. Pressing the 'Like' button or sharing content and commenting on others' posts are considered action, engagement. This kind of attention is very calculated when it comes to politics. On the one hand, this online activity absolves them from the responsibility to act or even of the responsibility to make a decision on their own. But comments bring with them a greater emotional charge and somehow a greater involvement, at least at the level of the participant in the discussion. Of course, commenting is not the same as acting, but publicly expressing an opinion can at least bring reactions of approval, disapproval, empathy or perhaps sympathy from people you know. Sometimes, comments can create real social movements or paradigm shifts when the opinions are widely shared. In this case, the overwhelming majority of the comments were negative towards the President and the position he adopted when faced with a political crisis, which only added to the health, medical, economic, educational, etc. crisis.

## CHARACTERISATION

- Cynical politicians wearing the mask of reformism![5]
- Claiming to care for Romanians.
- You are the first to blame for the situation!
- Lack of conscience
- (Educated) Romania in three words: Sad but true!
- You are totally disconnected from the country by inviting us to play golf.
- You have no achievements; Romania is today more uneducated than seven years ago and with forests

---

5    All comments were in Romanian; translation ours.

more deforested by your friends than when we elected you President.
- You are a sad but true President ...
- You are ineffective and miserable and have done nothing good for the country.
- You are a failed President in a State that deserves to be saved from the patent mediocrity of your clique!
- You are the source of all the crises of the last six years or so in Romania, that is the truth.
- For me, you are a failed project!
- We have a failed President who has bankrupted the country.
- The most hated President for whom we queued to vote.
- For those who lived here from 2014 to the present, the word "iohannis", a common noun, has become synonymous with "lazy", "lazy" and "greedy", but the list is not definitive.
- Mr Iohannis, you are the biggest disappointment in politics, you beat both Constantinescu and Băsescu, you are the death of hope that this country will have a leader who truly loves and protects it!

## OPINIONS:

- Sad but true is that you have continued and encouraged baronial and discretionary politics after the PNL became the main party in the ruling alliance.
- Sad but true is that I will hear you in a few days about how you want to give another chance to PSD.

- For a whole month, you have kept this zombie government alive just to win some elections in PNL (what does that have to do with the country?)
- How can you vegetate for seven years doing nothing? All that's left in your wake is the gnashing of a rusty jaw.
- You have managed to lead the country into total chaos, health, economic, and political crisis.
- At this moment, all the politicians in Romania have shown that you are only interested in your political games. In the middle of the health crisis, you are all passing responsibility around!
- I understand that you have decided to be the President of supermen only. It's okay, we'll manage somehow down here among the mortals.
- Man has no certainty of tomorrow, for we must toil to get justice, health is rather in our hands, education increases stupidity, the pocket cries after we pay taxes.
- NO Education, NO health, NO economy, NO infrastructure, NO justice
- Jobs are not there, and those who work are mostly working for the minimum wage of 400 euros.
- The health system is appalling; people who had their lives ahead of them are dying because we have no facilities (now everyone is dying of covid burned alive in intensive care).
- Children's education is also defective.
- The Romanians understood that they had already been abandoned by the President.

## ACTIONS:

- Distribution of public money without objective criteria
- Dismissing competent people, replacing them with incompetent politicians, creating new and useless posts in the state), this is a cynical politician!
- What have you actually done for seven years? You played golf, you looked down on the country when the hospitals were burning, you shrugged helplessly when serious leaders of the PNL sanctioned your self-sufficiency (I'm thinking of Ilie Bolojan), you surrounded yourself with incompetence.
- People are dying in hospitals, and you are not doing anything about it. How many more innocent people have to burn in hospitals in Romania for anything to change?
- By next week, people will die in hospitals because there are no beds and medicines.

## EXPECTATIONS

The 38,000 comments show us, first of all, by the extremely high number of contributions for a (political) post, that the President's position has intrigued many of his (Romanian) followers and that the effects of his actions will be seen quite quickly on the quality of life of those who commented and, of course, on the lives of Romanians. Each contribution, almost without exception, represents a hard stance against the statements made by the President, describing them in terms of where we are (achievements) and/or where we should be (expectations) from the point of view of mere citizens who should be protected by the state, have the right to healthcare, education, and obviously should, in a democratic state, be able to rely on the state, so that they can have a fair life, according to the efforts they make. All these standards seem far from what the Romanians actually receive, as the lines below clearly show. We have selected 20 comments that are representative of the thousands of comments that present pretty much the same expectations that Romanians have from their political leaders regarding the quality of life in Romania. We have grouped the comments according to the three criteria considered in the Achievements subchapter, namely: Characterisations, Opinions / Feelings and Actions.

## CHARACTERISATIONS:

- Our country is in constant crisis, and you act as if you are always on holiday.
- You are bound to ensure normality for all, to guarantee balance, to give us hope.
- You will appoint a prime minister...I don't know who, but it is your duty as President to know who is capable
- Common sense and respect for the Romanians are just empty words.
- No strategy, no vision!

- Mr. President, don't you really feel any responsibility for the failed state, the fourth wave of the pandemic, or the current government crisis?
- But for the rest, it may be too late …
- Do you assume your rightful role as a mediator? Is this permanent crisis situation you are part of doing the Romanians any good?
- I've been waiting for the right thing since I voted for you twice and nothing …
- I think we were all expecting a government solution, not a new accentuation of the fault line that made the last government impossible.
- Romanians want evolution, projects, and concrete solutions, not stories about scapegoats.
- Where is the concern for the citizens of this country?

## ACTIONS:

- Mediate fairly!
- There's time, perhaps, for a look in the mirror and a moment of honesty, until next week...
- Next week?! It's like our house is on fire, and we're thinking so maybe next week the fire department will be ready so let's call them then. In business, any leader would be fired for such slow crisis management.
- If you had cared in the slightest about our nation, you would have called the parties to consultations to

form a new government tomorrow, not next week! But you probably have some golf games scheduled for next week!

- Are you really interested in a quick end to the political crisis? If so, we are waiting for facts and realism.
- Let's get back to accountability and maturity - at least at the 11th hour.
- Price caps on gas, electricity, RCA insurance, masks, Covid tests. Ensure free, high-quality education for our children. Ensure a decent healthcare system!!!

## FINDINGS

Expectations and achievements in terms of quality of life are reflected in the social media discourse, all the more so as the topic is a sensitive one, namely POLITICAL. Because we are all aware that the way a country is run affects the quality of life to a large extent, politics is also widely discussed on social media. On the one hand, the exposure is enormous compared to the usual political gatherings (which range from a few people to a few thousands, to congresses or mass actions). On the other hand, the freedom of expression on social media, as well as the reaction speed, make the dialogue amplified through social networks a rich source of social interactions (including cyber conflicts, arguments, emotional reactions, violent reactions, etc.), characterisations (such as verdicts, solutions, responses, description of states of affairs through one's own and highly subjective view), opinions, feelings and actions that should be taken/behaviours that should be addressed.

We have chosen a symmetrical model for both dimensions explored, expectations and achievements, in order to mirror the topics addressed. The main subjects presented in the Romanian online discourse regarding life quality in terms of expectations and achievements are the crisis, the pandemic, social issues (labour market, medical system), and political decisions. By following these four main directions, it is easier to mirror the contributors' statements to the President's post on the postponement of consultations for the appointment of a Prime Minister and a cabinet of ministers.

Based on a purely political discussion, but with a decisive role for the country's development, and therefore on the quality of life of Romanians (at home or members of the diaspora that may still have relatives in the country or may intend to return), the comments posted are expectedly coordinated in the two directions, too few being neutral or considering the President's decision a correct one. We did not set out to judge/comment on the President's decision to postpone the call for party consultations, but we see very clearly this polarisation related to the quality of life: on the one hand, the present or past expectations that voters have from their President, on the other hand, the achievements, facts, actions, decisions which obviously impact the life of the Romanians. We have thus noticed that economic issues are among the most pressing ones, as well as the conditions in the health system, especially against the background of the pandemic and other particularly serious medical incidents (people burnt in hospitals or dying as a result of infection with various intra-hospital bacteria).

Against the backdrop of a crisis situation, the statements, questions, and characterisations made by the followers of the President's official Facebook account are bitter, sometimes ironic, with a sad undertone - this being one of the most frequent words, precisely because it would characterise the life (and therefore the quality of life) of the Romanians, but also because the President used it in his post from October 5, 2021. The tendency to mostly see negative life aspects (we notice the lack of positive or supportive comments) that are due, to some extent, to the political class and to the President, in particular, makes lack of achievements a key theme of the discourse. Thus, the word NO is also often present in association with EDUCATION, ECONOMY, INFRASTRUCTURE, HEALTH, JUSTICE, i.e. the very pillars of national well-being. Disappointment is shown not only through the high number of (negative) comments about the President, as it is not strictly related to the President's specific actions. However, it raises serious questions that not even those who supported him are satisfied with the way he governed or with the way he chose his partners in government so that he could be the President invested with so much trust.

This analysis shows that the President's public image went from being considered an icon of fairness, moderation or balance to being perceived as a political actor showing disregard for the country and the people, sharing resources only within the old political gangs, which he has failed to unite in order to direct them towards the good of the people, reflected in the standard of living, the ultimate goal of political power. The mediating President (expectation) has become the source of the crises of recent years. Instead of accountability and maturity (leading to economic stability and development in all economic sectors, education, etc.), an even greater gap has been created between those who lead and those who are led, which, in the first place, obviously results in economic discrepancies, but also into defective access to health services, education and especially justice. Instead of concrete projects and solutions, the Romanians can't even find a room in hospitals and die prematurely. This opposition between expectations and achievements becomes clearer with every comment posted, which leads us to the conclusion that perceived achievements are far below the expectations expressed years ago (at the time of the President's election). Considering the examples above, the quantitative discrepancy between the two sides of the scale is obvious because most opinions refer to achievements, which seem to be few to none, and, numerically, the actions correlated to achievements are at a considerably lower level. As for expectations, most actions are clearly said/claimed/named, so there is a need for action rather than opinions, consultations, and hesitations.

## 5. CONCLUSIONS

Almost a quarter of the world's population is now on Facebook, and more than half the people on earth now use social media[6]. Social network feeds are full of human (on-

6   https://datareportal.com/reports/more-than-half-the-world-now-uses-social-media (accessed on 2nd of February, 2022).

line) interactions, becoming more powerful as they grow. Social media has come to tremendously influence most of the communication processes, but also politics, business, world culture, education, careers, innovation, and more. Social media offers both opportunities and challenges in how people communicate and interact.

Thanks to the internet, everybody with online access and a social media account can shape reality – create memes, publications and comments, increase their visibility, provide explanations, express rejection, share information (from jokes to racial offences) and access the mainstream narrative.

As for the references to the quality of life through political social media discourse, this sample of political communication gave us the opportunity to tackle some of key aspects, positive and negative. The 38,000 comments on President Klaus Iohannis's post from the October 5, 2021 are a good barometer of the quality of Romanian life. They all came to the same conclusion, that the president's decision to postpone the political consultations for a few days is a symbol of the way he and the rest of the politicians handle public affairs in Romania. There is an enormous gap between expectations and achievements, and this awareness process led to a very sad and disturbing conclusion: that the country needs another kind of political class in order positively impact the quality of Romanian life.

Ultimately, sharing is about getting people to see and respond to content. This is also happening with political communication on social media. Politicians and groups of politicians are promoting and making themselves known, sometimes only in one (positive) direction, and can stay in touch with a larger public, thus weaving their influence. As for the content, relevant or non-relevant, it seems not to be the main stake of online political communication. Because the world constantly hungers for information, it is important for public persons or organisations to use social media and keep publishing.

Changes made by the internet and by social media in particular are affecting the way we see the world, the way we perceive reality, and even more, the way we conceive our lives. Another important change that has occurred is that there is now no filter on the way we choose to represent reality or on the way we speak: ironically, directly, by giving false or partially true information, etc. But, when the citizens' well-being is in danger, all the good and all the bad things can be reflected in social media, without caring for language, but more for the ideas voiced for the whole world to hear.

## REFERENCES

Bakardjieva, M. (2009). Subactivism: lifeworld and politics in the age of the Internet. The Information Society, 25(2), 238-257

Bode, L. (2012). Facebooking it to the polls: A study in online social networking and political behavior. Journal of Information Technology & Politics, 9(4), 352-369

Dimitrova, D., Shehata, A., Strömbäck, J., & Nord, L. (2014). The effects of digital media on political knowledge and participation in election campaigns: Evidence from panel data. Communication Research 41(1), 95-118.

Duggan, M., Ellison, N. B., Lampe, C., Lenhart, A., & Madden, M. (2015). Social media update 2014 [PDF]. Retrieved from https://www.pewresearch.org/internet/wp-content/uploads/sites/9/2015/01/PI_SocialMediaUpdate20144.pdf

Ellison, N. B., Steinfield, C., & Lampe, C. (2011). Connection strategies: social capital implications of Facebook-enabled communication practices. New Media & Society, 13(6), 452-471.

Matsa, E. K., & Michell, A. (2014). 8 key takeaways about social media and news [online] Available at: https://www.pewresearch.org/journalism/2014/03/26/8-key-takeaways-about-social-media-and-news/ [Accessed 10 January 2022].

Sasu, Constantin & Androniciuc, Andra (2017). How do Romanian Politicians Communicate Online? An Emphasis on Facebook, "Ovidius" University Annals, Economic Sciences Series, Volume XVII, Issue 2 /2017, 461-466.

Serazio, M. (2014). The new media designs of political consultants: Campaign production in a fragmented era. Journal of Communication, 64(4), 743-763.

Vergeer, M., Hermans, L., & Sams, S. (2013). Online social networks and micro-blogging in political campaigning: the exploration of a new campaign tool and a new campaign style. Party Politics 19(3), 477-501.

Acknowledgments: This research is supported by the project GI 3624/30.09.2021, Project Manager: Dr. Mariana Carmelia Dragomir-Bălănică

# Factors Determining the Composition of Means and Methods Of Strength Training of Athletes Specialising in Sports Wrestling

**MANOLACHI Veaceslav** Cross-Border Faculty, "Dunărea de Jos" University of Galati, veaceslav.manolachi@ugal.ro

**MANOLACHI Victor** Cross-Border Faculty, "Dunărea de Jos" University of Galati victor.manolachi@ugal.ro

The most important direction in the development of the knowledge system and enhancing the effectiveness of practical activities aimed to improve the strength of athletes specialising in wrestling is approaching strength training by observing some principles of utmost importance. The main ones, as shown in this chapter, are:

- the principle of designing strength training in accordance with a set of factors and mechanisms that determine the level of development of various strength qualities;
- the principle of adapting the means and methods of power training to the kinematic and dynamic structure of the motional techniques and actions typical for wrestling;
- the principle of ensuring the appropriate selection and integration of the impact of the strength training means and methods during the training process;
- the principle of connecting the means and methods of strength training with the dynamics of the func-

tional state of athletes and the peculiarities of the energy supply of motor actions during competitive fights.

The implementation of these principles requires a comprehensive assessment of the structure and features of the musculoskeletal system's functioning: features of the skeletal muscles; factors that determine the level of development and manifestation of various types of power qualities; features related to the manifestation of power qualities, their place and role in the effectiveness of the main motor actions necessary to perform competitive activities; means of selective and integrative influence on various aspects of strength training; interaction of power qualities with other motor qualities, as well as the features of energy supply of various types and manifestations of power qualities.

The use of such an approach should be based on the achievements of modern science in the field of both the general theory of athletic training and the theory and methods of wrestling training, as well as advanced sports practice. Equally important is the broad reliance on the achievements of sports areas of medical and biological disciplines – physiology, biochemistry, anatomy and morphology, kinesiology, which have accumulated a large amount of empirical material, that allows to significantly expand and objectify the level of knowledge in this area.

In recent years, numerous studies have shown the possibilities of nervous adaptation to increase the level of strength and identified the most important neuroregulatory components that reflect various adaptive reactions from the nervous system. However, the vast majority of these studies are based on simple motor actions and do not take into account the exceptional complexity and diversity of power manifestations in various sports activities. Moreover, the results obtained in this area were not reflected in the specialised literature and sports practice, which is largely built on the stereotypes characteristic of the athletes' strength training methods dating back to the 1950s – 1970s.

Therefore, further research is needed in this area, designed to expand the empirical material, extract the general principles and apply them into practice. So far, many mechanisms responsible for the activation of muscle activity, the development and manifestation of strength qualities in all their diversity and in relation to the conditions of modern sports have not been explored. Researchers have yet to expand on processes of nervous adaptation, especially at the level of spinal reactions, and its role in the development of various types of strength, potentially significant types of morphological adaptations, the role of various types of connective tissue, the features of the manifestation of strength in the interaction of various muscles and their motor units, as well as on the processes associated with complex interaction in real motor actions of muscle activity of a concentric, eccentric, isometric, plyometric, and ballistic nature.

It is clear that most of the research in this area is focused on a long-term perspective. However, the already available empirical material, a number of identified patterns of adaptation of the nervous and muscular systems to power loads, the achievements of modern practice in elite sports and recreational sports provide grounds for a serious expansion of ideas in the field of athletes' strength training, putting forward promising hypotheses and theoretical generalisations that can have a significant impact on the optimisation of this process, especially in relation to sports with a complex structure of motor actions and a variety of requirements for different types of strength qualities.

Many empirical facts, patterns, theoretical generalizations accumulated by sports physiology, morphology, biochemistry, sports medicine, as well as best practices can contribute to the optimization of the process of developing the strength qualities of athletes, leading to a systematic correlation between the methodology of strength training and the achievements of modern sports science.

For a more visual consideration of a wide range of issues related to the problem of strength training in general and in wrestling, in particular, it serves our research to first present the well-known information related to the general structure and functions of skeletal muscles, which will support the analysis in this paper.

## SKELETAL MUSCLES IN THE HUMAN MUSCULOSKELETAL SYSTEM

The human skeletal musculature is formed by skeletal muscle tissue capable of contracting under the influence of nerve impulses. Skeletal muscles and associated connective tissue make up about 40% of body weight (often up to 50% in athletes).

Skeletal muscles, together with the skeleton, joints, tendons, and ligaments, make up the human musculo-skeletal system which performs various functions. Among them, the movement of the body in space, the movement of body parts relative to each other ensuring the static-dynamic stability of the body. Skeletal muscles are also involved in the processes of external respiration, movement of blood and lymph, and temperature regulation. They are a depot of energy substrates, enzymes, water, and salts. They carry muscles and a protective function, protecting internal organs and bones from damage.

Considering the structure of the musculoskeletal system from functional positions, it can also be attributed to the motor nerve centres of the brain and spinal cord, in which the bodies of motor neurons that transmit nerve impulses to muscle cells are located. The branched processes of a neuron are dendrites, which play a major role in the perception, integration, and processing of information. Dendrites are the receptive parts of the neuron that perceive input impulses. Another part of neuron processes are axons, that carry the output impulse to the innervated organs or other nerve cells. In the final part, the axon branches form terminals that are in contact with muscle fibres through synapses, the place of contact and transmission of excitation.

Axons are covered with myelin, a substance that forms an electrically insulating myelin sheath of nerve fibres, which is interrupted only at the nodes of Ranvier. The presence of the myelin sheath, which allows the passage of ionic currents only in the area of the nodes of Ranvier, leads to a sharp increase in the rate of transmission of nerve impulses, which is 5-10 times higher in myelinated fibres than in non-myelinated ones. The development of the myelin sheath of axons, as well as the performance of the support (supporting the axon) function, is provided by Schwann cells, which are auxiliary cells of the nervous tissue located along the axons (Seely R.R. et al., 2007).

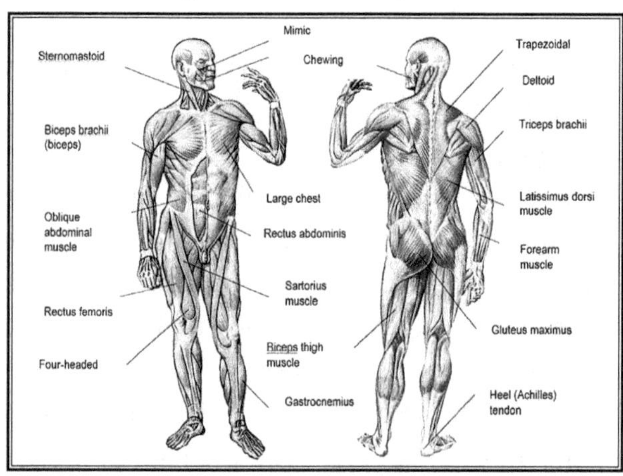


Fig. 1 Skeletal Muscles in the Human Musculoskeletal System
Source: https://reader.lecta.rosuchebnik.ru/demo/8244-65/data/Chapter19.xhtml

In response to the stimulation of a neuron, a wave of excitation spreads, transmitting information from muscle receptors to the nervous system or from the nervous system to muscles. The speed of nerve impulse conduction can vary from 1 to 100 or more m/s. Depending on the stimulation, the pulse frequency can range from 50 to 1,000 or more pulses per second. The propagation speed of impulses depends on the type of nerve fibres: in thin fibres, it can be 1-3 ms, in thick ones, up to 100 or more. The speed of propagation of impulses also depends on the thickness of the myelin sheath: the larger it is, the higher the speed of impulse conduction (Macintosh B.R. et al., 2006).

Skeletal muscles are characterised by certain physiological and physical properties. Physiological ones include excitability, conduction and contractility, excitability referring to the ability to respond with excitation to the arrival of a nerve impulse, conductivity to the ability to generate and conduct an action potential along and deep into the muscle fiber while contractility is the property of muscle tissue to change its length and tension following excitation.

Physical properties include extensibility (the property of muscle tissue to increase the length not only to the natural state of rest, but also exceeding it), elasticity (the ability of a stretched muscle to return to its resting length), and the ability to exert force. Muscle strength is determined by the ability to lift a load, overcome resistance.

## SKELETAL MUSCLE STRUCTURE

Skeletal muscle is formed by muscle cells - cylindrical muscle fibres containing a number of nuclei located on the peripheral part of the fibre near the plasma membrane. Each muscle fibre is surrounded by a thin fibrous connective tissue called endomysium. Muscle cells have different lengths – from a few millimetres to 10-12 centimetres and a diameter of 10 to 100 microns. In small muscles, there are mainly small fibres, and in large muscles, large ones. In small muscles, a single fibre may extend the full length of the muscle. In longer muscles, their contraction and stretching are provided by a group of consecutively adjoining fibres.

Groups of muscle fibres are combined into bundles, also surrounded by connective tissue - remysium. Skeletal muscle bundles can contain from several tens to several hundreds of muscle fibres. All fibres combined into one bundle have identical morphofunctional properties. Many muscle bundles form a muscle, which is also surrounded by a connective tissue (fascia) called epimysium.

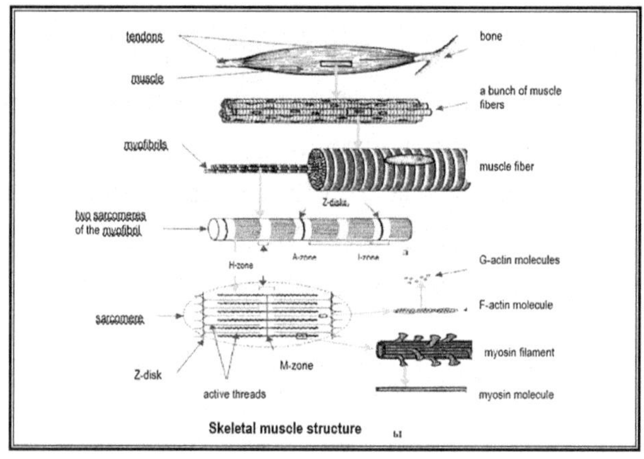


**Fig. 2** Skeletal Muscle Structure
Source: https://en.ppt-online.org/525593

All types of connective tissue of the muscle pass into the connective tissue of the tendons, which are connected to the periosteum of the bone.

The regulation of muscle activity is carried out by motor neurons located in the motor zones of the brain or spinal cord. At the level of the remysium, neurons branch into axons, each of which innervates one muscle fibre. A neuron with a group of axons stimulates the muscle bundle, forming the motor unit of the muscle.

Arteries and veins, together with nerves, pass to the skeletal muscle fibres through layers of connective tissue. The branches of the arteries form a capillary network that surrounds the muscle fibres and supplies them with blood, and the branches of the veins ensure the return of blood to the venous bed.

Muscle tissue also contains specific muscle cells – myosatellites (satellite muscle cells) – mononuclear adult muscle stem cells located between the basal lamina and the cell membrane (sarcolemma) of the skeletal muscle fibre. These cells are not involved in muscle contraction, and their role is reduced to participation in the regeneration process of damaged muscle fibres (Brownsgard J.C., 2010).

Each muscle fibre has a shell (sarcolemma, cell membrane), sarcoplasm and sarcoplasmic reticulum. The sarcoplasm is a jelly-like colloidal solution containing proteins necessary for the synthesis of the contractile elements of the muscle fibre – actin and myosin, attachment of actin myoflaments to Z-lines, etc.; enzymes that activate muscle fibre contractions (ATPase), stimulating the breakdown of creatine phosphate with the formation of ATP (creatine kinase) and glycolysis (phosphorylase and phosphofructokinase). The sarcoplasm contains non-protein substances that provide energy to the contractile elements of the muscles: glycogen, ATP, ADP, AMP, creatine phosphate, creatine, etc. (Macintosh B.R. et al., 2006; Kraemer W.J. et al., 2017).

The sarcoplasm has a sufficiently high viscosity, which increases internal friction and makes it difficult for myofibrils to shorten and elongate during muscle tension and relaxation. Around the muscle fibre, there is a specialised membrane network - the sarcoplasmic reticulum, which plays a key role in the regulation of muscle contractile activity.

Along the muscle fibre, there are myofibrils - thin filaments of actin and thick myosin - proteins that are the contractile apparatus of muscle fibres. Actin and myosin myofilaments are ordered in sarcomeres, which, cover the entire length of myofibrils when connected to each other. The separation of one sarcomere from another is provided by Z-lines – thread-like networks of a specific protein that form a disc-shaped structure to which actin myofilaments are attached. Between the actin filaments attached to each of the Z-lines, myosin filaments are, as it were, in a suspended state.

The actin myofilament consists of two intertwining filaments of globular actin and tropomyosin molecules, to which troponin molecules are attached. At rest, tropomyosin protein molecules are arranged in such a way as to prevent the attachment of myosin molecule heads to the active sites of actin molecules and the formation of so-called transverse bridges that provide shortening of sarcomeres and muscle contraction. The myosin filament consists of 300 – 400 myosin molecules, the fibrillary tails of which form the core of the filament. Above the surface of the rod, myosin heads are spirally arranged with a tail part that ensures their mobility.

Hypertrophy of muscle tissue under the influence of strength training is mainly the result of myofibrillar hypertrophy, which involves both an increase in the volume of myofibrils and an increase in their number as a result of hyperplasia. Myofibular hypertrophy is mainly affected by fast-twitch muscle fibres of group B (BS-II), and groups BS-I to a lesser extent (Wilmore J.H., Costill D.L., 2004).

Another type of hypertrophy, defined as sarcoplasmic hypertrophy, is characteristic of all types of muscle fibres, to the greatest extent for slow-twitch ones. This type of hypertrophy covers the non-contracting part of the muscle fibre - sarcoplasm and manifests itself in the expansion of the capillary network, the volume of mitochondria, an increase in the amounts of aglycogen, phosphocreatine, sarcoplasmic proteins – myoglobin, various enzyme proteins that stimulate oxidative phosphorylation, glycolysis, lipid metabolism, etc. (Kenney W.L. et al., 2012).

## TYPES AND FUNCTIONALITY OF MUSCLE FIBRES

Skeletal muscles have various types of muscle fibres, which differ in a large number of parameters - size, colour, excitation threshold, strength and speed of contraction, metabolism, glycogen storage, capillary density, enzymatic activity, energy supply features, fatigue, endurance, ability to hypertrophy, etc. These characteristics predetermine the division of muscle fibres into three main groups:

slow-twitch (red, oxidative) muscle fibres (ST), fast-twitch (fast oxidative) muscle fibres (FT-I), fast-twitch (fast glycolytic, white) muscle fibres (FT-II).

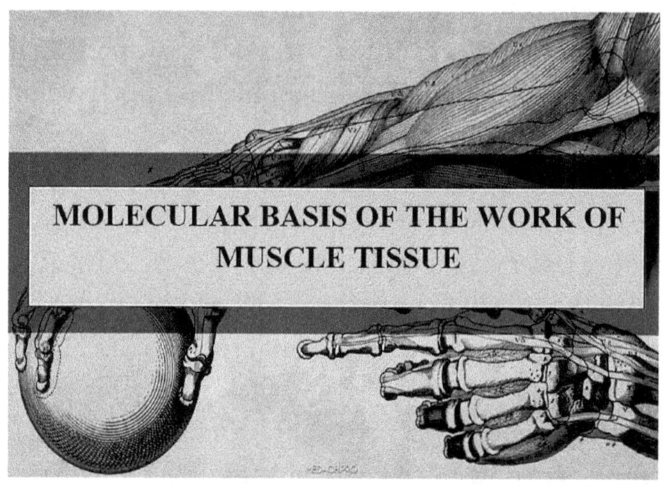


**Fig. 3** Molecular basis of the work of muscle tissue.
Source: https://medach.pro/post/1338

In muscle tissue, chemical energy is converted into mechanical work. As a source of energy for chemical bonds, ATP is used, which is obtained by muscle cells as a result of metabolic processes.

Slow-twitch muscle fibres (ST) are characterised by a low excitation threshold, a large number of mitochondria, and a large number of enzymes that ensure the oxidation of glucose and lipids with the formation of ATP. A wide capillary network and intensive blood supply give these fibres a red colour and provide conditions for aerobic energy supply to their activity. All this predetermines the resistance of slow-twitch fibres to fatigue and their main role in ensuring endurance in prolonged work. Only at maximum loads these fibres are capable of being involved in anaerobic glycolysis with the formation of lactate and the use of lactate as an energy source. Lactate from the bloodstream and intermediate tissue between muscle fibres is converted into pyruvate, which is oxidized in mitochondria (Hoffman J., 2002).

ST fibres provide posture retention of the body and bones of the skeleton. Postural muscles that ensure the stability of the lumbopelvic complex, the soleus muscle, etc., consist of fibres of this type (Macintosh B.R. et al., 2006)

Fast-twitch glycolytic muscle fibres (FT-II) are distinguished by their large thickness, increased sizes of the neurons innervating them, high excitation threshold, high speed of impulse conduction and speed of contraction, increased concentration of ATP and CrP, high power of anaerobic energy supply systems, high concentration of glycolytic enzymes, high strength, and speed-strength capabilities (McComas A.J., 2001; Kraemer W.J. et al., 2017).

The main energy pathways for these fibres are the ATP and CrP stores contained in the fibres and the glycolytic pathway for the formation of ATP for strength production by using muscle glycogen to form lactate. These fibres have a small number of mitochondria, a low ability to oxidize lactate and an exceptionally high ability to accumulate lactate – up to a 30-fold increase in relation to muscles at rest, which ensures high strength and speed of muscle contractions (Baechle T., Earle R., 2008).

Fast-twitch fibres of the intermediate type (FT-I) are distinguished by an increased ability for oxidative metabolism and endurance compared to FT-II muscle fibres. However, they are inferior to them in the speed of nerve impulse conduction, the possibilities of alactate and lactate energy supply systems, speed, speed-strength, and strength potential (Behnke R.S., 2001).

Compared to ST, FT-I muscle fibres are distinguished by a higher excitation threshold and speed of nerve impulse conduction, greater anaerobic and speed-strength capabilities. At the same time, they are characterised by lower oxidative capabilities, faster fatigue, and lower endurance for long-term work (Wilmore J.H., Costill D.L., 2009).

It should be noted that the division into muscle fibres of the three noted types is relatively arbitrary since there are fibres of an intermediate type – between ST and FT-I and between FT-I and FT-II (Kraemer W.J., 2017).

The rate of muscle fibre contraction depends on the myosin isoform characteristic of contractile fibres of various types. The contraction of fast-twitch fibres is provided by fast myosin, an isoform characterised by a high activity of ATPase, which determines the high rate of their contraction. The myosin isoform with low ATPase activity (slow myosin) is characteristic of slow-twitch muscle fibres (Guerrero M. et al., 2008). Thus, the properties of fast and slow muscle fibres are determined to a certain extent by the predominance of one or another isoform of myosin heavy chains in them, i.e., myosin phenotype (Shenkman B.S., 2016).

The heads of fast myosin molecules are characterised by enzymatic activity, which ensures the splitting of ATP with the formation of energy 4-5 times faster than the heads of slow myosin. Therefore, muscle fibres containing a large amount of fast myosin are able to contract with a short cycle of movement of the transverse bridges - in less than 0.1 s. Fibres with slow myosin are distinguished by a much longer cycle of transverse bridges and are able to contract only for 0.3-0.4 s (Shenkman B.S., 2016). Intensive splitting of ATP by fast myosins and a short cycle of movement of transverse bridges determine the high-speed strength capabilities of BS muscle fibres. However, there is no direct relationship between the number of fast twitch muscle fibres and the level of maximum or explosive strength, as there are a number of other factors that affect the manifestation of strength. The most important of them are the ability to involve a large number of muscle motor units in muscle activity and the frequency of their impulses (He ZH et al., 2000; Billeter R., Hoppeler H., 2003), the amplitude of movements and the breadth of the zone of interaction of actin and myosin myofilaments ( Sealey R.R. et al., 2007), the activity of muscle spindles and Golgi tendon organs (Dintiman G., Ward B., 2003), the level of muscle cell activation in the phases of transition from eccentric to concentric muscle work (Gamble P., 2013 ) etc.

In humans, the percentage of muscle fibres of different types can vary significantly in different muscles, which mainly depends on their function. For example, the muscles of the upper and lower extremities, the torso, which provide strength and power for motor actions, contain a large number of fast muscle fibres. In contrast, tonic muscles, which provide postural stability, are predominantly composed of slow-twitch muscle fibres. The ratio of muscle fibres of different types of muscles is genetically determined and does not change under the influence of training, which is extremely important for choosing a sports specialisation, working out models of competitive activity, the ratio of various means and methods of strength and speed training, and developing endurance (Wilmore J.H., Costill D.L., 2004; Platonov V.N., 2015; Kraemer W.J., Vingren J.L., 2017).

Features of the activation of motor units are determined by the amount of resistance (weight) and the speed of its overcoming. Minor burdens, movements at low-speed lead to the activation of only slow-twitch fibres. An increase in weights, speed and power of movements can ensure the involvement of fast-twitch fibres and, at the same time, suppress the activity of slow-twitch fibres that can adversely affect the speed and power of movements (Chu D.A., Myer G.D., 2013; Lloyd R.S., Oliver J.L., 2014). It is important to note that in movements and with heavy weights, the activation of motor units occurs gradually from small ones, with a low excitation threshold, to large ones, with a high excitation threshold (Kraemer W.J., Vingren J.L., 2017). When the threshold excitation reaches the level necessary for the activation of muscle fibres, all fibres of the motor unit are activated; if the threshold is not reached, none of the fibres is activated. However, this rule (the all-or-nothing law) applies only to the motor unit and not to the entire muscle (Sealey R.R. et al., 2007).

Muscle fibres of different types are characterised by different ways of energy supply. The contraction of fast-twitch fibres is provided mainly by the potential of the alactate (ATP and CRF) and lactate (anaerobic glycolysis) energy supply systems. These fibres have a larger diameter and are characterized by high activity of glycolytic enzymes, a significant amount of glycogen, an underdeveloped capillary network, low activity of oxidative enzymes, and a small number of mitochondria. Lactic acid formed as a result of glycolysis is excreted into the intercellular space.

Slow-twitch muscle fibres are small, contain a lot of myoglobin, and are surrounded by a dense capillary network. A large number of mitochondria of these fibres are characterised by a high activity of oxidative enzymes. All this predetermines the aerobic mechanism of ATP formation.

Characterisation of the structural and functional features of muscle fibres of various types should underlie the rational construction of training aimed at improving various strength qualities. Knowledge in this area reveals the possibilities of various muscle fibres for adaptive restructuring, which determines the level of development of speed (explosive and sprint) and maximum strength, strength endurance. It is possible to preferentially stimulate the speed of the flow of a nerve impulse both in a neuron and a muscle cell, aimed at the development of myofibrillar or sarcoplasmic hypertrophy, the effect on strengthening the actin and myosin filaments of myofibrils, the strength and speed of the interaction of actin and myosin myofilaments in sarcomeres, expanding the energy potential of muscle fibres, which determines both the level of manifestation of maximum and speed strength, and different types of strength endurance (Macintosh B.R. et al., 2006; Wilmore J.H., Costill D.L., 2009; Lloyd R.S. et al., 2014; Kraemer W.J. et al., 2017).

It is important to note that, despite the genetic predetermination of the structure and functions of muscle fibres of various types, the training process of a significant orientation can lead to a certain restructuring of muscle fibres and a change in their functionality. In particular, intense aerobic work, leading to pronounced fatigue, involves not only FT-I muscle fibres but also FT-II muscle fibres in its performance, stimulating adaptive reactions in them that are characteristic of ST fibres (Bouchard C., Rankinen T., 2001). In these fibres, the capillary network expands, the activity of enzymes that stimulate oxidative processes increases, etc. At the same time, processes that provide the speed-strength potential of fast-twitch fibres are suppressed (Carl D., 2008). Such changes can negatively affect the sprint capabilities of athletes and reduce the effectiveness of actions that require the manifestation of high power (Platonov V.N., 2017).

On the contrary, a large number of speed-strength exercises associated with the manifestation of the power of movements in a wide range of speeds, weights and muscle work modes, including plyometric and ballistic, leads not only to a significant increase in the speed-strength capabilities of FT-I muscle fibres, but also to noticeable changes in the level of maximum and speed strength of the ST of muscle fibres (Platonov V.N., 2017). At the same time, the leading role in the restructuring of muscle fibres is played by changes in the nature of motor neuron impulses, leading to the restructuring of the myosin phenotype of muscle fibres (Shenkman B.S., 2016)

## MUSCLE CONTRACTION

The nervous system regulates skeletal muscle activity by transmitting electrical impulses from axons to muscle cells. Impulses which are sufficient to excite muscle fibres form action potentials.

The first stage of muscle contraction is the emergence of an action potential, which propagates at a speed of several meters per second and becomes an irritating source for the muscle fibre membrane. The second stage covers the propagation of the action potential from the cell membrane to sarcomeres – the contractile elements of the muscle fibre. In the third stage, the electrical signal of the action potential is converted into a chemical signal, and the processes of interaction between actin and myosin myofilaments take place. Muscle contraction is provided by sliding of actin filaments along myosin filaments. When the sarcomere is activated, actin and myosin filaments are connected in the form of transverse bridges. These bridges are formed by myosin heads, which attach to the myosin-binding sites of the actin myofilament and, due to the hinged nature of the myosin neck, propel the actin filament to the centre of the sarcomere. The pulling movements of the myosin head pull the thin sarcomere filaments together, which pull the Z-lines along, causing the sarcomere to contract. In the process of contraction, the cross bridges repeatedly attach, bend, and create force, moving the thread along the thread, then detach and re-attach. The force developed by the muscle is proportional to the degree of mutual overlap of the myosin and actin filaments and their interaction in the overlapped area. The leading role in this process is played by myosin heads, which work like miniature paddles, using the energy of ATP hydrolysis present in the muscle cell (Shenkman B.S., 2016).

Sarcomeres can shorten by 20-50% during maximum muscle contraction. This shortening is provided by the convergence of the sarcomere membranes as a result of the sliding of actin and myosin filaments relative to one another and their mutual overlap. At the same time, the length of thick and thin threads does not change (Kenney W.L. et al., 2012).

Thus, the production of force is the main function of muscle fibres – large cells 80% filled with a contracting organelle - myofibrils, which often cover the entire length of the muscle fibre and represent a linear series of sarco-meres. Sarcomeres are contracting units consisting of lon-gitudinal thin and thick filaments, located between the so-called Z-discs. The main protein of thick filaments is myosin (60-65% of muscle protein), thin – actin (20-25%

of muscle protein). The interaction of these proteins underlies muscle contraction. Among the myosin filaments that work in muscles, there are fast and slow filaments. Fast filaments, characteristic of fast twitch muscle fibres, provide a faster and stronger contraction. Slow threads are characterised by lower contractility and greater endurance. They predominate in slow-twitch muscle fibres. The simultaneous sliding of thousands of sarcomeres leads to a change in the length of the muscle fibre and the development of strength in this cell (Kenney W.L. et al., 2012).

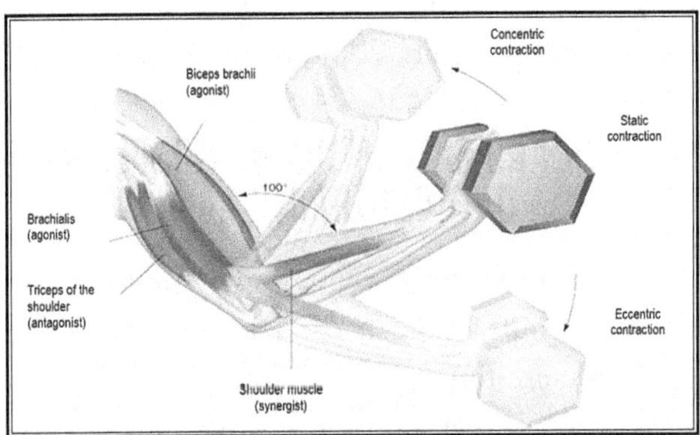


**Fig. 4** Muscle Contraction
Source:https://ro.pinterest.com/pin/472315079646632983/?amp_client_
id=CLIENT_ID(_)&mweb_unauth_id=&from_amp_pin_page=true

Coordination of the contraction of millions of muscle fibres in the skeletal muscle is achieved by combining muscle fibres into functional units (motor units), controlled by the central nervous system through the motor nerve, the body of which is located in the motor areas of the brain or spinal cord, passes into a long axon that reaches the muscle and expands at the end, innervating many muscle fibres. The innervation of each fibre is carried out through a single nerve ending (synapse) located approximately in the middle of the muscle fibre. An electrical impulse propagating along the axon at a speed of several meters per second leads to a series of reactions, the end result of which is the contraction of the muscle fibre. The energy for muscle contraction is provided by the breakdown of ATP by the enzyme ATPase. The energy released in this reaction allows the myosin heads to attach to the actin myofilament, forming transverse bridges, and to ensure its sliding over the myosin to the centre of the sarcomere (Billeter R., Hoppeler H., 2003; Sealy R.R. et al., 2007).

## EXCITATION AND SUMMATION OF MUSCLE MOTOR UNIT CONTRACTIONS

Excitation of a muscle by a single stimulus causes a single muscle contraction in the structure, with the following phases: excitation phase, latent phase, contraction, and relaxation. The strength of stimulation determines the number of motor units of muscles covered by excitation. The greater the force of stimulation, the greater the number of muscle fibres that respond by contraction.

Under natural conditions, the muscle contracts under the influence of no single but constantly arriving impulses, leading to tetanic contraction (tetanus). There is dentate and smooth tetanus. When the next impulse enters the relaxation phase of the muscle, dentate tetanus occurs. Smooth tetanus occurs when the next impulse coincides with the contraction phase. Smooth tetanus is optimal for the manifestation of strength, providing an increase in muscle excitation with each next nerve impulse (Sealy R.R. et al., 2007).

The duration of the phase of depolarization of the cell membrane of a muscle cell as a result of the development of an action potential that provides contraction of the muscle fibre is very short and is only 3–5 ms. In this phase, the muscle fibre membrane is in a state of reduced excitability. Then comes repolarization - the process of returning the potential difference on the membrane of the muscle cell to the level that preceded its depolarization. Until the state of the muscle cell returns to its original level, it is immune to the next stimulus.

Considering that muscle shortening in response to the generation of an action potential is several times longer than the "depolarization-repolarization" cycle, against the background of developing contraction on the muscle fibre membrane, it is possible to induce next cycles of excitation leading to the appearance of a summing contraction (Kraemer W.J. et al., 2017). The ability to intensify the process of receipt of nerve impulses from motor neurons to the motor units of the muscles, leading to the summation of the waved efforts, significantly increases the force of tetanic muscle contraction.

## ACTIVATION OF MUSCLE MOTOR UNITS

An exceptionally important factor determining the level of various types of strength qualities is the ability of the nervous system to activate the maximum number of muscle motor units involved in a particular movement. Each activated motor unit, consisting of one type of fibre, produces force. Non-activated motor units move passively, following the activated ones, not only not facilitating but also, to some extent, preventing the manifestation of force (Kraemer W.J., Vingren J.L., 2017).

The ability of the neuromuscular system to recruit the maximum possible number of muscle motor units, which ensure the efficiency of motor actions, plays a major role in the development of strength per unit of muscle cross-sectional area. At the same time, all components of the muscles and connective tissue are strengthened, contributing to resistance to injury and overstrain, as well as accelerating recovery reactions (DeLuca C.J. et al., 1982; Sealy R.R. et al., 2007).

Numerous studies have shown that under the influence of rationally organised strength training, the ability of athletes to mobilize the number of motor units of agonists and synergists can increase significantly. In people who are not involved in sports, when performing exercises that require the maximum level of manifestation of strength, 50–60% of the motor units of the working muscles are involved in the work (Hoffman J., 2002; Platonov V.N., 2017). As a result of training, this amount can reach 90% or more (McComas A.J., 2001; Alter M.J., 2001; Kenney W.L. et al., 2012).

An increase in the number of agonists and synergists involved in the work, which is a consequence of training, is closely related to an increase in the strength capabilities of athletes (Sale D.G., 1992; Fujii S. et al., 2009) and an improvement in intermuscular coordination. This manifests itself in most cases both in a decrease in the activity of antagonist muscles and an increase in the efficiency of work – with standard power loads, qualified athletes have less muscle activity (Kato K., Kanosue K., 2015).

Features of activation of motor units determine both the peak level of manifestation of strength and the rate of development of strength (Huber A. et al., 1998; Becker S., Awiszus F., 2001). The excitation process of muscle motor units can include various levels of regulation – from the spinal cord to the motor cortex (Sale D.G., 2003). Motor unit activation deficiency is different in different muscles and for different modes of their activity – isometric, concentric, eccentric (Westing S.H. et al., 1990; Sale D.G., 2003). These differences may be due to many factors of biomechanical, morphological, and psycho-emotional nature, the volume and content of previous muscle activity (Herbert R.D., Gandevia S.C., 1999).

The lack of muscle activation is manifested to a much greater extent in complex motor actions compared to simple ones. In simple motor actions (for example, the bench press), untrained individuals, compared with trained individuals, have a smaller activation deficit than in complex ones that require the involvement of large muscle volumes in the work with various types of muscle activity and different speeds of movement.

An important point in the improvement of neuroregulatory manifestations of strength is a decrease in the activation of antagonists, which accompanies a high level of tension of agonists and synergists. However, when performing complex movements with maximum or close power loads, the increased activity of agonists and synergists is often accompanied by an increase in the activation of antagonists (Aagaard P. et al., 1996). This effect is due to the provision of stability in the joints, statodynamic stability of the body as a whole, the achievement of a rational direction of force application, as well as a warning reaction in relation to the risk of injury to muscle and connective tissues (Sale D.G., 2003).

The speciality literature pays a lot of attention to the means and methods that contribute to increasing the ability to activate the largest possible number of muscle motor units. It has been shown that an increase in weights is accompanied by an intensity of neural stimulation of muscle motor units. Activation of motor units with a high threshold of excitation, consisting of FT muscle fibres, requires a lot of muscle tension, which determines the number of weights – 60-70% or more. High tension, involving fast-twitch muscle fibres into work, also activates slow-twitch ones, which have a low threshold (Schuenke M.D. et al., 2013). The maximum possible activation of muscle tissue for a particular person is caused by exercises with near-limit weights (90% or more of the maximum available), performed in the form of several series (4-6) of 6-8 repetitions each and with a short rest between series (usually about 1 min) (Kraemer W.J. et al., 2017). Also, a series of exercises lead to the depletion of energy sources for muscle contractions, the accumulation of intermediate metabolic products in them, severe fatigue, often to injury of muscle fibres, nervous and connective tissues

(Wilmore J.H., Costill D.L., 2009). It is clear that under such conditions, the maximum available activation of muscle motor units is also noted (Kraemer W.J. et al., 2017). However, such work, typical for bodybuilding, is inappropriate for martial arts and other sports as it limits speed-strength capabilities, does not allow mastering effective technique, negatively affects endurance, agility, and coordination, and is fraught with serious injuries (Platonov V.N., 2017). Therefore, when it comes to developing the ability to activate motor units in wrestlers, research should be carried out in the direction of using methods and means that allow the development of the maximum power of movements and motor actions with a high manifestation of both speed and power components, reflecting the specifics of motor actions. As evidenced by numerous indirect data, there are several ways to activate muscle activity (Hoffman J., 2002; Clark C.B., Taylor L.J., 2011; Platonov V.N., 2017). In this regard, the use of plyometric and isometric methods can be especially effective (Kawamori N. et al., 2006; Lloyd R.S. et al., 2011; Moir G.L., 2012; Chu D.A., Myer G.D., 2013).

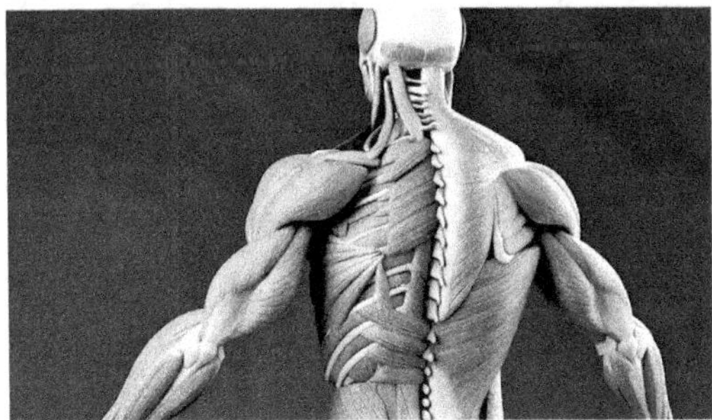

Fig. 5 Human muscular system of the back
Source: https://justsport.info/fitness/tipy-myshechnykh-volokon

Each type of muscle fibre is trained in a specific way. The more fast-twitch fibres in the athlete's muscles, the higher his sprint capabilities.

Muscle spindles and Golgi tendon organs in the manifestation and development of strength qualities are the two most important neuroregulatory mechanisms of muscle activity, without which it is impossible to provide effective training that promotes the development of these qualities. These mechanisms are provided by the action of mechanoreceptors located in the muscles and tendons. Muscles contain receptors (muscle spindles), which are specific muscle fibres that are excited during rapid muscle lengthening. These fibres, which can be up to 10 cm long, are attached to and located between ordinary muscle fibres. When muscles are rapidly stretched, muscle spindles send appropriate signals to the spinal cord and cause a response that causes the muscles to contract reflexively, preventing them from stretching, ensuring against injuries and overloads (Kraemer W.J., Vingren J.L., 2017). In this regard, it is clear that in real conditions of sports activity, which require high-speed movements with the corresponding stretching and contraction of muscles, this mechanism restrains the amplitude of movements, does not allow effective performance of motor actions using the plyometric mode, and limits the manifestation of strength qualities (Chu DA et al., 2006; Platonov V.N., 2017). Therefore, it is quite natural that in the process of developing strength qualities and flexibility, attention should be paid to the danger of this reaction in relation to restraining muscle stretching, with its subsequent limiting effect on the amplitude of movements and the level of force manifested in the depreciation phase (transition from muscle stretching to muscle contraction) and the concentric phase following it (Chu DA et al., 2006).

Special training allows to blunt the activity of this neuroregulatory mechanism and increase the range of motion, creating the necessary prerequisites for the transition from eccentric to concentric work. It becomes possible to obtain the effect of accumulation of elastic energy of stretched muscles and connective tissue, as well as a number of advantages due to the plyometric nature of the manifestation of strength qualities (Korff T. et al., 2009).

Such training is based on a systematic increase in the speed-strength characteristics of movements, taking into account the age characteristics of those involved, their skill level, and previous motor experience. A variety of exercises, resistance values, and speed characteristics with a systematic complication of training programs underlies training that limits the protective reaction and, at the same time, ensures muscles and connective tissue from injuries (Platonov V.N., 2017).

Limitation of power manifestations can also be associated with the reactions of tendon mechanoreceptors. These receptors, called the Golgi tendon organs, are located in the zone of transition of muscle fibres into tendons. In the case of high muscle tension, which is fraught with their overload and injury, the Golgi tendon organs send signals to the spinal cord that cause a defensive response - a reflex decrease in the activity of tense muscles and activation of antagonist muscles that limit their contraction (Sealy R.R. et al., 2007).

Experts believe that a special training focused on minimising the protective activity of the muscle spindles and Golgi tendon organs, which limit the manifestation of strength, may be effective for the manifestation of strength qualities (Kraemer W.J., Vingren J.L., 2017). However, this requires the development of an appropriate methodology for the development of such abilities since it is clear that monotonous work with heavy weights, which contributes to the development of maximum strength and power of movements with appropriate muscle tension and mobilisation of the nervous system, cannot have a significant restraining effect on the activity of mechanoreceptors of muscles and tendons.

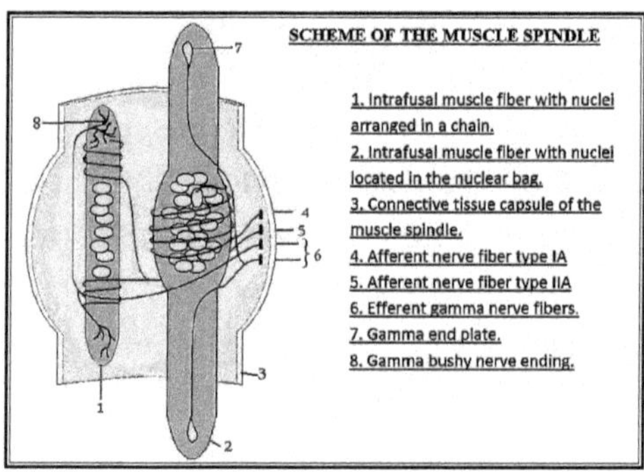


**Fig. 6** Scheme of the muscle spindle
Source: https://ru.wikipedia.org/wiki.jpg

## MICROTRAUMA OF MUSCLE TISSUE AND ACTIVATION OF MYOSATELLITES

Specialists researching strength training, especially in association with muscle hypertrophy, have a very peculiar attitude towards injury to muscle and connective tissues caused by maximum power loads. Injury to muscle fibres, pain and loss of function are often perceived as a natural stimulating response, causing intense adaptive processes that contribute to the restoration of damaged tissues.

Excessive power loads lead to damage of muscle fibres, leading to a change in their structure and functionality. The membranes of the muscle fibre and sarcomeres are damaged, which leads to the destruction of myofibrils. The sarcoplasmic reticulum is also damaged. These injuries, accompanied by tumours, inflammatory processes, significantly affect strength capabilities and also stimulate the breakdown of damaged myofibrillar proteins and their removal from the structure of myofilaments (Guerrero M. et al., 2008).

The elimination of these symptoms within a few days after the injury is perceived as a normal reaction to the training process, leading to changes in muscle tissue, increasing its volume and level of maximum strength. Only chronic and severe damage to muscle and connective tissues is perceived as a problem requiring medical intervention (Kraemer W.J. et al., 2017; Harmon K.K. et al., 2017).

Injury to muscle fibres (destruction of cell membranes and sarcomeres, inflammatory processes, tumours, etc.) is mostly associated with the use of maximum weights (1–2 RM) in concentric work and 120% of 1 RM in eccentric work. Serial performance of exercises with heavy weights and short pauses is also traumatic, for example, 6 series of 6–8 repetitions with a load of 90% of the maximum and pauses between sets of 30-60 s (Gamble P., 2013).

The adaptation-stimulating effect of muscle micro-trauma is perceived as an important part of the training methodology aimed at developing strength and increasing muscle mass (Fragala M.S. et al., 2011; Lewis P.B. et al., 2012). Experts see the problem only in finding the boundary between "good" and "bad" micro-trauma and inflammation. However, the very need for muscle injury, which causes a complex of protective reactions, seems necessary (Kraemer W.J., 2017). Moreover, the so-called "destruction theory" of muscle tissue is developing and gaining popularity in practice (Protasenko V., 2013), muscle injury being perceived as the main stress that stimulates hypertrophy and leads to success in competitions, despite the fact that the damage to muscle tissue is based on mechanical, not metabolic mechanisms (Nicol C., Komi PV, 2003). The disorganisation of the processes occurring in the muscle fibre, the destruction of myofibrils as a result of hydrolysis of the structural proteins of actin and myosin filaments, sarco-tubular systems and other disorders are the result of excessive muscle tension, causing a complex and multi-stage reaction of the immune system, designed to limit the area of damage, restore structure and function, cleanse the injured area of microorganisms and decay products of damaged muscle cells (McBride K. et al., 2002; Nicol C., Komi PV, 2003).

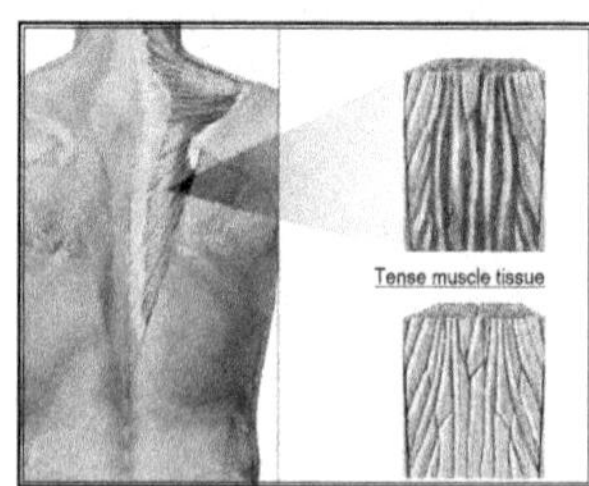


**Fig.7** Muscle crepitus. Who is to blame, and what to do?
Source: https://fotostrana.ru/public/post/231906/1403557692/

The main mechanism for the regeneration of damaged muscle tissue and the development of adaptive reactions under the influence of power loads is the activation of satellite cells (myosatellites) located on the outer surface of muscle fibres. Usually, they are inactive and are activated only when the muscle fibres are injured. These cells multiply and are attracted to damaged areas of the muscles, promoting their regeneration, transferring their nuclei and increasing the amount of contractile proteins. An increase in the number of myonuclei in myosatellites precedes the development of muscle hypertrophy (Bruusgaard J.C. et al., 2010). Even a single training session with a large total load of a power nature, leading to muscle microtrauma, can activate satellite cells and involve them in the process of regeneration and hypertrophy of muscle fibres (Blaauw B., Reggiani C., 2014).

Significant response of muscles subjected to excessively intense load, leading to microtraumas and involvement of myosatellites in adaptation and rehabilitation processes, is a significant increase in the satellite cells themselves in the skeletal muscle. Thus, the hypertrophy of injured fibres, due to the inclusion in the process of their rehabilitation, is supplemented by hypertrophy caused by the appearance of new satellite cells (Kadi F., 2008).

The mechanisms that cause the activation of satellite cells, as well as the processes of their fusion with damaged muscle fibres, are not yet fully understood. However, this does not pose issues related to the strength training of athletes. For this, it is enough to understand that myosatellites have a huge potential for regeneration and hypertrophy of skeletal muscle. Still, there is uncertainty to how expedient it is to use this potential in sports and how its use affects the structure of sarcoplasm and myofibrils, contractile capabilities of sarcomeres, neuroregulatory activation of muscles, automatisms of motor actions, and various types of coordination abilities. These questions clearly arise when we turn to the practice of bodybuilding, where the training methodology is largely based on overload and microtrauma of muscle tissue in order to activate myosatellites, as the most important reaction that stimulates the regeneration and hypertrophy of muscle tissue.

It is impossible not to see the negative impact of excessive muscle hypertrophy, achieved by non-specific motor actions which to not follow strict technical and tactical principles, the inevitable violation of muscle memory, which largely determines the effectiveness of training and competitive activities of athletes. It is known that muscle fibres have their own memory, closely related to their nuclear structure, the restructuring of which, under the influence of the activity of accompanying cells and the processes of regeneration of muscle fibres, cannot but affect the regulation of muscle activity (Brownsgard J.C., 2010).

Noting the huge role of muscle micro-trauma, its role in muscle regeneration and hypertrophy of myosatellites, which is characteristic of athletes specialising in bodybuilding, one cannot help but see the low performance of these athletes in all matters related to speed, speed-strength, coordination abilities, various types of endurance, which results in the numerous but unsuccessful attempts of bodybuilders with huge muscle mass and maximum strength to prove themselves in weightlifting, wrestling or track and field throwing (Platonov V.N., 2004, 2015).

Therefore, when it comes to the strength training of athletes specialising in wrestling, there is a need to develop a methodology that leads to an increase in strength, the development of moderate but not excessive hypertrophy, without muscle injury, and the subsequent process of muscle tissue regeneration.

## THE HORMONAL STATUS OF THE ATHLETE'S BODY AND ITS USE TO INCREASE THE EFFECTIVENESS OF STRENGTH TRAINING

The development of various strength qualities cannot be considered without taking into account the hormonal environment that accompanies the training activity and finding ways to use it to increase the effectiveness of the training process. Naturally, it is important to consider hormones that affect the regulation of protein metabolism in muscles and the entire spectrum of neuroregulatory, morphological, physiological, biochemical, and contractile processes that ensure the level of development of strength qualities – testosterone, somatotropic hormone, insulin-like growth factor 1 (IGF-1), insulin, and cortisol. It is clear that we can only talk about the natural hormonal environment associated with active training activity and not its artificial formation by introducing artificial drugs related to doping agents into the body of athletes and subject to a strict ban on their use.

Optimisation of the hormonal status aiming an increase in the level of anabolic hormones associated with muscle mass and strength capabilities (testosterone, insulin, somatotropin, insulin-like growth factor (IGF-1), a decrease in the level of catabolic processes caused by an increase in the concentration of cortisol, contribute to the formation of hormonal reactions that stimulate the synthesis protein and an increase in the contractile capabilities of muscle tissue (Volek J.S., Sharman M.J., 2008), as well as the activation of a wide range of other reactions associated with an increase in the neuroregulatory and contractile capabilities of muscle fibres (Kenney WL et al., 2012; Kraemer et al., 2017).

Adaptive processes in muscle, connective and bone tissues in response to hard work of a power nature are largely determined by hormonal reactions in response to the training programs used. Resistance exercises designed to develop strength stimulate hormonal responses that promote muscle, connective, and bone tissue remodelling. Despite the lack of clear evidence about the role of various hormones in the adaptation processes associated with the development of strength qualities, their influence on the effectiveness of the training process is obvious (Wilmore J.H., Costill D.L., 2004; Platonov V.N., 2015).

The magnitude of hormonal activity is closely related to the training load, the volume, and the intensity of work. It has been established that the intensity of the hormonal response is directly related to the volume of muscles involved in the training. This effect is manifested in relation to any muscle group. For example, hypertrophy of the muscles of the upper extremities will be significantly higher if exercises for the muscles of the arms are performed in parallel with exercises for other muscle groups (Ronnestad B.R. et al., 2011).

The highest hormonal response that stimulates hypertrophy of muscle cells is provided by fairly large weights (80% or more), series of strength exercises (3-4 sets of 6-12 repetitions), relatively short pauses between sets (1-2 minutes) and exercises involving large muscle volumes (Kraemer W.J., 2017).

Great physical activity leads not only to high hormonal activity during exercise but also determines a pronounced hormonal response in the recovery period, especially during the first hours after exercise (Eliakim A., 2008).

It is clear that increased hormonal activity both during training sessions and in the recovery period after them can be used to purposefully increase the effectiveness of the training process, in particular, in relation to strength qualities. A large amount of evidence is already available in this regard, indicating the effect of the concentration of insulin, testosterone, growth hormone, insulin-like growth factor 1 on protein synthesis, muscle hypertrophy and increase in the level of maximum strength, as well as the effect of cortisol on muscle catabolism caused by excessive loads, ways of ensuring the predominance of anabolic processes over catabolic ones (Viru A., Viru M., 2008; Vingren J.L. et al., 2010; Damas F. et al., 2015).

**Fig. 8** Bodybuilding Trainer
Source: http://izhevsk-news.net/other/2019/11/16/157514.html

**Testosterone.** Testosterone is a male sex hormone synthesized by the testes, in a small amount by the ovaries in women, and also by the adrenal cortex of men and women. Testosterone provides virilisation processes and promotes the development of muscle and bone tissue. Strenuous exercise of a power nature leads to the penetration of testosterone into the muscle cell, where it binds to androgen receptors located on DNA in the nuclei of the muscle fibre, providing anabolic signals that stimulate an increase in the size of the muscle fibre (Wilmore J.H., Costill, D. L., 2009).

The action of testosterone is androgenic and anabolic in nature. Androgenic properties of testosterone are manifested in the development of secondary sexual characteristics while anabolic in an increase in muscle mass. Testosterone in its natural form is rapidly degraded.

For many years, including recent years, active research work has been going on to find a drug that works like testosterone but remains in the body for a long time and is also characterised by increased anabolic activity and does not suppress androgenic activity. Manufactured steroids with reduced androgenic activity are defined as "anabolic", while those with increased androgenic activity are considered "androgenic".

The main effect of steroids on the muscle cells is to increase protein synthesis and counteract the decomposition of muscle proteins. Steroids suppress the activity of cortisol, which has a catabolic effect, and also intensify the process of synthesis of CrF in the muscle cell, increasing the potential of the anaerobic alactic system; inhibits lipid consumption, stimulates lipolysis, and also activates some other processes associated with functional readiness (Viru A., Viru M., 2008).

Testosterone activates the secretion of insulin-like growth factor I (IGF-1) and erythropoietin, thus indirectly affecting athletic performance. Undoubtedly, the influence of testosterone on the psyche of athletes – aggressiveness, irrational confidence in one's invincibility, overcoming a feeling of severe fatigue – gives undoubted advantages in competitive activity in many sports (Fridl, 2008).

A single exercise that requires a high level of strength and power does not lead to a significant increase in the concentration of testosterone in the blood. However, a series of several approaches (from 3-5) already causes a significant increase in the content of testosterone in the blood – from 20 to 40% (Schwabetal., 1993; Viru A., Viru M., 2008). However, the greatest answer is given by the total impact of the magnitude of power loads in each exercise and a fairly large total amount of power work of both concentric and eccentric nature in the lesson (Fleck,

Kraemer, 1997; Durandetal., 2003). Despite the fact that the mechanisms of testosterone action require further study, and many aspects of its influence are at the level of assumptions, the intense effect of testosterone on neuroregulatory and metabolic processes that determine the level of strength is obvious.

The increase in testosterone concentration stimulated by physical exercises of a strength nature is temporary, so that an hour after the end of the exercise program, it begins to return to the initial level and may even fall below it, returning to final values after 24-72 hours (Hackney, 1996; Remy, 2008). Aerobic exercise does not significantly increase serum testosterone levels (Kraemer, 1992).

The effectiveness of adaptive reactions caused by an increase in testosterone concentration after strenuous training sessions is closely related to the availability of metabolic substrates, which determines the importance of the nature of nutrition and the relationship of food consumption with training programs and the recovery period (Remy, 2008; Vingren J.L. et al., 2010).

**Somatotropic hormone.** This growth hormone (somatotropin) is secreted by the anterior pituitary gland and belongs to the group of polypeptide hormones. In children, adolescents, and young people, it has a pronounced acceleration of growth, mainly due to the tubular bones of the limbs. It enhances protein synthesis and inhibits its decay, promotes an increase in muscle and a decrease in adipose tissue, stimulates the absorption of calcium by bone tissue, and the growth of cartilage tissue. Participation in carbohydrate metabolism is manifested in an increase in blood glucose levels (Viru A., Viru M., 2008; Vingren J.L. et al., 2010).

The effects of the somatotropic hormone are associated with a series of adaptive reactions that contribute to the manifestation of strength – an increase in growth and the strengthening of bone tissue, its regeneration after injuries, an increase in the ratio of lean tissue to fat, an increase in the muscle mass and connective tissues (Fridl K.E., 2008; and others.). There is reason to believe that an increase in the concentration of the somatotropic hormone can promote the development of fast myosin isoforms, which can increase the speed-strength potential of BS-II muscle fibres (Kadi F., 2008).

## SYMPTOMS OF TESTOSTERONE DEFICIENCY

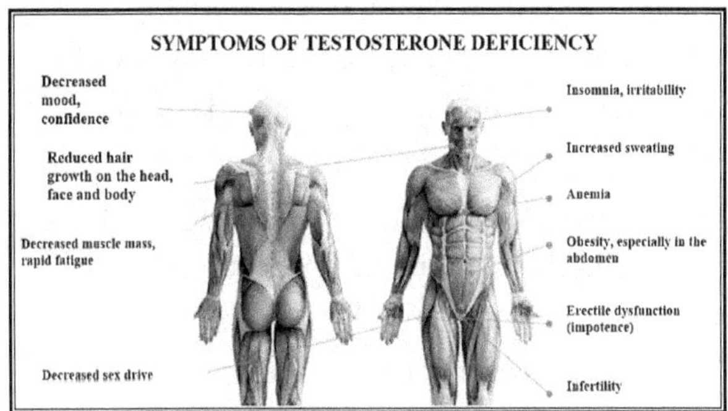


**Fig. 9** Symptoms of testosterone deficiency
Source: https://mordex.net/news/kak-povysit-testosteron-u-muzh-chin-i-u-zhenshchin

The secretion of somatotropin is closely related to the intensity and duration of physical activity. Short and low intensity exercise (up to the level of the anaerobic metabolism threshold) cannot cause a metabolic effect to stimulate the secretion of somatotropin. On the contrary, training with heavy loads of a power nature, as well as loads of anaerobic glycolytic nature, leading to a decrease in blood glucose levels, intensifies the release of somatotropic hormone both during training sessions and in the immediate recovery period after their completion. On the contrary, carbohydrate saturation, leading to an increase in the concentration of glucose in the blood, reduces the concentration of somatotropic hormone in tissues. Under the influence of loads, as well as drugs that stimulate the secretion of growth hormone, its concentration in the blood can increase by 10-15 or more times relative to the baseline (Kraemer et al., 2017).

Stimulation of somatotropin secretion by physical activity already manifests itself 10-15 minutes after the start of the session, and by the end, it reaches its maximum values (Wideman et al., 2000; Veltman et al., 2008). At the same time, a linear relationship is noted between the level of somatotropin secretion and the intensity of work (Pritzlaff-Roy et al., 2002; Nindl et al., 2003). An increased amount of growth hormone can persist, gradually decreasing, for a long time – up to 24 hours (Veltman et al., 2008).

The anabolic action of somatotropin manifests itself synchronously with the action of insulin, a reduced level of which limits the action of growth hormone, and suppresses the anabolic effect of somatotropin and cortisol, a steroidal glucocorticoid hormone secreted by the adrenal cortex (Rootetal, 1998).

Athletes are interested, of course, in the ability of the growth hormone to increase muscle mass and promote fat burning.

**Fig. 10** Growth hormone

Source: https://sportivnoepitanie.ru/somatotropin-gormon-rosta-i-proporcij/

**Insulin-like growth factor 1 (IGF-1)** is an insulin-like anabolic protein. IGF-1 is secreted by the liver, muscles, and other tissues largely under the influence of the somatotropic hormone and contributing to the implementation of its function (Eliakim A. et al., 2008). IGF-1 is similar in its action to somatotropin. Both hormones promote protein synthesis and increase muscle mass and strength, bone mass and density. That is why these hormones are often presented in the form of the "GH-IGF-1 system".

Stimulation of this system by motor activity leads not only to an increase in protein synthesis but also increases the activity of the cardiorespiratory system, providing a close correlation between the level of VO2max and the blood levels of growth hormone and IGF-1 (Eliakim A. et al., 2008), increases glucose uptake, suppresses lipolysis (Siddalsetal., 2002; Nindle, Rierse, 2010).

The use of IGF-1 secreted by the liver is problematic in relation to the processes occurring in the muscles. Therefore, IGF-1, expressed in muscles in response to mechanical stimuli, is designated as a mechano-dependent growth factor (MPF), which has specific features that require it to be characterised separately from liver IGF-1, despite their certain similarity. At the same time, it can be expected that MFR produced in specific muscles will stimulate effects in the muscles that produced it (Goldspink et al., 2008).

An increase in the level of IGF-1 in the blood is observed already 10 minutes after the start of intense physical activity, i.e., much earlier than it happens with the somatotropic hormone. Unlike somatotropin, the content of which fluctuates significantly, the concentration of JGF-1 during and after exercise is quite stable (Kadi F., 2008). An increased content of IGF-1 in the blood after exercise is observed much longer than in the case of the somatotropic hormone (Schwantzetal., 1996; Kraemeretal., 2000).

Interestingly, the recovery of IGF-1 levels after a period of strenuous training occurs in parallel with the self-assessment of physical condition and is one of the criteria for an athlete's readiness for competition or strenuous training. A stable decrease in the level of IGF-1 in the blood can be considered as one of the factors indicating the development of overtraining and, in young athletes, a slowdown in growth processes (Eliakim A. et al., 2008).

Insulin is a peptide hormone secreted in the pancreas and has a wide spectrum of action on metabolic processes. The hormone activates the consumption of amino acids, stimulates protein synthesis and prevents its breakdown, promotes an increase in glucose transport and glycogen synthesis (Volek D.S., Sharman M.D., 2008; Kraemer

W.J., 2017). It is important that the stimulating effect of insulin on protein synthesis is manifested only in the presence of a sufficient amount of amino acids (Kimbal et al., 2002). Motor activity significantly enhances the effect of insulin, which stimulates hypertrophy, energy and contractility of the muscle cell, a short-term increase in muscle protein synthesis (Ho et al., 2008). A decrease in insulin levels leads to a sharp increase in the intensity of lipolysis (Kersten, 2001).

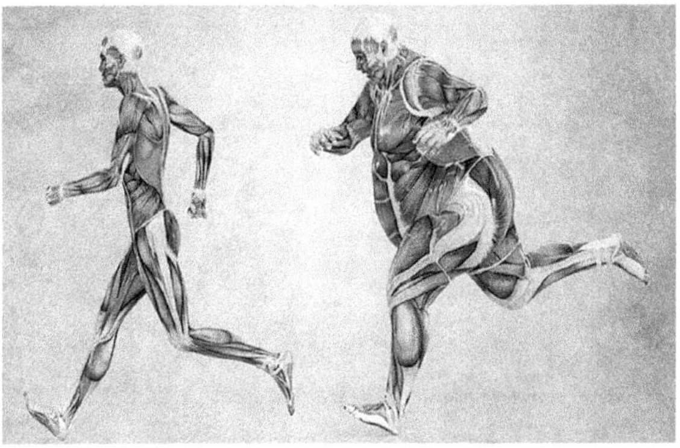

**Fig. 11** Insulin builds muscle. Insulin stimulates protein synthesis by activating its production by ribosomes.
Source: https://www.nanonewsnet.ru/articles/2016/gormon-insulin-vsechto-vam-neobkhodimo-znat

**Cortisol** is a glucocorticoid hormone of a steroid nature, secreted by the adrenal cortex and contributing to the conservation of energy resources in the body, providing an increase in the amount of glycogen in the liver, a decrease in the breakdown of glucose in the muscles, and involvement of adipose tissue in energy supply. Cortisol limits protein synthesis, its action is associated with protein catabolism, limiting muscle hypertrophy. Cortisol is a hormone that responds to stress and stimulates gluconeogenesis, that is, the formation of glucose from free fatty acids and amino acids, and it inhibits the consumption of glucose by body cells. High cortisol concentrations are characteristic of excessively strenuous training, imbalance between exercise and rest, overwork, and recovery. Its action can block anabolic processes in the muscles and develop overstrain, leading to the predominance of catabolic processes over anabolic ones (Spiering et al., 2008; Szivak et al., 2013).

**Fig. 12** Cortisol in bodybuilding
Source: https://genetics.uz/ru/gormon-stressa-kortizol/

## HORMONAL ENVIRONMENT AND FOOD INTAKE

The most important direction of using the hormonal response to physical activity as a factor stimulating adaptive reactions is the study of its relationship with the composition and orientation of training means and methods, food consumption. Research on this issue, in relation to the development of strength qualities, is presented in a fairly large number of publications of a consistent nature, mainly reflecting the relationship between the activity of

122

anabolic hormones (insulin, testosterone, somatotropic hormone, insulin-like growth factor 1) and protein synthesis, muscle hypertrophy and maximum strength. The influence of cortisol, a steroid hormone of the adrenal glands, which stimulates protein breakdown and the development of catabolic processes, was also studied. Unfortunately, a wide range of processes and mechanisms that reflect the manifestation and development of strength qualities in areas not related to protein synthesis and muscle hypertrophy has been left without due attention. However, despite this, as well as the fact that most of the studies conducted were carried out on the simplest motor material, far from the specific manifestations of strength qualities in real sports activity, the facts obtained and theoretical generalisations quite clearly determine the relationship between the direction and magnitude of loads, hormonal activity, and nutrition.

Modern scientific data quite convincingly indicate the need for an organic relationship between increased hormonal activity caused by strength loads, the composition of food products and the mode of their consumption (Kimball, Jefferson, 2002; Kraemer W.J. et al., 2017). Despite the fact that the volume of research in this area is very limited, and sports practice is generally far from realising the possibilities of improving the quality of the training process hidden in this direction, one cannot help but see that there are significant reserves for increasing the efficiency of the process of developing strength qualities.

The issue of using increased hormonal activity caused by the use of intense training programs of a strength nature is organically related to the composition and amount of food and the time of its intake relative to physical activity. Appropriate products can be consumed prior to the start of training programs, during the sessions themselves, as well as in the recovery period after them, both immediately after exercise and within 1-2 hours after or up to 24 hours or more. The coincidence of increased hormonal activity with the presence of substrates that contribute to the proper adaptive reactions of those who caused it is of undoubted interest from the standpoint of optimising conditions for the development of strength qualities (Biolo et al., 1995; Damas F. et al., 2015).

Intense strength training stimulates both synthesis and degradation of muscle protein. The predominance of protein synthesis over its degradation, characteristic of rational training, leads to an increase in muscle mass and strength. The effectiveness of adaptation in relation to muscle hypertrophy and strength increase depends on the magnitude and nature of the training loads, the quantity and quality of macronutrients (protein, carbohydrate, fat), food intake patterns, hormonal response to exercise, and the interaction of hormones with muscle cell receptors (Kraemer WJ et al., 2017), immediately after the end of the session, especially intense during the first few hours, gradually fading over 24-48 hours (Damas F. et al., 2015). The consumption of protein with food both during training sessions and within a few hours after their completion stimulates metabolism, increases the rate of supply of amino acids and their utilization in the muscles.

The intensification of this process is also facilitated by the simultaneous consumption of carbohydrate foods with a high glycaemic index (Kraemer W.J. et al., 2017).

Muscle protein synthesis involves 20 amino acids that differ in properties and molecular structure. Nine of them are essential, cannot be synthesized in the body and must be obtained from food. The rest can be synthesized in the body from essential amino acids. Products with a high biological value (eggs, meat, fish) contain all essential amino acids. The proteins contained in grain products and vegetables are considered incomplete since they do not contain all the amino acids. The main regulators of muscle protein synthesis are essential amino acids (Dmitriev, Gunina, 2019).

Branched-chain amino acids (leucine, isoleucine, and valine) are essential acids that play an extremely important role. Leucine contributes to the formation of protein in the muscles and liver, is a source of energy, counteracts protein catabolism, and also maintains a high level of serotonin, counteracting the development of fatigue. Isoleucine is actively involved in cellular processes, being a source of energy for muscles, as well as a means of counteracting a decrease in blood sugar levels and loss of muscle mass. Valine is also an energy source for muscles and maintains high levels of serotonin. Branched-chain amino acids become the most important sources of energy in case of depletion of muscle glycogen stores. The action of these amino acids promotes the production of insulin, an anabolic hormone closely associated with glycogen formation and protein synthesis (Tipton et al., 2001; Kagu, 2008).

The availability of nutrients and hormones during strength exercises enhances the transport of amino acids and glucose into muscle cells, creating favourable conditions for anabolic processes. The availability of nutrients during intense physical and increased hormonal activity is crucial for the effective course of anabolic processes and the predominance of protein synthesis over its breakdown (Wolek J.S., Sharman M.J., 2008).

The introduction of amino acids during and immediately after training sessions, especially if combined with carbohydrate intake, stimulates the synthesis of major muscle proteins and reduces the intensity of protein breakdown, which is largely due to an increase in insulin concentration as a response to carbohydrate intake (Vingren J.L. et al., 2010). Experimental researchers (for example, Rasmussen et al., 2000) proved that the use of protein-carbohydrate supplements (6 g of essential amino acids and 35 g of sucrose) during the first three hours after the exercise of the power orientation sharply intensifies the process of protein synthesis. The same reaction is caused by the consumption of similar mixtures before exercise: there is an increase in the transport of amino acids to muscle cells and the total synthesis of muscle proteins. However, these changes take place only with the consumption of essential amino acids, which are the main regulators of muscle protein synthesis (Tipton et al., 2001; Kimball and Jefferson, 2002; Bohe et al., 2003).

The increase in protein synthesis compared to resting levels, due to increased hormonal activity, is noted, gradually fading within 1-4 hours after the end of the session (Biolo et al., 1995; Philips et al., 1997). It is during this period that the greatest availability of amino acids for protein synthesis is observed (Kadi F., 2008). Therefore, the use of protein and carbohydrate food supplements immediately and within two hours after the exercise of the power orientation leads to an increase in the level of somatotropin and its participation in the course of adaptive reactions (Kraemer W.J. et al., 1998; Volek J.S., Sharman M.J., 2008). Thus, it is with the next recovery period that the most effective adaptive reactions in muscle tissue associated with an increased hormonal response are associated (Damas F. et al., 2015; Kraemer W.J. et al., 2017).

Strength training sessions with high loads leading to the accumulation of lactic acid in the muscles, if they are not accompanied by the consumption of protein-carbohydrate foods, leads to the production of cortisol by the pancreas, which suppresses protein synthesis and creates a negative balance in which protein breakdown exceeds its synthesis. Consumption of carbohydrates with a high glycemic index inhibits the release of cortisol, which limits protein synthesis and thus promotes protein synthesis (Kraemer W.J. et al., 2017).

Thus, during and after intense power loads in the body of those involved, there is an increased hormonal activity (insulin, testosterone, somatropin, insulin-like growth factor), which contributes to the synthesis of contractile proteins. Effective adaptation requires an appropriate diet during and immediately after training sessions: protein intake to ensure the availability of amino acids, a small amount of carbohydrate to stimulate insulin and fluid intake to prevent dehydration (Eliakim A. et al., 2008; Kraemer W.J. et al., 2017).

It is quite natural that practitioners would like to receive clear, unambiguous recommendations on the nutrition of athletes and the expected effects of sports training. Unfortunately, it is extremely difficult to offer algorithmic recommendations; in some cases it is impossible. We have to take into account many contradictory patterns, and on a number of issues in science, there is still no exact data. Nevertheless, we present such interpretations that can be used in the theoretical, conceptual, and applied basis of sports training technologies.

Sports training, competition are always physical activities of high intensity (power) and greater or lesser duration. Depending on the power (intensity) of loads, energy is provided through various biochemical processes.

There are fundamental differences between anaerobic and aerobic energy supply of physical activity. Anaerobic processes in muscles actually proceed in a closed system: the total amount of energy that can be used is predetermined by the internal reserves of energy substrates (ATP, CF, glycogen). What does this mean for real workloads? 1. If training and (or) competitive exercises in terms of power level are possible only due to endogenous substrates of muscle energy, then, therefore, there are no external sources of energy in principle: only what is contained in the muscles. In training, the problem is solved relatively simply: breaks between loads are accompanied by the resynthesis of anaerobic energy sources. In a continuous competitive exercise, this possibility does not exist. Intermittent competitive loads (in games, martial arts, etc.) partly allow restoring of the substrates of anaerobic energy.

Continuous competitive competitions (all kinds of sports of the locomotor type) lasting more than > 2.5 ... 8 minutes, and many other activities of longer durations also require reserves of anaerobic energy sources: solving tactical problems, accelerating, climbing uphill and finishing. To successfully solve the problems of competition, the anaerobic substrates present in the muscles must be spent sparingly since their recovery under continuous loads is impossible.

The functioning of the muscles during competitive aerobic exercises is an open system. Muscles are supplied with blood during exercise and, in this way, are obtained from other organs, systems, compartments (compartments) of the body: C2. If one gets rid of such metabolic products, one receives energy supply substrates.

It is useful to remember the above fundamental differences constantly and build the entire technology of sports training, taking into account such differences.

During aerobic exercise, the capabilities of the muscles themselves and the "import" of the necessary gases, substrates from other compartments of the body are combined. From the point of view of bioenergetics, the organism acts as a holistic, integrative system.

Under any load, it is necessary to take into account the uneven distribution of energy substrates between muscle fibres of different types. At different stages of muscular work, at different capacities, different types of fibres act.

When analysing applied problems, we have to consider the presence of three types of muscle fibres: white, intermediate and red. Such differences due to the different content of myoglobin in the fibres are noticeable even visually. Research makes a more detailed classification, depending on the methods used: electron microscopy, histochemical characteristics, biochemical processes in pieces of biopsy preparation. Here we restrict ourselves to the main three groups of fibres.

In mammals and humans, skeletal muscles are like a mosaic of fibres of all three types. White fibres and fibres of an intermediate type are "fast" in their contractile characteristics, and red fibres are "slow".

White fibres are large (sarcomere diameter up to 100 A), poorly capillarized, with few mitochondria, and a highly developed sarcoplasmic reticulum. Red fibres are surrounded by an abundant capillary network, the sarcoplasmic reticulum is less developed, and the number of mitochondria is very large. Red fibres are 3-4 times thinner than white ones. Fibres of the intermediate type also belong to the fast ones; they are also capable of both anaerobic and aerobic metabolism (F.D. Golnik, L. Germansen, 1982).

White fibres, due to their characteristics, are adapted to carry out short periods of high power operation, but these periods must be separated by long recovery periods. Red ones are designed for long-term work of medium intensity. Intermediate ones are capable of aerobic-anaerobic work (Holloshi J.O., 1982).

In this section, we will focus on the bioenergetic use of fat substrates, considering, first of all, red and intermediate muscle fibres.

Red and intermediate fibres contain endogenous energy substrates – glycogen and especially a lot (in the energy sense) of triacylglycerols. As mentioned above, during aerobic exercise, the muscles, namely the red, intermediate fibres, are an open system. During exercise, it is possible to "import" substrates from other depots (adipose tissue, liver), substrates that have entered the blood from food.

The reciprocal relationship between glucose and fat metabolism is already known. When the energy breakdown of fats is activated, glucose oxidation decreases and vice versa. Meanwhile, exact reciprocity is not always, and perhaps not often observed. More and more data are accumulating on the simultaneous breakdown of glucose and fats during prolonged and intense muscle work in aerobic conditions (Khochachka P., Somero J., 1988).

Carbohydrate reserves in humans are able to maintain work close to maximum load for ~ 20-30 minutes. The reserves of fat are such that a sufficiently intense work could continue for several days. But the rate of energy production, and hence the power (intensity) of work when using only fats, is about half compared to when carbohydrates are broken down together with fats. The reasons for such differences in energy capacities are not yet fully understood (Table 1).

**Table 1** The maximum possible power of human skeletal muscles when using various substrates and catabolism pathways (Khochachka P., Somero J., 1988, p. 100)

| Substrate and metabolic pathway | Power, µmol ATP/1 g (wet weight) /1 minute |
|---|---|
| Fatty acid oxidation | 20.4 |
| Glycogen oxidation | 30.0 |
| Anaerobic breakdown of glycogen | 60.0 |
| Hydrolysis of creatine phosphate and ATP | 96.0 – 360 |

The reasons for the lower power of exercise when using fatty substrates may be as follows. With the onset of fat catabolism in the muscle cell, intracellular fat is used. As it is exhausted, the muscles are forced to switch to "imported" sources: NEFA of blood plasma. As described above, their penetration into the cell is a rather complex, problematic process. It is this mechanism that may be the limiting factor in sufficient supply of the substrate.

It has also been shown above that when there is a lack of carbohydrate substrates, the concentrations of intermediate products of the Krebs cycle and in particular oxaloacetate decrease. ß – oxidation of fats supplies sufficient amounts of acetyl – CoA in exchange, but due to a decrease in the concentration of oxaloacetate, it cannot be introduced into the terminal stage of oxidation, i.e., to the citric acid cycle. These two mechanisms seem to reduce the level of exercise power.

Wrestling is always a desire to increase the power (intensity) of physical activity, which predetermines the further growth of sports results.

The highest power (intensity) of aerobic exercise is possible due to the metabolism of carbohydrates (glycogen). Since glycogen stores are limited, both glycogen and fats begin to be used as intensive work continues. Even longer work leads to the exhaustion of the available funds of carbohydrates, and then the body switches to providing energy only at the expense of fats. But... equivalently, the peak power output is reduced to about 60% of the aerobic power provided by the carbohydrate substrates (Table 1). With such loads, a very important point is associated with the need to maintain an acceptable level of blood glucose. It is absolutely necessary for the energy of some tissues and organs.

How are these mechanisms implemented during aerobic training? With purely aerobic training, hypertrophy of "working" muscle fibres does not occur. This means that improving fitness simply by "producing" additional muscle mass does not take place. There are also no re-arrangements of the existing muscle fibres, for example, from white to red, which, of course, would be beneficial for purely aerobic exercise. Moreover, with aerobic training, the differences between the fibres are even amplified.

During aerobic training, the stores of glycogen and fats increase in the muscles and, above all, in the red muscle fibres. Fitness increases simply due to the quantitative accumulation of substrates. This factor alone is clearly not enough. After all, we can easily accumulate significant reserves of glycogen and triacylglycerols in the muscles with the help of special diets and acceptable loads for untrained people. In general, it will be useful, and it may demonstrate a slightly better personal achievement than before. But this does not mean at all that we have achieved high fitness with such methods.

A trained person must use the accumulated substrates with the highest efficiency possible. In a sense, the effectiveness of bioenergetics in aerobic training can be higher and more diverse than in anaerobic training. The differences are explained by the fact that the effectiveness of anaerobic training is an improvement in the use of the only energy mechanism - glycolysis.

Aerobic energy supply is the simultaneous and interconnected implementation of several metabolic pathways. All of the above, from the digestion of food in the gastrointestinal tract, to absorption and transport by the blood, metabolism in the liver, muscles, fat depots can and do improve under the influence of aerobic training.

There are positive changes in the following metabolic pathways: activation, transfer, oxidation of fatty acids; increased use of ketone bodies in the Krebs cycle; apparently, the "power" of the Krebs cycle increases; the quantitative and qualitative bioenergetic functions of mitochondria increase significantly.

It has been reliably established that aerobic training is accompanied by an increase in the size and number of mitochondria; there is an increase in the total content of mitochondrial protein. The capillarization of aerobic muscle fibres increase is also very important.

Characteristically, such training improves not only aerobic metabolic mechanisms but also increases the activity of glycolysis enzymes, in particular, the most significant of them, hexokinase. The biological meaning is that during the implementation of aerobic loads, there are always episodes of the required increase in power. And this is possible only through more efficient use of carbohydrates through glycolysis. In other words, high fitness in aerobic sports is not only about increasing endurance but also about increasing anaerobic power, which is required in real sports.

A trained athlete must be able to use carbohydrate substrates extremely sparingly; their capacity is negligible compared to the practically unlimited reserves of fat substrates.

Thus, continuous, long, super long competitive exercises are accompanied by the improvement of carbohydrate metabolism, together with fats. As carbohydrate substrates are exhausted, muscle fats and fatty substrates from the blood, liver, and fat depots are mobilized.

Considering the above-mentioned principles, trainers should consider that fat supply of energy for physical activity is typical only for long and super-long sports, at the level of a powerful component of $\approx$ 60% of that with carbohydrate substrate provision; this is just a marathon (and even then, partly), long-distance running, multi-day bike races, marathon swimming, super triathlon, etc. It turns out that all this is relevant only for the listed exotic sports and does not apply to classical, Olympic sports. First of all, this is indeed a fair conclusion, but only in the sense that, using the examples of energy-prolonged and super-long loads, the mechanisms of mixed bioenergetics (carbohydrates + fats) and the purely fat covering of energy costs were most clearly understood in the form of ideal models. Secondly, bioenergy fat substrates are used for life processes during recovery periods, with very light loads (for example, very long walking, not intensive physical labour during the whole working day) and during periods of sleep.

However, there is a much more difficult problem in elite sports, where daily training is practised two or three times a day. With their methodological developments, and the original elaboration of training programs, trainers seek to minimise adverse changes in the body due to previous training sessions.

From the point of view of the substrate supply of bioenergetics for daily and repeated trainings, unfortunately, this is not possible. In any case, the means of training used are accompanied by the consumption of carbohydrate substrates: anaerobic, aerobic-anaerobic, mixed modes of aerobic exercise (carbohydrates + fats). Meanwhile, it is known that with conventional diets, complete recovery of carbohydrate substrates and the most labile fatty substrates (i.e., intracellular triacylglycerols) takes up to two days. And this means that the next workout is carried out against the background of a clear under-recovery of carbohydrate reserves. And this is why there is a "fat shift" in the working supply of the muscles.

Let's assume that we train athletes in sports where the power and the duration of the competition obviously fall into the class of loads provided by carbohydrate substrates. If we give examples of running (due to convenience and better data), then these are classic distances from short (100 m) up to 5-10 km. It is not so important that at short distances, anaerobic glycolysis prevails ($\approx$ 100...1000 m), and at stayer distances, aerobic bioenergy prevails. But everywhere, the main and only substrates of bioenergetics are the carbohydrate substrates of the muscles and the body as a whole.

Meanwhile, in the real practice of elite sports, we train these people against the background of a clear under-recovery of the carbohydrate substrates required for the type of sport. Consequently, de facto, we are training these people with completely different bioenergetic mechanisms. Namely, bioenergetic mechanisms with mixed substrate supply (carbohydrates + fats) or even pure fat substrate supply. Logically, we come to the conclusion that there is a real paradox in the sport of the highest achievements. The implied and officially declared goals of sports training do not correspond to the real ones.

What are the possible ways to resolve the paradox?

1. There are methods of accelerated and maximum saturation of the body with carbohydrate substrates.
2. Data is accumulating on the improvement of enzymatic systems of carbohydrate metabolism when utilising a mixture of carbohydrates and fats, and even with a purely fatty substrate supply. The above-

cited facts refer to a significant increase in the activity of a number of key enzymes of glycolysis, especially hexokinase.

3. The methodological achievements of coaches are focused on such sports training technologies that reduce the consumption of carbohydrates to the maximum extent in training sessions, during non-training time and in a rationally developed system of competitive behaviour.

## PROSTAGLANDINS

In the introduction to this work, we already mentioned that dietary lipids supply the body with essential fatty acids. They are important ingredients in many plastic processes: building cell membranes, preservation of reserve fats in a liquid state of aggregation. Polyunsaturated fatty acids serve as precursors to a relatively recently discovered whole class of bioregulators – prostaglandins.

If at least an unsaturated fatty acid with 2 unsaturated bonds, for example, linoleic, comes with food, then the biosynthesis of arachidonic acid from it inside the body is possible, as specified above. Such biosynthesis out of monounsaturated acids is impossible.

The nutritional problem with polyunsaturated fatty acids appears to be simple when mastering the relevant knowledge and, of course, the relevant nutrients. But this problem is complex and simple at the same time. It is complex because none of the dietary fats fully meets all the requirements, taking into account their biological value, in particular for essential fatty acids, but also simple because by simply combining quite affordable food products, you can always (in all seasons of the year) provide the body with irreplaceable ingredients.

In terms of availability, prevalence, a special role belongs to vegetable oils, especially sunflower. Many unsaturated acids are found in linseed, hemp, soybean, and corn oils. To fully meet the needs, it is enough to receive 15-20 g of these oils per day.

Using the same example, it is useful to remember, as it were, some food paradoxes. For example, olive oil, which is very valuable in other respects, in this respect is significantly inferior to sunflower oil and, as it is not surprising at first glance, even pork fat. It is for the purpose under discussion that we should not spend more money on the purchase of olive oil that is less accessible to us. Another example would be that of cocoa butter and coconut oil, expensive and scarce products, not suitable for the purpose under discussion. These are solid oils, which means they are made up of saturated fatty acids.

These examples were purposefully cited since it is useful to remember that one can spend a lot of money on food, get exotic products and still eat inappropriately. Fortunately, due to the reasonable combination of quite affordable products, it is possible to provide balanced, adequate, and targeted nutrition. Knowledge saves money.

Endogenous synthesis and (or) ingested arachidonic acid is, at first glance, the simplest chemical compound: the total formula is $C_{20}H_{32}O$, i.e., has 4 double bonds –
$CH_3 - (CH_2)_4 - (CH = CH - CH_2)_4 - (CH_2)_2 - COOH$.
Spatially, this long molecule "bends into a loop", forming CIS – an isomer of arachidonic acid, represented below:

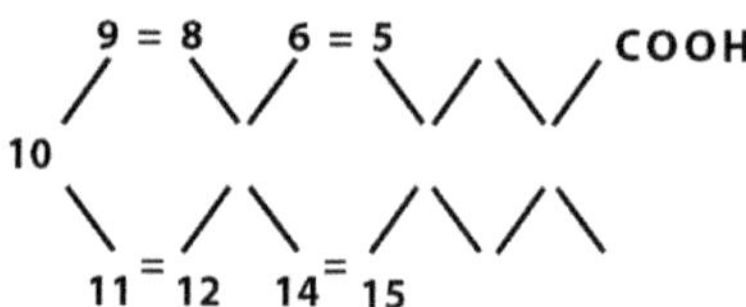


The numbering of carbons begins with the carboxyl group – COOH, the C numbers between which are double bonds, and the bend into a "loop" occurs at the level of 10 carbon atom. In this spatial form, the acids are prepared for the direct biosynthesis of prostaglandins.

Essentially, the biosynthesis of prostaglandins is the oxidation of arachidonic acid, the cyclization (formation of a closed structure) of the hydrocarbon skeleton and the reduction of the hydroperoxide group (-OOH) to the hydroxy group (-OH). All this happens in the region of the "loop", and the ends of the arachidonic acid molecule remain virtually unchanged.

An important point is that prostaglandins are spatially, chemically complex, and original compounds, but they consist only of carbon (C), oxygen (O) and hydrogen (H) atoms. So to speak, other important chemical elements inherent in the complex substances of the body: nitrogen (N), sulphur (S) or some metals are absent in their molecules.

A visual representation of the biosynthesis of prostaglandins and the structural formulas of the individual ones are presented in Figure 1.

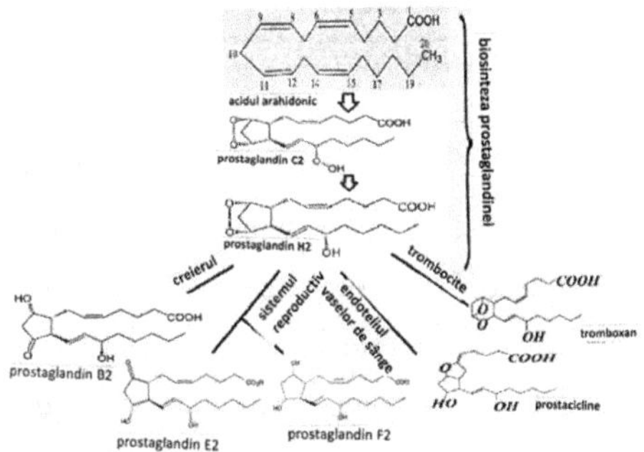



**Fig. 13** Scheme of the two-step conversion of arachidonic acid into prostaglandins (Varfolomeev S.D., 1986)

The purpose of the above scheme is reduced only to the general development of the structure and biosynthesis of these most important hormone-like bioregulators. Given the development of generalised knowledge about prostaglandins, we will make a brief presentation of the history of their discovery.

Special merit in the discovery of prostaglandins belongs to the famous Swedish scientist Ulf von Euler (Nobel Prize winner). Back in the 30s and 50s of the last century, he perfected biological methods for detecting the effects of various extracts from tissues and organs. In the course of such tests, he found that extracts from the prostate, seminal vesicles, seminal fluid contain a certain substance that can lower blood pressure and cause uterine contractions. He also established that this substance behaves like a fat-soluble acid and not like a protein. He gave this substance the working name "prostaglandin" (according to the organ of extracts) and stopped research at this point. At that time, there were no opportunities to obtain the identified substance in a crystalline form: there were no methods, and its concentrations were vanishingly small. Nevertheless, Euler's merit does not end there. Whether due to scientific luck or due to extraordinary scientific insight, Euler extracted a substance he called "prostaglandin" from the vesicular glands and prostate of a ram. Only later, it turned out that the biomaterial from sheep contains the highest concentrations of the target product in comparison with all other animals. Another merit of the forerunner is that he handed over all the materials on the substance he was looking for, as it turned out later, to his outstanding student Suna Bergström (Karolinsky U-ty).

In 1960, Bergström, with the cooperation and financial support of the American pharmaceutical company Upjohn, managed to isolate the first milligrams of pure crystalline prostaglandins from several tons of frozen vesicular glands of sheep and their seminal fluid. It is clear that the material had to be taken from many slaughterhouses. Even this simple fact demonstrates the enormity of serious biological scientific projects and the means and organisation required for this. Moreover, at the very initial stage, far from being obvious in terms of the expected positive results.

Only in 1962-1965, after the development of the latest research methods, it was possible to determine the chemical structure of the first compounds of this class. Considering the nature of the extracts from the mixture, the substances were named: prostaglandin E (extraction with ether – Ether); prostaglandin F (phosphate buffer – Fosfate). These terms are preserved in the modern classification. The first tests of isolated prostaglandins gave stunning results: millionths of a gram of these substances had a strong effect on almost all cells of the body.

Between 1968 and 1970, there has been a real research boom in the comprehensive study of prostaglandins. A specialised journal, The Prostaglandins, was published, and Upjohn publishes complete, up-to-date bibliographic information. A group of researchers, including S. Bergström and especially his student Bengt Samuelson, established two pathways for the formation of arachidonic acid: a pathway for the synthesis of a whole class of prostaglandins and a pathway for the biosynthesis of thromboxanes (in platelets).

English researcher John Wayne discovered a third biosynthetic pathway into prostacyclins, the site of synthesis in endothelial blood vessels (Figure 3.1).

In 1979, B. Samuelsson, together with his graduate student, P. Barzho, discovered an original pathway for the biosynthesis of arachidonic acid in leukocytes under the influence of the enzyme lipoxinase. In this case, another class of bioregulators is formed – leukotrienes A – E (Figure 3.1).

All the above discoveries in the field of metabolism of arachidonic acid in the body make it possible to speak at present about the cascade of arachidonic acid metabolites, about their versatility as a natural food substrate. Naturally, the scientific community of the world was more than inclined, immediately after such impressive discoveries, to award the authors of the Nobel Prize. The award was somewhat delayed due to the fact that S. Bergström, being the Rector of the Karolinska Institute in Stockholm, simultaneously served as chairman of the Nobel Committee. At such a high level of the scientific world establishment, the principle of "one's own hand is master" is impossible.

Finally, in 1982, the prize was awarded to the three above-mentioned researchers in the field of a new, gigantic group of bioregulators of most functions of cells, organs, tissues (Yudaev N.A., Pivnitsky K.K., 1983). They briefly cited the history and circumstances of the discovery of prostaglandins in order to focus on a seemingly elementary nutritional requirement – the systematic provision of the body with sources of polyunsaturated fatty acids.

The science of prostaglandins is in a state of exponential growth. As new biological effects are being identified, synthetic analogues are being created, some of which are used in various branches of medicine.

Apparently, no such achievements could be used as doping or as some kind of energizers for sports. In a healthy body, they perform other functions: extracellular, organ, tissue bioregulators of normal life processes.

Practitioners focusing on sports training need knowledge only about the obligation to supply the body with polyunsaturated fatty acids.

In this paper, we aim to present a rather complex approach to patterns, facts, and their interpretation in a form that would be both accurate and accessible for sports practitioners, without the ambition of being exhaustive.

To proceed with our historical approach, we will make a step-by-step presentation of the process of discovering new bioregulators carried out by American biochemist Nathan Applezweig under the name "The Saga of the New Hormone".

The saga began when the world learned about the discovery of three miracle drugs by three leading pharmaceutical companies. Upon closer examination, it turned out that all three drugs are the same hormone. If you're curious about how the same chemical compound gets several different names, let's follow the chain of events leading up to the creation of the miracle cure.

The physiologist usually discovers it first by accident in pursuit of the other two hormones. He gives it a name that reflects its function in the body and predicts that the new compound could be useful in treating a rare blood disorder. After processing one ton of fresh bovine tonsils, delivered directly from the slaughterhouse, he extracts 70 grams of pure hormone and sends them to a physical chemist for analysis.

The physical chemist discovers that 95% of the hormone purified by the physiologist is made up of various kinds of impurities, and the remaining 5% contains at least three different compounds. From one such compound, he successfully isolates 10 milligrams of pure crystalline hormone. Based on the study of its physical properties, he predicts the possible chemical structure of a new substance and suggests that its role in the body, most likely, does not coincide with the predictions of a physiologist. He then gives it a new name and forwards it to an organic chemist to confirm his assumptions about the structure of the compound.

The chemist does not confirm these assumptions and instead finds that the new compound differs by only one methyl group from the substances recently isolated from the melon peel, which, however, is biologically negative. He gives the hormone a strict chemical name, quite accurate, but too long and therefore unsuitable for widespread use. For the sake of brevity, the name invented by the physiologist is retained for the new substance. In the end, the organic chemist synthesizes 10 grams of a new hormone but informs the physiologist that he cannot give a single gram because all these grams are absolutely necessary for him to obtain derivatives and further structural studies. Instead, he gives him 10 grams of the compound that is isolated from the melon peel. Here, a biochemist, who has joined in the search, suddenly announces that he has discovered the same hormone in the urine of pregnant sows. Based on the fact that the hormone is easily broken down by a crystalline enzyme recently isolated from the salivary jellies of the South American earthworm, the biochemist insists that the new compound is nothing more than a type of vitamin B16, the deficiency of which causes shifts in the acid cycle in annelides. And it changes its name. The physiologist writes a letter to the biochemist asking him to send a South American worm. The food specialist finds that the new compound works exactly the same as the "PFF factor" recently extracted from chicken manure and therefore advises adding it to white bread in order to increase the vitality of future generations. To emphasize this extremely important quality, the food worker comes up with a new name.

The physiologist asks the food worker for a piece of the "PFF factor". Instead, he gets a pound of raw material from which the "PFF factor" can be made.

The pharmacologist decides to test how the new compound works on grey rats. With dismay, he is convinced that after the first injection, the rats go completely bald. Since this does not happen with castrated rats, he concludes that the new drug acts by promoting the sex hormone testosterone and is therefore antagonistic to the gonadotropic factor in the pituitary gland. From this, he concludes that the new remedy can serve as excellent drops for instillation into the nose. He invents a new name and sends 12 bottles of drops along with a pipette to the clinic. A clinician receives samples of a new pharmaceutical product to test on patients with frontal sinus colds. Drops into the nose very little, but he is surprised to see that three of his cold patients, who still suffer from a rare blood disease, are suddenly cured.

And so, he wins the Nobel Prize. The text of the saga is an adapted version from the book "Almost Natural Medicines" by Nikiforovich G.V., 1986, p. 198-200.

## FAT-SOLUBLE VITAMINS

The nutritional aspects of lipids are interrelated with the body's supply of fat-soluble vitamins. Firstly, they are found in natural foods containing lipids, and, secondly, their digestion in the gastrointestinal tract and absorption are carried out through the same mechanisms.

The group of fat-soluble vitamins is characterised by a number of features compared to water-soluble vitamins. For example, for some of them, negative consequences of an overdose are possible. Therefore, both the manifestations of deficiency, the actual avitaminosis, and the manifestations of toxicity with excessive consumption are studied.

With normal diets, overdoses are unlikely. They are possible due to the uncontrolled consumption of pharmaceutical preparations or the same vitamin complexes that are intensively promoted on the market of nutritional supplements. This is yet another case that shows the approach "the more, the better" is unacceptable. In this work, we strongly emphasize the inadmissibility of such an approach since especially "concerned" citizens often allow such violations: those who want to instantly lose weight, who suddenly decide to become healthy, coaches, athletes who want to instantly improve sports results through "magic means".

For modern civilized life, at first glance, there should be no problems with vitamins at all. Many people are sufficiently aware of the need and importance of these nutritional ingredients. Also, in general terms, the most problematic seasons of the year are well-known, when the development of avitaminosis is very likely.

The modern food industry takes into account and actually implements saving technologies, including vitamins, or they add them to finished products. The world production of vitamins, either as medicines or as food supplements, has reached such proportions that any need for vitamins can be completely satisfied. However, problems with vitamins are not miraculously solved. Some of the most common ones among athletes are:

- Classic, clinical forms of vitamin deficiency in athletes, as in other citizens who eat more or less balanced, do not occur. However, hidden forms of beriberi or overdose phenomena are likely.
- The benefits have increased vitamin demand. At the same time, the exact values of such an increased need are established in a fairly wide range. With regard to clarifying individual needs, such tasks are still beyond the scope of practical implementations.
- Surprisingly, the mechanisms of the biological effects of vitamins, their interactions, competitive relations, and the impact on physical performance are far from being fully known.
- Research continues to identify the biological effects of other substances, which are conditionally called vitamin-like compounds.

In this work, the priority, of course, is given to the nutritional aspects of providing the body with all the required ingredients, including vitamins.

Despite the impressive achievements of the pharmaceutical industry, absolute preference must be given to natural foods. No pharmaceutical preparation is equivalent to a natural product yet. In natural food, each vitamin is accompanied by a whole "escort" of biologically active substances (BAS). BAS in natural foods are also essential,

as well as more thoroughly researched nutritional ingredients.

**Vitamin A.** Relatively similar biological effects are
characteristic of vitamin A and some carotenes, especially
ß-carotene, from which vitamin A can be synthesized in
the body.

Chemically, vitamin A is a cyclic compound containing a ß-ionic ring, two isoprene residues, and a primary
alcohol group:

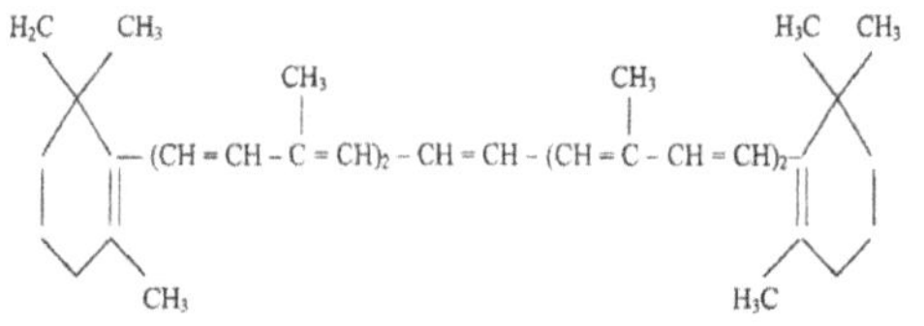

**Fig. 14** Retinol (Vitamin A)

The structure of ß-carotene has a symmetrical shape –
two rings and, as it were, a doubled hydrocarbon chain:

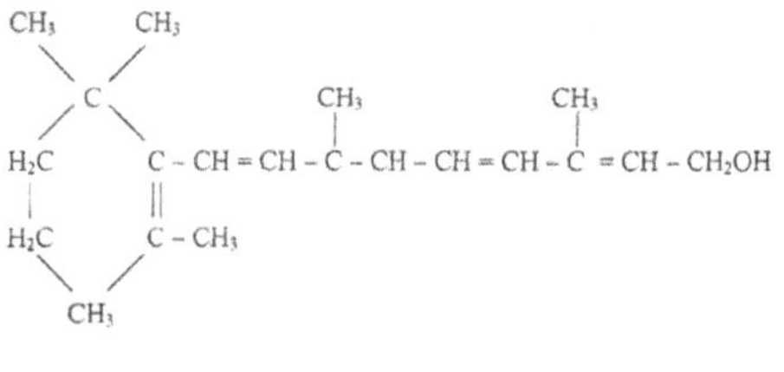

**Fig.15** ß – carotene

Two molecules of retinol are formed from symmetrical
ß-carotene in the body, ά-carotene, γ-carotene. Cryptox-
anthin has only one ring, which is found in retinol. When
taken with food, they are half as effective (on a weight
basis) as retinol or ß-carotene. Other carotenoids, such as

lipokene or xanthophyll, which do not have a ring structure, or one other than that of γ retinol, do not have vitamin A activity. This does not mean that they do not have biological activity at all. Carotenoids are a large group of biologically active substances that have been extensively researched for their A vitamin activity alone.

The presence of unsaturated double bonds in the molecules of carotenoids and retinol is always fraught with slight oxidation (both in food and in the body). Saturation of such bonds is accompanied by a loss of vitamin A. In natural products, oxidation is prevented by the presence of antioxidants, such as vitamin E.

Daily requirements and guidelines in weight units are presented by many studies. For example, the doses of vitamin A (retinol) recommended for athletes: 2-4 mg/day. Nevertheless, it is more accurate to express the needs in international units (IU) of ingredients A of vitamin activity (retinol and (or) ß-carotene). One IU biological activity is equivalent of 0.6 μg ß-carotene.

In the accompanying documentation of vitamin preparations (medical, food supplements), the content in weight units and activity units (IU) may be given.

In the case of vitamin A, it is not very important in what form the body is supplied with this important ingredient. In some respects, an advantage can be given to the consumption of ß-carotene. The reason for the preferences is very simple: the effects of overdose, so to speak, poisoning due to excessive consumption of ß-carotene are not observed, within known, reasonable limits. It has long been known that with excess consumption of carotene-containing vegetables, fruits, juices from them, yellowing of the skin may occur due to the deposition of excess carotenoids in its cells – carotenoid xeroderma.

Metabolism of dietary ß-carotene begins in the intestinal mucosa, here retinol is synthesized from it, or a part of ß-carotene is absorbed, and the transformation process is completed in the liver cells. In the liver, there is an accumulation of reserve depots of vitamin A. The most well-known signs of vitamin A deficiency are eye damage – xerophthalmia. In young animals and children with severe deficiency, growth arrest and keratinizing metaplasia of epithelial cells of all organs are observed.

Distinct, diagnosable manifestations of avitaminosis A are observed primarily in children.

The liver stores of vitamin A in normal, well-nourished adults are sufficient to meet biological requirements even if dietary intake is insufficient for several years. But this is a purely theoretical assessment since a normal diet, of course, is accompanied by the intake of either retinol or ß-carotene.

The problem of latent forms of vitamin A deficiency is not entirely clear. Studies have been conducted on volunteers on a diet poor in vitamin A for more than two years. Of the actually recorded changes, a deficiency of dark adaptation was found, i.e., dimly expressed signs of "night blindness" in some subjects.

Such data can be interpreted as follows: a. normal nutrition for all food ingredients, as it were, makes it possible to economically spend available resources of retinol and (or) be content with an involuntary intake, for example, of ß-carotene, which the experimenters failed to control. The studies were done on volunteers, not prisoners; b. in a number of sports, the slightest, most insignificant changes in the functions of vision can be limiting factors in sports performance (shooting, sports games). Therefore, the hidden forms of avitaminosis A are unacceptable; c. other biological effects of vitamin A are far from clear. It is likely that other functions of this indispensable nutritional ingredient will become clear in the expected periods of time.

Thus, the control of the sufficiency of the intake of retinol and (or) its precursor (3-carotene) with food is directly related to the tasks of sports nutrition.

Questions of overdose, vitamin A toxicity should also be in the field of interest of sports nutrition. The main reason is that there are no mechanisms in the body to excrete excessively absorbed amounts of vitamin A. The control of excess intake is only at the level of absorption in the gastrointestinal tract: excessively fatty foods or excessive intake of ß-carotene can be excreted naturally, through diarrhea, and for especially fatty foods, steatorrhoea (fatty stools). In all other cases, toxicosis develops from an excess of vitamin A. With normal nutrition, toxic effects due to an excess of vitamin A are almost unbelievable. Nevertheless, the gullible attitude to advertising recommendations and the extraordinary availability of all vitamins do not exclude such a possibility. Dangerous doses can be considered exceeding $\approx>$ 500,000 IU daily. The consequences are fragility of bones, calcification of the ligamentous apparatus, headaches, nausea, weakness, dermatitis.

The issue of vitamin A overdose is a biological puzzle. The main depot of vitamin A reserves is the liver. In humans, these reserves are ≈ 500 – 1000 IU/g. In fish, ≈ from 2000 to 100,000 IU / g, most of all in the liver of cod, shark, halibut. "Champions" in this sense are polar bears and bears in general. Indigenous peoples of the Sub-Arctic simply throw away the liver when butchering the carcasses of bears since its consumption is invariably accompanied by poisoning. Why these differences exist is not known.

Apart from the topic under discussion, there is the problem of carotenoids, in the broad sense of the term. ß-carotene is a precursor of vitamin A and it is taken into account in the tasks of rational nutrition.

There are many more individual chemicals related to food carotenoids. Related studies are carried out in a broader sense and not only as substances that are precursors for the synthesis of vitamin A. An overview of the data on a comprehensive study of carotenoids is given in the monographs of T.W. Goodwin 1984; V.N. Karnaukhova, 1988. Works of this type develop ideas about the direct participation of carotenoids in the supply, transfer, and use of oxygen, in addition to the main pathways of oxygen exchange. It also proves the participation of carotenoids in oxidative processes, in addition to mitochondrial mechanisms. If the studies of this cycle are confirmed, then this will lead to a number of alternative ways of solving the problems of extremely high levels of energy supply.

At the current level of evidence, slightly higher doses of carotenoids in the form of natural foods can be recommended to athletes as a guaranteed way to provide vitamin A and other presumed beneficial biological effects.

Vitamin D. The pathological consequences of a deficiency of this vitamin have been known to mankind for a long time by the symptoms of a disease called rickets, which was common in less sunny climatic zones.

Experimental rickets in animals is obtained by feeding them with food poor in calcium. If the food was irradiated with ultraviolet light, then this prevented the development of rickets. The UV-sensitive compound was identified as 7-dehydrocholesterol. One of the compounds after irradiation, calciferol, was named vitamin D2, the other cholecalciferol - vitamin D3.

These transformations also occur in human skin, under the influence of natural light or UV sources: skin 7-dehydrocholesterol is transformed into calciferol (vitamin D2).

Commercial preparations of vitamin D are obtained by irradiating ergosterone.

The biological antirachitic activity of calciferols is expressed in international units (IU). One IU is equivalent to 0.01 ml of average medical cod oil, which corresponds to $\approx$ 0.05 µg of calciferol.

Dietary guidelines for adult athletes usually do not list daily requirements for vitamin D since conventional diets contain the required doses of calciferols and/or precursors that are converted to vitamin D when skin is irradiated. Although this is unlikely, attention should still be paid to the danger of excessive consumption of vitamin D preparations. Commercial advertising, the availability of a variety of supplements, etc. can provoke gullible individuals into their own "experiments".

With an excessive intake of vitamin D, bone demineralisation occurs. Moreover, the leached calcium is not excreted from the body but is redeposited in many soft tissues, including leading to the formation of calcium kidney stones. Negative effects mutually reinforce decalcification of bones and calcification of internal organs and tissues.

**Vitamin E.** A larger number of vitamins were discovered according to the protocol: clearly detectable changes in the body (clinical picture), elimination of changes due to the addition of supposed essential substances, isolation, and identification of the desired vitamin.

In contrast to this scheme, vitamin E was first discovered in experimental studies. Rats whose diet consisted of cow's milk lost the ability to bear offspring. With the addition of vegetable oils, pathological changes disappeared. Accordingly, substances were isolated from these oils, which were called vitamin E. The largest quantities are isolated from wheat germ oils. They are called tocopherols, as they are a mixture of substances. Of these, a-tocopherol has the greatest biological activity; beta, gamma, and delta tocopherols are characterised by less activity:

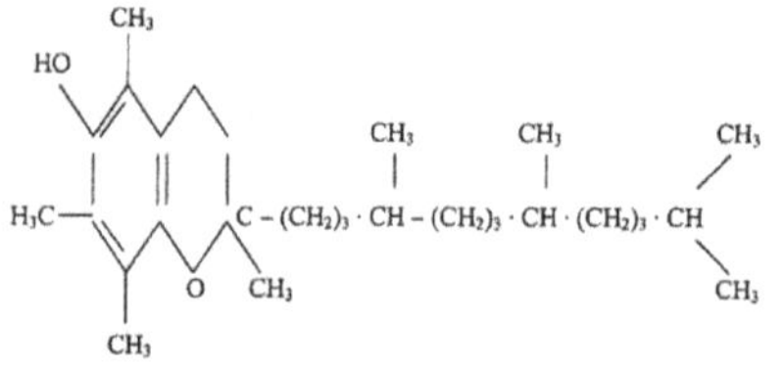

**Fig. 16** A – tocopherol (vitamin E)

A – tocopherol (5, 7, 8 – trimethyltocol), other tocopherols have a smaller number of methyl groups: ß – 5.8 – dimethyltocol; γ – 7.8 dimethyltocol, Δ – 8 – methyltocol.

A large amount of experimental material has been accumulated on changes in various processes with a deficiency of tocopherols in different animals. In humans, isolated cases of beriberi E have been described with severe lipid malabsorption and cirrhosis of the liver. Changes are quite formidable: muscle weakness, dystrophy, hemolysis of erythrocytes, changes in cell membranes. The introduction of tocopherols was accompanied by the normalisation of processes.

The deficiency of tocopherols is characterised by a polymorphic pattern of changes. Currently, the mechanisms of deficiency are interpreted in terms of the role of tocopherols as antioxidant agents of peroxidation of unsaturated fatty acids. Naturally, the antioxidant system of the body includes many substances, both supplied with food and synthesized endogenously. But tocopherols are obligatory in this antioxidant defence system.

Tocopherols also ensure the stability of unsaturated fatty acids and vitamin A during food storage. As noted above, most tocopherols are found in wheat germ oil, as well as in vegetable oils, whole grain seeds, nuts, and leafy greens. The daily requirement for speed-strength sports: 15 ... 30 mg; in the species of the endurance group, it is slightly more than ≈ 30-45 mg (Samoilov A.V. et al., 1993).

No toxicity in overdose has been identified, but one must be aware of the competitive relationship in the process of absorption with vitamin K. An excess intake of tocopherols also cannot be due to the limited absorption of natural vegetable oils containing them.

Vitamin E is heavily advertised as a dietary supplement, and many other effects are attributed to it, in particular those related to the sexual sphere. In fact, if we have in mind the general and particular tasks of sports nutrition, then such supplements should be considered as a means of normalising nutrition.

Of the available supplements, capsules under the very pretentious name "Viardot" can be recommended. Capsules contain 100% wheat germ oil, developed by Diod (Russia). Irwing Naturals supplements are commercially available but extremely expensive. Bread based on whole sprouted wheat grains, Helal SRL, enters the trade network irregularly. One must always remember the most important rule of the science of nutrition: natural foods are always preferred.

**Vitamin K.** This is a whole group of biologically active naphthoquinones:

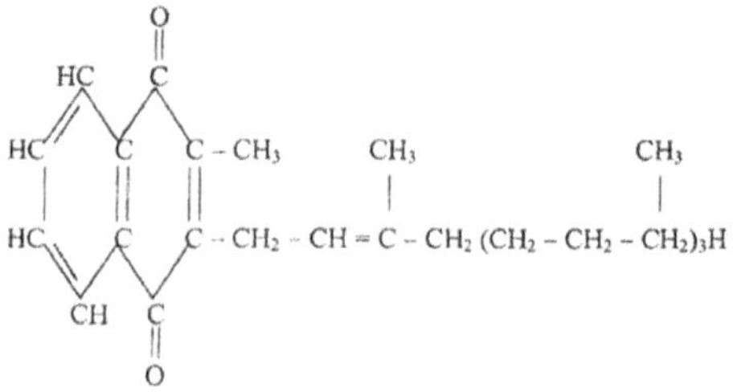

**Fig. 17** Vitamin K1 (2 – methyl – 3 – phytyl – 1.4 – naphthoquinone)

A number of analogues of vitamin K that contain naphthoquinone are known, the only difference being the length of the side chain.

Vitamin K deficiency leads to a deficiency in the formation of prothrombin, which plays a key role in the process of blood clotting. Vitamin K deficiency in humans is extremely rare: with rather serious lipid absorption disorders and gastrointestinal dysbacteriosis. The intestinal flora synthesises vitamin K, which is absorbed by the intestines.

The supply of this vitamin is actually the control consisting of lipid absorption and the normal state of the intestinal microflora. The need for this vitamin is not standardised.

## PLANT SOURCES OF DIETARY LIPIDS

The preceding sections substantiate the key role of vegetable fats for adequate, balanced human nutrition, including special population groups, in particular athletes. This means that food consumers, nutritionists, doctors and trainers should have similar information about the sources of vegetable fats, the technological aspects of preserving their quality, the composition of lipids from different plants and the antimetabolites in some of them.

The purpose of the data below is precisely to provide interested readers with information on the issues listed. At the same time, an attempt was made to characterise a large number of sources of vegetable fats. This means the need to implement the most important principle of nutrition science – the use of as many sources of essential nutrients as possible (the principle of optimal diversity). In simple terms, if we have even a very valuable source of dietary fat, then this does not mean that the adequacy of the diet is decided only due to this, albeit a very valuable product. Diverse sources are always required for any food ingredient.

Vegetable fats largely cover the body's needs for unsaturated fatty acids, fat-soluble vitamins, and biologically active substances. Therefore, it is required to comply with all technological methods for the complete preservation of the quality of the listed valuable food components.

The real food consumer needs to be informed about simple ways to control the quality of food products, in particular in the form of nut kernels, fruit and berry seeds, oil seeds.

At present, sources of vegetable fats that were previously perceived as exotic and/or were extremely scarce have become quite affordable. Due to this, food consumers can become "victims" of aggressive advertising in the sense that, if there are no scarce foods, then a balanced diet is impossible. Meanwhile, due to a rational combination of quite affordable, local food sources, the rationality of diets can be achieved. This is why more information is needed about a large number of sources of vegetable fats, both local and available on our market.

We do not use individual, chemically pure food components but natural foods that have been cooked. This paper also considers the development of the necessary additional information, nutritional problems, the metabolism of the individual, and the nutritional, metabolic aspects of lipids.

This section analyses the consumption of whole nucleoli of nut-bearing, oil-bearing, and partly stone fruit plants. People periodically, in any case, episodically consume a certain amount of nuts, seeds, stone fruit kernels without their culinary processing. It is these cases that are analysed in this chapter.

Naturally, in this case, not only the lipids contained in them but also high-quality vegetable proteins, as well as biologically active substances (BAS) enter the body. The intake of proteins, biologically active substances, is analysed here from the point of view of interaction with lipid consumption.

### *Nut plants*

Cultivated and wild types of walnut plants are known and widely cultivated. Many of them play a prominent role as very valuable foodstuffs, are used in the preparation of various food products (confectionery, etc.), as additives to dishes (sauces, etc.) or are consumed directly.

Direct consumption requires careful chewing since the entry of solid micro pieces into the gastrointestinal tract makes it difficult for further digestion and absorption of the nutrients contained in them.

### *Walnuts (Juglans regia L.)*

The walnut's place of origin is Central Asia, where it can still be found in the wild. In our territory, it spread from Greece, where its name comes from. The systematic name (Juglans) was assigned due to the release of a special substance, juglone, from its leaves. Juglon is toxic to other plants and insects, therefore, in the vicinity of the bark of trees, vegetation is practically absent or oppressed.

Walnut leaves can be figuratively called a biochemical combination, consisting of caffeic acid, vitamin E, serotonin, calcium pectate, a high concentration of vitamin C and even nicotine. These valuable properties of the leaves are used in folk medicine. In walnuts, the fruits have a green outer shell, which cracks and falls off when ripe. True maturity is the moment when this green shell falls off. Accordingly, after that, the inner layer of the pericarp, the so-called endocarp, in everyday language, the nutshell, turns out to be outside. Botanists call the fruit of the walnut a drupe. Unlike typical juicy drupes (cherry, plum, peach, apricot), walnut is a dry drupe. Inside the drupe, there is the nucleus, the surface of which resembles the convolutions of the brain. The kernel of the nut is a seed with two very peculiar large cotyledons, each of which is divided into two lobes. The nut kernel is covered with light brown skin, the colour of which makes it easy to determine the quality of the kernel. Well-preserved nuts, including the most delicious and fatty ones, are covered with a light film with a golden hue.

The Research Institute of Nutrition of the Russian Academy of Medical Sciences considers the norm for the consumption of nuts by an average person ≈ 2.4-3.0 kg/year, i.e., about one walnut or 2-3 hazelnuts a day. Consumption of a larger quantity is acceptable, as the recommendation emphasises something else: the desirability and even the need for their systematic consumption.

For athletes, the quality of this product is of exceptional importance.

Beyond compliance with the nutritional recommendations, it is important for athletes to independently, actively and consciously resolve any issues of their nutrition, i.e., constantly improve the level of their nutritional culture.

The composition of walnut kernels is exceptional: 60 – 75% fat (depending on the specific variety and growing conditions). Oil, with a greenish tint, pleasant smell and outstanding taste, is extremely rare and is produced only for very special purposes: confectionery needs, medical needs, fatty base of artistic paints. There is no need to try to find such a scarce product because it can be completely and adequately replaced by the nuts themselves.

Naturally, walnut oil is balanced in terms of the content of essential mono- and polyunsaturated fatty acids.

Depending on the variety and growing conditions, walnuts contain ≈ 9-16% proteins that contain all the indispensable (essential) amino acids. For this reason, walnuts are included in all vegetarian diets. They also contain fat-soluble vitamins, B1 B2, PP, carotene; trace elements: iron, cobalt, iodine; tannins.

Walnuts have the disadvantage of being low in vitamin C, but this applies to fully ripened drupes. The green, still soft fruit contains up to 3% ascorbic acid, which is much more than in blackcurrant and wild rose. In areas where walnuts are grown in large quantities, compotes and jams are cooked from green fruits, ground with sugar to preserve and preserve the above highest concentrations of vitamin C (Plant World of Moldova, 1986; Cretsu L.G., Domashenko L.G., Sokolov M.D., 1990).

Although it is possible, in principle, to have an overdose of walnuts, which means consumption of a quantity of nuts that exceeds the enzymatic and absorption capacity of the intestines, the consequences are insignificant: nausea, diarrhoea, "fat" stools are possible.

Nevertheless, the main nutritional problem is the choice, the selection of walnuts of good quality and the constant inclusion of this most valuable product in the diets of athletes.

### *Common hazelnuts (Corylus avellana L.)*

The homeland of hazel is considered the Black Sea European and Asian regions, where this plant is cultivated or has grown wild until now, including in the territories of Moldova. It is not entirely clear whether the hazel is a cultivated or wild plant. Even in ancient times, people actually cultivated wild thickets of hazel: they left bushes with the largest, thin-skinned nuts and planted them in yards, hedges, etc. Through folk and later scientific selection, on the basis of especially large-fruited hazel, many species of hazelnuts (interspecific hybrids of the most valuable lines of hazel) were bred.

Hazel, hazelnuts in the botanical sense, are real nuts [see above walnuts: dry drupes].

Naturally, the composition of nut kernels differs due to varietal characteristics and growing conditions. However, this composition is, in any case, exceptionally favourable: ≈ 60-70% high quality oil, with a balanced ratio of unsaturated fatty acids; ≈ 15...20% of complete proteins; a noticeable amount of anti-anaemic microelements (iron, copper, cobalt); vitamins of the tocopherol group and group B. Vitamin C is found in immature nuclei but decreases significantly during ripening.

The nutritional aspects come down to choosing the right quality nuts. These rules are similar to those for choosing walnuts.

When choosing hazelnuts for consumption, special attention should be paid to the following aspects: fully ripened nut, properly dried, with white kernels and no signs of mould.

Of course, hazelnuts are the best product to cover the required quotas of vegetable oils in the diets of athletes. For such cases, it is preferable to consume nuts directly since some culinary technologies can alter some of the initial qualities of the product, including chemical interactions of the components: fat, protein, carbohydrates.

Among adherents of vegetarianism, hazelnuts are rightly recognised as the best source of complete vegetable proteins.

The Research Institute of Nutrition of the Russian Academy of Medical Sciences recommends the consumption of nuts ≈ 2.4-3.0 kg/year, which can also be compensated by hazelnuts: a few nuts daily or more in 2-3 days. It is highly desirable to use hazelnuts in the nutrition of athletes, observing all the rules for the selection of good quality products (Artamonov V., 1989; Kretsu L.G., Domashenko L.G., Sokolov M.D., 1990).

### *Common almonds (Amygdalus communis L.)*

The birthplace of almonds is Asia Minor, North Africa. Later, this plant spread throughout the Mediterranean, Transcaucasia, and Central Asia, growing wild or being cultivated. This is the oldest cultivated plant (in Greece, Rome, and eastern provinces of the Roman Empire).

The importance of this culture is so great that breeders are making efforts to promote it to northern regions. In particular, this was done for the conditions in Crimea. In Moldova, great work was carried out by the famous breeder E.S. Temples to create varieties resistant to spring frosts. Unfortunately, these successful selection works were not realised on an industrial scale. However, local almonds are also sold in small quantities in the markets. The rest of the needs of the food and confectionery industries are met through imports. Small amounts of almonds are added to finished products, in particular to confectionery. When drawing up very precise diets, it is possible to consume this product in the form of ready-made food products, for example, in the form of chocolate-covered almonds, etc. But, at the same time, you need to take into account the quotas of consumed nutrients: sugar, etc. In other words, if almonds are required for a balanced diet, then the best alternative is the direct use of good quality nuts (see above for the same quality requirements for other nuts – walnuts, hazelnuts).

Almonds are among the valuable and scarce food products, as they have a unique taste and a unique combination of useful nutrients and, above all, the best combination of unsaturated fatty acids.

Depending on the variety, and growing conditions, nuts contain 50-60% fat, which is characterised by the best composition of unsaturated fatty acids, the saturated ones being only 3-5%. Since they also contain natural antioxidants, almond oil does not go rancid even during long-term storage. This ability of almond oil is exploited in medicine in the manufacture of oil injections.

The nutritional problem of almonds is closely related to their scarcity and economic factors: there is insufficient production in traditional cultivation areas, and even more so in the northern regions.

However, this valuable food requires careful attention to its characteristics. It is appropriate to always remember that many foods of plant origin may contain so-called antimetabolites and even toxic substances. Therefore, it is necessary to have the knowledge and culinary processing methods that neutralise the shortcomings of the original products.

There are two varieties of almonds - forma amara (bitter) and forma dulcis (sweet). Outwardly, these forms do not differ but they can be differentiated organoleptically. Bitter almonds cannot be consumed unless cooked. Almonds or bitter seeds should be thoroughly ground in a mortar with the addition of water. This slurry must be sniffed. All bitter nuts, seeds, and stone fruit kernels have a characteristic almond smell. It is due to the presence of hydrocyanic acid (HCN) and benzaldehyde ($C_6H_5CHO$).

It is useful for all nutritionally cultured people to know such a smell, distinguish products and taste as mandatory knowledge for the prevention of poisoning.

When rubbing the seeds of bitter almonds, apricots, peaches, wilted cherries, cherries, seeds of apples, pears and some other fruits and adding water due to the emulsin enzyme, the amygdalin molecules contained in them break down. Amygdalin ($C_{20}H_{27}O_{11}N$) is a modified disaccharide (more precisely, a glycoside) built from two glucose units linked to each other. Moreover, one of the groups – OH of the glucose link is replaced by a benzaldehyde group containing a cyanide group – CN.

If nuts, stone fruit kernels, and seeds are subjected to heat treatment, the above enzymatic reaction does not occur due to the degradation of the emulsin enzyme. Amygdalin itself is not toxic; it decomposes very slowly in the body.

Hydrocyanic acid and benzaldehyde have been associated with poisoning. In fact, people quite often deal with the presence of hydrocyanic acid derivatives in very common foods and drinks. Often this happens unintentionally; in other products and drinks, such microadditives are introduced on purpose. For example, many people know the smell and taste of drinks like Amaretto. In home-made jams from seeds and kernels, micro doses of amygdalin derivatives pass into the product, especially when making jams from quince (without prior removal of seeds). A similar extraction occurs in the manufacture of liqueurs from cherries, sweet cherries, cornelian cherry, plums, apricots and even grapes. Slivovitz in the form of strong drinks is popular, among other things, because of the almond smell and taste.

There are many data indicating the formation of cyanides in the human body under physiological conditions. Cyanides of endogenous origin are found in biological fluids, exhaled air, and in urine. It is believed that their normal level in blood plasma can reach 140 mcg/l. It should also be understood that vitamin B12 is chemically a polycyclic compound with a cobalt atom in the centre of the molecule, to which a CN group is attached (Oxengendler G.I., 1982).

It is logical to assume that this endogenous synthesis of cyanides (these are, of course, toxic compounds) is associated with the existence in the body of special mechanisms for their detoxification. And such processes have actually been discovered, and their molecular mechanisms have been deciphered. These mechanisms of detoxification are effective both for endogenously synthesised cyanides and for those coming from the outside (with food, drinks, or air). It is quite clear that natural detoxification mechanisms are effective within certain limits (doses of these toxic substances).

There are significant differences in this regard between species. Cold-blooded animals are highly resistant to hydrocyanic acid poisoning or its derivatives. Warm-blooded animals, on the contrary, are characterised by high sensitivity to cyanide poisoning.

People are more resistant to cyanides than warm-blooded animals. For the first time, such a fact was established in an auto experiment by the famous English physiologist Barcroft. He exposed himself and the experimental dog to HCN gas at a concentration of 1:6000. The experiment continued until the dog fell into a coma and had convulsions. The researcher actually had no symptoms of poisoning except for nausea and some impairment of attention and speech.

Nevertheless, Chinese giant panda bears can be considered "champions" in cyanide resistance. They are herbivorous, feeding exclusively on leaves and shoots of bamboo (this is a rare example of monophagy among higher animals). Meanwhile, in the leaves and shoots of bamboo, cyanide substances contain ≈ up to 0.15% of the wet weight. Therefore, cyanide detoxification mechanisms function best in pandas. It has been stated above that a person is relatively resistant to cyanide poisoning, in particular, amygdalin glycoside. But this does not mean at all that the indicated resistance has no limit. Fatal poisoning occurs due to ≈ 1 g of amygdalin. This means that eating 10 to 15 bitter almonds is dangerous, as are the bitter kernels of apricots, peaches, plums, sweet cherries, cherries, apple seeds, pears, quince, and other foods containing amygdalin.

The mechanism of action of cyanides was established quite a long time ago by Otto Warburg (20s of the XX century). Cyanides penetrate into cells, in particular, into mitochondria, and block the enzymes of the Krebs cycle. Characteristically, this blockade has a precise molecular "address". In particular, there is inhibition of the second link of cellular oxidation, which ensures the transfer of electrons to oxygen through the enzymatic chain of cytochromes. Electrons sequentially pass from one cytochrome to another, from them to cytochrome oxidase, and then to oxygen. This final stage of cellular oxidation can be represented schematically as two reactions:

It is in the given oxidation link that cyanides act. CN ions have a special chemical affinity for ferric iron. Accordingly, they selectively interact with oxidized molecules of cytochrome oxidase. Consequently, the normal process of tissue respiration is inhibited, and this prevents the cells from producing the main energy "currency" - ATP. At significant doses of incoming cyanides, blockade of the functions of cytochrome oxidase leads to an almost complete cessation of oxygen uptake by cells. The venous blood flowing from the tissues acquires a scarlet colour, corresponding to that of the arterial blood. This state of tissues is an example of histotoxic (tissue) hypoxia. In severe cases of poisoning, symptoms of suffocation, severe cardiac disorders, convulsions, and paralysis develop. Mild forms of poisoning are characterised by a metallic taste in the mouth, redness of the skin, mucous membranes, dilated pupils, vomiting, shortness of breath, and headache.

When vanishingly small amounts of amygdalin (amygdalin-containing nuts, nucleoli, grains) are taken with food, there are no symptoms of poisoning. This, of course, does not mean that the minimum dose of cyanide in such cases does not affect respiratory enzymes (cytochromes). In any case, SI ions interact with the ferric iron of oxidized cytochrome oxidase, thereby turning off a certain proportion of these enzymes from oxidation processes. But the overall, so to speak, "power" of the enzymatic system of oxidation is so significant that cyanide micro poisoning is at the level of the organism's adaptive capabilities.

The reversibility of cytochrome exclusion by cyanides from the oxidation process should also be taken into account. Over time, due to antitoxic natural processes, enzyme functions are restored completely. In other words, cyanides do not turn off cytochromes forever. In addition, not all cyanides that enter the body interact with respiratory enzymes. Some of them are excreted unchanged with exhaled air and are detoxified with the formation of harmless products in the blood due to biochemical reactions with sugars, sulphur compounds (cystine, cysteine, methionine, glutathione) and oxygen. These processes protect the body from the cumulative effects of cyanide intake. Subtoxic doses of cyanide are effectively neutralized within the adaptive capacity of the body.

There are problems of cyanide poisoning, which are solved within the framework of medical measures, but there are also problems with the dietary intake of cyanides, in particular in the form of amygdalin, in subtoxic doses. It is this case that concerns the meaning and content of this section.

In principle, it is possible to model the states of histotoxic (tissue) hypoxia through the use of amygdalin as an alternative to mid-mountain hypoxia. Of course, such modelling of hypoxic conditions must be performed at a high methodological and methodological level.

The need for careful control of nuts and other nucleolar products, which can be damaged by mould, has been emphasized several times above. The likelihood of mouldy nuts is associated with violations of harvesting, storage and unsuccessful drying regimes. It is appropriate here to pay attention to the inadmissibility of consumption of all other food products that are affected by mould.

The danger of such food is that there is a possibility of the development of microscopic fungi that produce mycotoxins. Not all mycotoxins have been studied in detail, but some of them are certainly hazardous to health and can be present in many common foods (not just nuts).

Among the most studied toxic metabolites of mould fungi are aflatoxins – toxic metabolites of some strains of Aspergillus flavus and Aspergillus parasiticus, which have a strong hepatotoxic effect, up to the development of liver cirrhosis and even the development of tumour diseases.

Aflatoxins accumulate in a wide variety of foods when stored at high temperatures and humidity. From this point of view, peanuts deserve special attention. Peanuts have become quite an affordable food, but we never know under what conditions they were grown. If there is an alternative substitute (walnuts, hazelnuts, etc.), then athletes should avoid significant amounts of peanuts.

It is useful to adhere to a simple rule of rational nutrition: in case of obvious or suspected spoilage of products, they should be discarded. It is better to temporarily starve than to expose your body to the effects of toxic metabolites from spoiled food.

The purpose of drying nuts and similar other oily products comes down to a few things: a. bringing the water content in the products to a level that would guarantee long-term preservation, allow you to consume the products directly or be ready for the extraction of fats, the isolation of proteins and biologically active substances without changing their native structure; b. proper drying protects products from mould (see above - mycotoxins); v. good drying preserves the food ingredients intact, and this ensures not only the quality but also the outstanding taste of nuts and similar nucleolar products.

At first glance, it seems that drying is a very simple technological technique, and from the point of view of the goals of this work (nutrition of athletes), it is completely indirectly related to the practical interests of sports specialists. We will try to show that at least minimal knowledge about drying is directly related to the goals of this work.

- Nuts, stone fruits and seed fat products should be harvested when they are fully ripe. Unripe nut products during storage and drying cannot serve as sources of food ingredients for special nutrition, in our case, for the nutrition of athletes.
- Harvested crops should be stored (before drying) in dry rooms, air-permeable containers, at low humidity and in places where there is good air exchange (a light breeze is better). The listed storage conditions provide the initial stages of drying and prevent moulding of products.

- Depending on the technical equipment, such technological methods of drying are chosen that are technically accessible and do not worsen the quality of the finished product.
- There is an ideal way to dry herbal products: freeze drying – vacuum removal of water. Naturally, freeze-drying requires special equipment and is possible for small-volume products. For special nutrition needs (cosmonautics, alpine tourism, extreme travelling), freeze-drying is used mainly for delicate fruits. Accordingly, in sublimated products, all natural components are preserved for a long time in their native form. As you can see, this is an extremely expensive technology. It is not used for drying nuts and many other plant products.

Meanwhile, to a certain extent, mankind has been using the idea of sublimation drying in a meaningful way for a long time, based on thousands of years of empirical experience. In this case, two mechanisms are exploited: low temperature and removal of vapours, microcrystals of water due to intensive air exchange at low humidity. For these purposes, people have always used cold attic rooms, wicker dryer barns, for example, for corn in heads, etc. Wet linen in dry frosty weather is also dried by the freeze-drying mechanism.

Nevertheless, heat is really necessary for drying nut fruits. To do this, solar-air drying is carried out in well-ventilated places and with constant stirring of the dried products. Since mass harvesting and, accordingly, the required drying takes place in autumn, it is usually not possible to completely dry nuts and similar products using the solar-air method. Namely, thermal drying methods are required so that the moisture content of the finished product is at the level of $\approx$ 10 ... 13%. To the touch, well-dried nuts are perceived as light, and, for example, apricot pits are cracked. The presence of at least 10 - 30% cracked apricot pits indicates their good drying. On the other hand, cracked nuts, stones should be especially protected from high humidity - the risk of mould.

Thermal post-drying should be carried out at as low a temperature as possible, with such heating which excludes the denaturation of proteins of nuts, nucleoli, and seeds. Denatured protein degrades the quality of these natural foods, but not only. Protein denaturation is a modification of its three-dimensional structure: reactive carboxyl and amino groups act on the outer surface of the molecules. These groups of protein molecules interact with sugars, especially glucose. Glucose-protein molecular crosslinks form polycyclic products from several molecules of protein and glucose.

The resulting compounds are dark in colour and resemble the characteristic colour of fried meat (meat fried crust). In the case of fried meat, the same compounds are formed: the protein-glucose complex. These reactions during high temperature drying of protein products and during frying of meat were described by the biochemist Maillard as early as 1912 in the article: "The reaction of amino acids with sugars: biological consequences." In science and practice, such food changes have come under the name: Maillard reactions; Mayar products. By the way, these are non-enzymatic changes and reactions; special enzymes are not required for this.

Substances of glycosylation of proteins sharply worsen the quality of both proteins and fats in nuts and seeds. The oil from such products comes out dark-coloured, which requires complex refining methods. Sometimes peasant sunflower oil of dark colour is sold in the markets. This means that too high temperature was used during pressing or extraction.

It should be noted that fried meat with a dark crust also cannot be considered a good technology for sports nutrition purposes.

Thus, rational drying should exclude the formation of Maillard products: a significant deterioration in the quality of these most valuable food products. We considered it necessary to bring these data, since in the food industry, home cooking, there are quite a few violations of drying technology.

Substances of glycosylation of proteins sharply worsen the quality of both proteins and fats in nuts and seeds. The oil from such products comes out dark-coloured, which requires complex refining methods. Sometimes peasant sunflower oil of dark colour is sold in the markets. This means that too high a temperature was used during pressing or extraction.

There is one more factor in drying technology, after-drying, which can worsen product quality. Proper drying, post-drying is the repetition of several cycles of heating to acceptable temperatures ($\approx 40°...50°C$), with immediate cooling (place in places with good ventilation). This is required for the reason that during spontaneous cooling, its own lipase enzyme is activated, which decomposes triacylglycerols into glycerol and fatty acids. The more products of this enzymatic reaction accumulate in nuts, seeds, the worse the quality of the final product. The quality of all oils or nuts and seeds is evaluated by the amount of fatty acids. This indicator is called acid number (AN). AN is the number of mg KOH, which is used for acid titration of 1 g of oil or for the corresponding mass of nuts, seeds.

If the oil is obtained through cold pressing technology ($\approx 40°...50°C$) or after refining, then the CN is $\approx 0.4$. Such oils are considered the best for nutrition or other delicate applications (cosmetics, pharmaceuticals). It is permissible to use oils (or their starting products) up to the level of CN – 2.5. With a higher acidity, oils can only be used for technical purposes.

They gave brief information about the drying technology and data on very likely violations of this, at first glance, the simplest technology. Apparently, such information will help consumers to consciously look for products that can actually be used for the nutrition of athletes.

This section is dedicated to one of the best nuts - almonds. Nevertheless, we found it expedient in this section to describe the dangers, ambiguities, and possible shortcomings that are characteristic and possible for this best kind of nuts.

Description of antimetabolites, toxic substances (amygdalin); the likelihood of mould (mycotoxins); violations of drying regimes (products of Maillard reactions; increase in acidity) applies to all types of nuts, fruit stones, seeds, and oilseeds. Accordingly, when characterising other lipid sources, all of the above will be implied.

### *Real pistachio (Pistacia vera L.)*

The homeland of pistachio is the Middle East and Central Asian regions. It is a shrub or a low tree. The fruit is a one-seeded stone, the core (seed) is light green. It belongs to the most delicate nuts. Since Turkey is one of the world's exporters, this rare type of nut is available in our markets, in the form of nuts themselves or in the form of salted snack kernels.

The seeds are high in complete proteins, moderate in carbohydrates, and high in fat, composed almost entirely of unsaturated acids. Pistachio as a food product has not been studied in detail. This is apparently due to small production volumes and the fact that pistachio can hardly be considered a food product. This is a typical example of a rare and expensive treat. If, for economic reasons, this nut is available to some, then occasional inclusion in special diets is certainly useful. It should be constantly remembered that the widest possible range of products is always required in nutrition, it is in this way that a balanced diet is easily ensured, and the body receives the full range of essential nutrients.

### *Common chestnut (Castanea sativa Mill.)*

This deciduous tree, up to 35 m high, with a spherical crown, belongs to the nut-bearing plants. Asia Minor is considered the homeland, but chesnuts are also widespread in France and Italy. In the cuisine of these countries, it occupies the 3rd-4th place after grapes, apples, pears, and citrus fruits.

The fruit is a nut with a hard, dry pericarp. Nuts are also enclosed in a leaf-shaped wrapper (plus), which opens when ripe.

The specificity of these nuts is that they are primarily rich in high-quality starch ($\approx 60\%$), contain small amounts of protein, fats and high concentrations of nutrients and microelements. In connection with this composition, these nuts are fried, baked, boiled, i.e., cooking is the same as for other high-starchy foods. Strictly speaking, sowing chestnuts should be analysed in terms of carbohydrates, but since chestnuts are nut-bearing, it was found expedient to consider them here, including due to the presence of a certain proportion of fats in them.

Our ornamental chestnuts are naturally inedible. They are called horse chestnuts. Nevertheless, a venotonic drug is obtained from them, which is widely used in ointments, gels, and other forms for the treatment of disorders of the venous system, including in sports practice.

### Siberian pine (Siberian cedar) Pinus sibirica Du Tour

The correct botanical name is Siberian pine, and the term Siberian cedar is most likely evidence of the reverence for this majestic, extremely useful plant of the Urals. Real cedars are Lebanese, Himalayan, Atlas, and Cypriot cedars (North Africa – Atlas Mountains; Middle East; Himalayas; o. Cyprus). The seeds of true cedar cones are inedible.

However, the term cedar pines is also used. There are four types of walnut cedar pines: Siberian pine (Pinus sibirica); Korean cedar pine (Pinus koraiensis – Far East of Russia, China, Korea and Japan); European cedar pine (Pinus cembra – artificially settled to the West from the Urals); Siberian pine dwarf (Pinus pumila – Eastern Siberia, Kamchatka, Sakhalin, up to the level of the coastal territories of the Arctic Ocean). The pine ones of all the listed pines contain edible pine nuts. It has been calculated that, if all these pines were harvested, and oil was squeezed out of them, then it would be possible to provide all mankind with vegetable oil. Such opportunities are realised to a very small extent.

Pine nuts contain ≈ 60% of oil, which is comparable in quality and composition to olive oil. Like all nuts, they contain complete proteins: ≈ 18%, similar in composition to the reference egg white. The content of the largest amount of the amino acid arginine is specific in the cedar protein, which is used when it is necessary to saturate the body with this particular amino acid. Nuts contain ≈ 12% of easily digestible carbohydrates, B vitamins, tocopherols (vitamin E); from biogens, trace elements – phosphorus, copper, iodine, cobalt.

Trade relations with Russia also create prerequisites for the possible supply of pine nuts and (or) the purchase of this delicacy during visits for competitional purposes.

In various other areas, other products of Siberian pine are also used. Pine resin does not crystallise and does not refract light in the optics – microscopic glass system. For this reason, it produces the best immersion oil for all microscopy techniques. Siberian pine wood is used to make a pencil stick and many other products.

### *European beech*

This plant deserves mention for several reasons. Beech belongs to the typical types of forests in Moldova. Due to the predominance of European beech in forests, Bukovina has had large areas of the Eastern Carpathians (Romania, Chernivtsi region of Ukraine). Beech can be classified as a wild nut-bearing plant.

Trihedral one-seeded beech fruits contain ≈ 50% oil, which has an undoubted nutritional value. The proteins of beech nuts are balanced in amino acid composition. They contain sugars, starch, malic, citric acids, and vitamin E.

Due to the higher content of carbohydrates, flour is made from peeled and obligatory roasted nuts in years of abundant harvest and is added to ordinary bread baking. Beech nuts must be toasted, because their nucleus contains a poisonous alkaloid fagin, which, when consumed raw, causes a severe headache. When roasting, the alkaloid is destroyed, and the nuts become suitable for nutrition.

The mention of this, like many other non-traditional food plants, is not limited to recommendations for their mandatory inclusion in the diet of athletes. The idea is different: a variety of food sources is the best alternative to getting as many nutrients into the body as possible: BAS, macro- and microelements, organic acids, and metabolic regulators. In other words, if possible, the diet of athletes should include beech nuts in the form of treats.

### *Oils from seeds of stone fruits, vegetables gourds, and grapes*

In modern theories of human nutrition, the principle is to use as many sources of nutrients as possible is of utmost importance in the implementation of a balanced diet and of targeted nutrition. Ensuring the principle of optimal diet diversity is especially important for the nutrition of special population groups and for people performing special types of work, including athletes.

Diversity applies to lipid requirements as well, and therefore prior sources of lipids and subsequent common and potential sources are described.

In the Republic of Moldova, extensive research and development are being carried out regarding food industry (including the uses of kernels, seeds of all processed plants), new products, new biologically active substances, etc.

The Polytechnic University, and, in particular, the group of Marchuk G.S., made inventions and prototypes of the required technical means. Unfortunately, for a variety of reasons, the above works have not yet reached the production level. This is largely due to the fact that, during the 60s-80s, in technologically advanced countries, there was progress on the methods for obtaining lipids from any plant material. Prior to this, oils were obtained by pressing in interaction with process steam or traditional lipid extractants (petroleum ether, hexane, etc. extractants). Currently, lipid extraction is carried out with liquefied and compressed gases. As such, the so-called freon extractants, chlorofluoro derivatives of hydrocarbons, are used, for example, freon 11 is CC13F, etc. Due to environmental requirements, halon extraction is gradually being phased out of production. The most widely used extraction is that with solid, liquid, gaseous carbon dioxide, CO2 – extraction.

Technologies based on CO2 – extraction have extraordinary advantages and technological flexibility in terms of the requirements of extraction from vegetable raw materials of a variety of target products: oils, esters, biologically active substances, etc. The problem of excessive heating, which deteriorated the quality of the target products due to Maillard reactions, completely disappeared (see above). Target products are isolated in their natural form and combinations (native products).

At present, they offer and sell an unusually large range of natural products from a wide variety of plant materials, including all waste from the food industry. In the vast majority of cases, these are obtained by CO2 – extraction. This technology is especially used in the production of food additives, pharmaceuticals, perfumes, and cosmetics.

These excellent CO2 extraction methods are not used yet in the Republic of Moldova because of the need for a complete technical, technological re-equipment of food industry enterprises, where significant investment is required. A higher level of production culture and the implementation of strict technological regulations are needed: high-pressure vessels, cheap ways to produce food CO2, etc. Successful in-house hardware development efforts are highly unlikely; in fact only turnkey imports of equipment from established manufacturers are possible, such as from the "Vereinigte Egelyntal-Werke" (Germany) company, which is extremely expensive. Naturally, with the availability of such technical means and the development of all production regulations, costs are sharply reduced, and product quality improves. Abroad, in this way, high-quality oils are obtained from raw materials with a low-fat content (soybean, corn, and even more so sunflower and (or) any others). The resulting oil does not require refining, deodorization, etc. works of traditional technology. Production costs are reduced by 4-6 times. Since $CO_2$ extraction is carried out at a low temperature, native proteins (without denaturation) and any other target products contained in plant materials are obtained along the way.

Here is a very brief summary of $CO_2$ extraction. Such data is required for the following reasons:

1. When choosing imported food products, food additives, biologically active substances approved for use, energizers, and medicines, it is necessary to pay attention to the country and the producing company. If the use of $CO_2$ – extraction is confidently assumed, then this is evidence of the native quality of the products.

2. The main idea of $CO_2$ – extraction is the extraction of target products from raw materials without changes during the technology process. Accordingly, a good alternative may be the direct consumption of plant products, with minimal cooking, for example, to neutralize amygdalin or other antimetabolites.

3. Modern food industry, in the light of the requirements of new data on nutrition, successfully intro-

duces more and more new plant sources of food, additives, biologically active substances, and metabolism regulators. From all points of view, such trends are economically justified and correspond to the main provisions of nutritional science.

The above-mentioned studies and the developments in the Republic of Moldova of new alternative sources of lipids concern the country's main agricultural crops. Cultivated and wild (zhardeli) varieties of apricots are grown in the Republic. The selection of cultivars is also carried out according to the requirements of the sweetness of their nucleoli to ensure the lowest possible content of amygdalin. Nevertheless, some varieties, especially roasts, have a bitter taste, and therefore they can be consumed only after heat treatment – inactivating the emulsin enzyme. Nevertheless, it is undesirable to consume bitter seeds since some bitter apricot kernels contain ≈ 4.0-8.8% of amygdalin.

Sweet apricot kernels' composition (oil, proteins, carbohydrates, nutrients, vitamins) is a very suitable alternative to the more scarce products, like almonds and walnuts. The main problem with apricots in general and their kernels is that the periods of mass ripening are very short (≈ 1.5-2 weeks). Therefore, during this time, it is necessary to process both the pulp contents and to separate and properly dry the kernels. The scourge of stone processing is mould, which prevents their use in human nutrition.

Peach pits are usually bitter; they usually contain a lot of amygdalin ≈ 4.0-8.8%. To obtain oil from them, this is not an obstacle. Seed oil for medical applications, regardless of the source (peach, apricot, plum), is officially called peach oil. The oil content of peach kernels is ≈ 44-46%.

At home, it is difficult to isolate peach nucleoli because of their hard shell. Taking into account the high concentrations of amygdalin, they are not of particular interest to the nutrition of athletes. Quite the opposite, one needs to be careful and avoid consumption.

The oil content of plum nucleoli is ≈ 40-48%, and the composition is similar to other nucleolar plants. The content of amygdalin is ≈ 1.0-1.8%, depending on the variety and growing conditions. In other words, poisoning is possible when consuming ≈ 50-100 g of thermally untreated nucleoli.

Plum pits accumulate in large quantities (as waste) in the manufacture of jams, marmalade; therefore, the emulsin enzyme is inactivated. Considering that the plum season is autumn, air-solar drying of the seeds is difficult, and thermal methods are required. In traditional rural conditions, plum stones were dried in attics near moderately heated chimneys. Previously, such pits served as valuable food supply during difficult periods of the year.

Moderate consumption of heat-treated, properly dried plum pits is acceptable as a supplement, a delicacy, but not in excess, precisely considering fat and (or) protein quotas of the daily diet.

The oil content of cherry nucleoli is ≈ 25-26%. In terms of oil content, this is a high percentage and therefore, oil can be obtained under production conditions. In ordinary nutrition, it is difficult to imagine crushing small bones in an attempt to saturate the body with vegetable oil. The content of amygdalin is moderate $\approx 0.8\%$, and yet this requires careful attention to liqueurs from raw berries with an almond smell.

Seeds from vegetable crops, especially from tomatoes, are also promising raw oil. Difficulties are associated with the need to develop special lines for washing and cleaning small seeds.

In this sense, a somewhat better technological situation is typical for melons: pumpkin, melon, and watermelons. They strive to obtain target products valuable in many other respects, not only as sources of oils. For example, pumpkin seed oil (Oleum cucurbitae rero) is promising for medical purposes, in particular for the treatment of prostate diseases. Medicines from them are widely used in medical practice. As a delicacy, pumpkin seeds are sold in the markets. The right choice of high-quality seeds is, first of all, high-quality drying.

Grape seeds, in principle, are also a promising raw material for oil production, but their oil content is low ~ 14-15%. Oilseed raw materials with a low content of the target product can only be processed by extraction methods.

Grape seeds are promising for obtaining tannin; from grape seeds it is called enotanine. The same seeds are being investigated as a promising source of various BASs.

### *Oilseeds*

The largest quantities of oils are obtained from plants whose selection is carried out for signs of high lubricity and the desired composition of these oils.

In some respects, oilseeds are not a botanical characteristic of plants but the content of the target product in them. With the development of new methods of extraction, especially $CO_2$ – extraction, vegetable oils are produced from almost all seeds of cultivated and wild plants. In particular, oils are obtained from plants that are cultivated for other purposes: cotton, soybeans, rapeseed, flax, mustard, corn, wheat germ and many other plants.

Sunflower oil (Helianthus annuu L) is consumed most readily and in the largest quantities under our conditions. Other regions of the world have their own dominant oil crops. For example, most of the Mediterranean countries produce olive oil. During the Olympiad, athletes are offered dishes cooked in olive oil.

Sunflowers are native to North America. In European countries, the plant was first grown for ornamental purposes, and only later were its seeds used as a delicacy instead of nuts. For this purpose, selection methods were carried out to obtain larger seeds. The tradition of using sunflower seeds as a substitute for nuts has survived. As mentioned above, roasted seeds are often sold, although there is a clear deterioration of quality (denatured protein, Maillard reaction products, increased acid number). For reasons of dignified social behaviour and because of the poor quality of the seeds, of course, their consumption is contraindicated for athletes.

Table 1 shows the composition of vegetable oils, including sunflower. This oil, as resulted from the table, is of excellent quality and contains a high percentage of unsaturated fatty acids, including essential ones, which are required for the biosynthesis of prostaglandins.

If it were possible, it would be advisable that sunflower oil, as well as other oilseeds, would be products obtained using $CO_2$ extraction methods. Such products fully preserve the native quality of the raw materials. This is equivalent to what a person receives from the direct consumption of properly dried sunflower seeds. Unfortunately, in our conditions, $CO_2$ extraction is not used.

The oils sold in the distribution network are obtained by traditional methods: cold pressing, hot pressing, and solvent extraction. Subsequently, the oil is subjected to refining and brought to the standard so as to meet quality requirements.

In the case of special nutrition, including for athletes, the oil fraction obtained by cold pressing is preferable, i.e., fractions are selected from the first press expeller. In the same way, pharmacopoeial fractions of oils are obtained from almonds, apricot kernels, and peaches. Naturally, at the same time, cake (makuha) contains residual amounts of oils. They are extracted on the next two expeller presses at high steam temperatures (protein denaturation, Maillard reactions, darkening of the oil). For general food purposes, these fractions must be refined.

For economic and production reasons, a mixture of all fractions of oils from three press expellers is sold into the distribution network, subjected to refining and other procedures for ensuring quality standards.

There is a lot of talk about the supposedly excellent quality of peasant butter. Usually, this is not true. Older generations of vintage butter churns used cold pressing at moderate temperatures. And if, more or less accidentally, a clear oil was obtained, then it could actually be considered peasant oil or, according to modern technology, the first fraction due to the cold pressing method. It is quite natural that the cold-pressed fraction or peasant oil must be consumed in its native form: additives to salads, etc. Roasting and other high temperature cooking techniques are possible with refined oils.

For many southern countries (Mediterranean, Africa, Asia, America), the main oil crop is that of the European olive (olive tree – Olea europae L.). The olive oil obtained from them is one of the most valuable oils. Unfortunately, the climatic conditions of the Republic of Moldova are not suitable enough for this more southern culture. In the southern regions of the Republic of Moldova, olive trees grow as ornamental trees, but their fruits do not ripen.

Most of the olive harvest is processed into oil. For delicate applications (medical oil, special nutrition), a fraction is obtained by cold pressing or by $CO_2$ extraction (see the same above for sunflower oil). For normal food purposes, olive oil is produced at higher pressures and temperatures. Since this technology was first implemented in the French province of Provence, the term Provencal oil has spread. What is sold here (at prices much higher than sunflower oil) is, of course, Provencal oil, according to manufacturing technology.

It is not necessary to insist upon the inclusion of olive oil in the diet of athletes. However, for Olympic athletes, it is necessary to ensure the testing of olive oil dishes to exclude the possible individual intolerance of such a product, albeit a very valuable one. For highly prestigious competitions, even mild symptoms of intolerance (diarrhea, etc.) must be absolutely ruled out.

It is necessary and advisable to use canned, pickled olives as flavouring additives. Preference should be given to fully ripened olives, i.e., black fruits. They have a spicy taste and crispy softness. Olives themselves contain useful nutrients and go well with a variety of dishes: salad, soups, hodgepodges, etc. They are also used as an independent snack with herring, onions, and butter. Olive pits are not used, as they contain noticeable amounts of amygdalin and have an unpleasant bitter taste.

Flax (Linum usitnlissium L.) belongs to the ancient oilseed crops. Through folk selection and subsequently scientific breeding, it was possible to create special oilseed varieties of flax (curly flax). The main varieties of fibrous flax, namely fibre flax, are not promising for oil production. Linseed oil consists of triglycerides of unsaturated fatty acids and is used as a food and for paintwork. Some medicines are obtained from flax seeds, in particular the drug linetol, used for the prevention and treatment of atherosclerosis. This plant's use proves the advantages of plant food sources, such as biologically active substances, micro-, macronutrients, vitamins and real or potential medicines.

In our current conditions, peanuts (Arachis hypogaea L.) are quite available in the form of nuts, as well as the products obtained from them: peanut butter. This plant is grown in large quantities in many countries of the world, so there are no shortages. Peanut seeds (nuts) contain oil rich in unsaturated fatty acids (linoleic, arachidic, oleic, linoleic, etc.). Peanut proteins contain all the essential amino acids (complete protein). Peanut nuts also contain digestible carbohydrates, fibre, saponins, pangamic acid, and lecithin.

Peanuts are highly nutritious, high-calorie products. It is assumed that the use of peanuts prevents the development of atherosclerosis since some components contribute to the removal of excess cholesterol.

We noted above that the choice of high-quality peanuts is difficult. Mouldiness must always be assumed, as it is grown and transported from areas with high temperatures and humidity. It seems appropriate to use peanuts in small amounts as a treat or as a flavouring addition to food pairings.

Non-traditional oil plants are also possible sources of plant lipids. For example, cotton-growing regions use cottonseed oil (Central Asia). Alimentary oil is obtained from the seeds of mustard, soybeans, rapeseed, etc. Oil and fat production technologies make it possible to obtain vegetable oils from raw materials with low oil content.

In the world as a whole, oil palm lipids are widely used, the absolute leader in world production and export being Malaysia (60-70% of world production). In accordance with the rules for concluding very large transactions, such as Russia – Malaysia (combat aircraft), there will almost certainly be counter deliveries of palm oil to Russia and re-export to the Republic of Moldova is possible. The specificity of palm oil, a semi-solid product in its raw form, is that it contains 50% saturated and 50% unsaturated fatty acids. Palm oil contains the largest amount of vitamin E. When oil is refined, vitamin E turns into a distillate of fatty acids and vitamin E is extracted from these, so to speak, waste products. Using a similar technology, vitamins E are obtained from soybean oil refining waste. The alleged anti-sclerotic properties of palm oil are being investigated.

The main sources of vegetable oils are described above. Each of them has some inherent advantage in terms of nutritional value and other applications.

Some vegetable oils are quite affordable for us, others are either scarce or extremely expensive. In the order of price and scarcity, vegetable oils are cocoa beans, pistachio, almond, nut (walnuts), olive oil. Strictly speaking, the chocolate tree (cocoa) (Theobroma casao L.) belongs with plants – a source of tonic substances, and not to oilseeds. Meanwhile, the most valuable oil in the world is obtained from the seeds of the chocolate tree (the common name for cocoa beans). It is used to make the best varieties of chocolate. Since cocoa butter is both scarce and expensive, various recipes for its substitution are being intensively developed in the world. Apparently, most types of chocolate available to us are made on the basis of more or less acceptable substitutes. There are firms in this sub-sector that produce the most adequate substitutes, for example, the Dutch firm Loders Kroklaan. Her products: Shoklin, Kroklaan special 499, Kroklaan special 555. In West Africa, people grow the shea olive tree. The oil obtained from them is valuable in itself and as an intermediate for substitutes of cocoa butter.

The world market of cocoa beans and by-products is a gigantic industry according to which the global economic situation is judged. Transnational giants, such as Uni Lever, Nestle, and others, carry out their business in this industry. The real success for Nestle came when its founder Arnie Nestle and his confectioner Daniel Peter invented a recipe for combining chocolate and milk. Solid chocolate then became the main product of this most important sub-sector of the global food industry.

Thus, the above characteristics of the main vegetable sources of oils, lipids in general, apparently help coaches, athletes, and nutritionists to make an adequate choice of the most important lipid nutrients. The combination of products from different oil-containing plants will ensure the implementation of the most important principle of balanced, adequate nutrition – the principle of optimal diversity of sources of basic nutrients (Vakhnovan P.S., Ilyin G.I., Lefter N.A., Manolaki V.G., Popushoy A.V., 2004).

In conclusion, modern sports physiology, kinesiology, biochemistry, morphology, and medicine have accumulated a large array of empirical knowledge, which can significantly expand the understanding of strength and strength training of athletes, in close relation to the mechanisms of muscle contraction, the structure and function of sarcomeres, myofibrillar and sarcoplasmic hypertrophy, and the structure and adaptation of different types of muscle fibres. This paper explores the possibilities of neuroregulatory adaptation of muscle motor units for the development and manifestation of strength qualities and the importance of taking into account and reducing the protective reactions of muscle and tendon mechanoreceptors. Moreover, this research tackles the role of muscle microtraumas and the activation of muscle fibre regeneration in the development and manifestation of strength qualities. The prospects for using the hormonal response to physical activity in organic connection with the processes of nutrition to increase the efficiency of the process of strength training have also been a key point of analysis.

Despite the still incomplete understanding of the factors and processes that determine the level of development of various types of strength, as well as of many reactions that reflect the adaptive processes occurring in muscles under the influence of training, previous studies can provide a sound support for the development of wrestlers' strength training, in line with modern achievements in sports areas of biomedical disciplines. For this to be achieved, various knowledge must be combined: the structure of motor actions, the features of the manifestation of power qualities and their relationship with technical and tactical mastery, flexibility, coordination, dexterity, endurance, adequate nutrition. The combination of scientific and practical achievements, which resulted in the contemporary perspective on strength training, can only lead to the formation of a system of knowledge in the field of strength training of wrestling athletes that meets the requirements of modernity.

# REFERENCES


Aagaard, P., Simonsen, E.B., Trolle, M., Bangsbo, J. & Klausen, K. (1996). Specificityoftrainingvelocityandtraining load on gains in isokinetic knee joint strength. Acta Physiologica Scandinavica 156, 123-129.

Baechle, T., Earle, R. (2008). Essentials of strength training and conditioning. 3st ed. Champaign, IL: Human Kinetics, 642 p.

Becker, S., Awiszus, F. (2001) Physiological alterations of maximal voluntary activation by changes in knee joint angle. Muscle and Nerve, 24, 667-672.

Behnke, R.S. (2001). Kinetic anatomy. New York: Human Kinetics, 281 p.

Billeter, R., Hoppeler, H. (2003). Muscular basis of strength. In: Komi, P.V. Strength and power in sport [2nd ed.]. Blackwell Science Ltd. p. 50-72.

Blaauw, B., Reggiani C. (2014). The role of satellite cells in muscle hypertrophy. J. Muscle Res. Cell Motil. 35(1):3-10.

Bouchard, C., Rankinen, T. (2001). Individual differences in response to regular physical activity. Medicine and Science in Sport and Exercise. 33 (Suppl.), S446-S451; discussion S452-S453.

Brounsgard, J.C. (2010). Mionuclei acquired by overload exercise presede hypertrophy and are not lost on detraining. PNAS, Vol. 104 (34). p. 1511-1516.

Bruusgaard, J.C. (2010). Mionuclei acquired by overload exercise precede hypertrophy and are not lost on detraining. PNAS, 104 (34): 1511-1516.

Carl, D. (2008). Balancing aerobic with anaerobic swim training. In: Swimming World, 1st ed. pp.40-41.

Chu, D.A., Myer, G.D. (2013). Plyometrics. Champaign, IL: Human Kinetics, 241 p.

Clark, C.B., Taylor, L.J. (2011). Age-Related Changes in Motor Cortical Properties and Voluntary Activation of Skeletal Muscle. Current Aging Sciencee, 4(3), pp.192-199.

Damas, F., Phillips S., Vechin F.C. and Ugrinowitsch C. (2015). A review of resistance training-induced changes in skeletal muscle protein synthesis and their contribution to hypertrophy. Sports Med. 45(6):801-807.

Dintiman, G., Ward, B. (2003). Sports Speed. 3rd ed. Champaign, IL: Human Kinetics, 272 p.

Dmitriev A, Gunina L. (2019). Modern pharmacological nutrients in the practice of training qualified athletes. Science in Olympic Sports; 2: 36-45.

Eliakim, A., Nemeth, D., Cooper, D.M. (2008). Physical activity, physical training and the STH-IGF-I system. In the book: Kremer W.J. and Rogol A.D., ed. Endocrine system, sports and physical activity. Kiev: Olympic literature. pp. 167-181.

Fleck S.J., Kraemer W.J. (1997). Designing Resistance Training Programs. 2nd ed. Champaign, IL: Human Kinetics.

Fragala, M.S., Kraemer, W.J., Denegar, C.R., Maresh, C.M., Mastro, A.M., Volek, J.S. (2011). Neuroendocrine-immune interactions and responses to exercise. Sports Med. 41(8):621-639.

Fujii, S., Kudo, K., Ohtsuki, T., Oda, S. (2009). Tapping performance and underlying wrist muscle activity of non-drummers, drummers, and the world's fastest drummer. Neurosci Lett, 459, pp.769-773.

Gamble, P. (2013). Strength and conditioning for team sports: sport-specific physical preparation for high performance. 2nd ed. Kindle, 304p.

Goldspink, J., Young, Shi Yu, Hamid, M., Harridge, S., Bulu, P. (2008). The role of MPF and other IGF-I variants generated by alternative syntherases in maintaining muscle tissue volume and hypertrophy. In the book: Kremer W.J. and Rogol A.D., ed. Endocrine system, sports and physical activity. Kiev: Olympic literature. pp. 182-195.

Golnik F.D., Hermansen L. (1982). Biochemical adaptation to exercise: anaerobic metabolism. In: Science and Sports. Moscow: Progress, pp. 14-59.

Guerrero M., Guin-Comadevall M., Cadafeau J., Parra J. (2018). Fast and slow myosins as markers of muscle injury. British Journal of Sport Medicine. V. 7. p. 581-584.

Harmon, K.K., Dunnick, D.D., Brown, L.E. (2017). Strength Assessment. In: Brown, L.E., ed. Strength training/National Strength and Conditioning Association. Champaign, IL: Human Kinetics. pp. 97-114.

Herbert, R.D., Gandevia, S.C. (1999). Twitch interpolation in human muscles: mechanisms and implications for measurement of voluntary activation. Journal of Neurophysiology 82,2271-2283.

Hochachka, P., Somero, J. (1988). Biochemical adaptation. Moscow: Mir, pp. 119-121.

Hoffman, J. (2002). Physiological aspects of sport training and performance. Champaign, IL: Human Kinetics, 343 p.

Holloshie, J.O. (1982). Biochemical adaptation to physical activity: anacrobic metabolism. In: Scicncc and Sport, Moscow: Progress, pp. 60-89.

Huber, A., Suter, E., Herzog, W. (1998) Inhibition of the quadriceps muscles in elite male volleyball players. Journal of Sports Sciences, 16, 281-289.

Kato, K., Kanosue, K. (2015). Muscle Relaxation and Sports. In: K. Kanosue, T. Nagami and J. Tsuchiya, eds., Sports Performance, 1st ed. Springer Japan, pp.67-78.

Kawamori, N., Rossi, S.J., Justice, B.D. (2006). Peak force and rate of force development during isometric and dynamic midthigh clean pulls performed at various intensities. Journal of Strength and Conditioning Research, 20, pp.483-491.

Kenney, W.L., Wilmore, J.H., Costill, D.L. (2012). Physiology of sport and exercise. Champaign: Human Kinetics, 621 p.

Korff, T., Horne, S., Cullen, S., Blazevich, A. (2009). Development of lower limb stiffness and its contribution to maximum vertical jumping power during adolescence. Journal of Experimental Biology, 212(22), pp.3737-3742.

Kraemer, W.J. (2017). How muscle grows. In: Brown, L.E., ed. Strength training / National Strength and Conditioning Association. Champaign, IL: Human Kinetics. pp. 29-48.

Kraemer, W.J., Hatfield D.L., Fleck, S.J. (2017). Types of muscle training. In: Brown, L.E., ed. Strength training / National Strength and Conditioning Association. Champaign, IL: Human Kinetics. pp. 49-73.

Kraemer, W.J., Vingren, J.L. (2017). Muscle anatomy. In: Brown, L.E., ed. Strength training / National Strength and Conditioning Association. Champaign, IL: Human Kinetics. pp. 3-27.

Kretsu L.G., Domashenko L.G., Sokolov M.D. (1990). The world of food plants. Chisinau: Timpul, 1990, pp. 290-292.

Lewis, P.B., Ruby, D., Bush-Joseph, C.A., (2012). Muscle soreness and delayed-onset muscle soreness. Sports Med. 31(2):255-262.

Lloyd, R.S., Faigenbaum, A.D., Stone, M.H., Oliver, J.L., Jeffreys, I., Moody, J.A., Brewer, C., Pierce, K., McCambridge, T.M., Howard, R., Herrington, L., Hainline, B., Micheli, L.J., Jaques, R., Kraemer, W.J., McBride, M.G., Best, T.M., Chu, D.A., Alvar, B.A. and Myer, G.D. (2014). Position statement on youth resistance training: The 2014 international consensus. *British Journal of Sports Medicine*, 48, pp.498-505.

Lloyd, R.S., Meyers, R.W., Oliver, J.L. (2011). The natural development and trainability of plyometric ability during childhood. *Strength and Conditioning Journal*, 33, pp.23-32.

Lloyd, R.S., Oliver, J.L., eds. (2014). Strength and conditioning for young athletes: science and application. London; New York: Routledge, 232 p.

Macintosh, B.R., Gardner, P.F., McComas, A.J. (2006). Skeletal muscle: form and function. Champaign, IL: Human Kinetics, 423 p.

McBride, K., et al. (2002). The model B6(dom1) minor histocompatibility antigen is encoded by a mouse homolog of the yeast STT3 gene. Immunogenetics, 54(8), pp. 562-569.

Moir, G.L. (2012). Muscular strength. In: T. Miller, ed., NSCA's guide to tests and assessments, 1st ed. Champaign, IL: Human Kinetics, pp.147-192.

Nicol, C., Komi, P.V. (2003). Stretch-shortening cycle fitique and influence on force and power. In: Komi, P.V. Strength and power in sport [2nd ed.]. Blackwell Science Ltd. p. 203-230.

Nindl, B.C., Kraemer, W.J., Marx, J.O., Tuckow, A.P., Hymer W.C. (2003). Growth hormone molecular heterogeneity and exercise. Exerc. Sport Sci. Rev. 31(4):161-166.

Platonov, V.N. (2004). The system of training athletes in Olympic sports. General theory and its practical application: a textbook for students of universities of physical education and sports. Kiev: Olympic Literature, 808 p.

Platonov, V.N. (2015). The system of training athletes in Olympic sports. General theory and its practical applications: textbook [for trainers]: in 2nd book, Kiev: Olympic Literature, Book. 2., 752 p.

Platonov, V.N. (2017). Motor qualities and physical fitness of athletes. Kiev: Olympic Literature, 656 p.

Protasenko, V. (2013). Super training without delusions. E-library.

Remy, J.N. (2008). Growth, development and hormonal changes during puberty: the impact of athletic training. In the book: Kremer W.J. and Rogol A.D., ed. Endocrine system, sports and physical activity. Kiev: Olympic literature. pp. 503-515.

Ronnestad, B.R., Nygaard, H., Raastad T. (2011). Physiological elevation of endogenous hormones results in superior strength training adaptation. *Eur. J. Appl. Physiol.* 111(9):2249-2259.

Sale, D.G. (1992). Neural adaption to strength training. In: P.V. Komi, ed., *Strength and power in sport*, 1st ed. Oxford: Blackwell Sci. Publ., pp.249-265.

Sale, D.G. (2003). Neural adaptation to strength training. In: Komi, P.V. Strength and power in sport [2nd ed.]. Blackwell Science Ltd. p. 281-314.

Samoilov A.V. et al. (1993). Study of the effect of the water-soluble form of fat-soluble vitamin E ($\alpha$ - tocopherol acetate) on physical performance. In: Theory and practice of physical culture, no. 9-10, pp. 25-56.

Schuenke, M.D., Herman, J., Staron R.S. (2013). Preponderance of evidence proves "big" weights optimize hypertrophic and strength adaptations. *Eur. J. Appl. Physiol.* 113(1): 269-271.

Shenkman, B.S. (2016). From slow to fast. Hypogravitational restructuring of the myosin phenotype of muscle fibers. ActaNaurae; Volume 8, No. 4 (31): 51-54.

Spiering, B.A., Kraemer, W.J., Anderson, J.M., Armstrong, L.E., Nindl, B.C., Volek, J.S., Judelson, D.A., Joseph, M., Vingren, J.L., Hatfield, D.L., Fragala, M.S., Ho, J.Y., Maresh, C.M. (2008). Effects of elevated circulating hormones on resistance exercise-induced Akt signaling. *Med. Sci. Sports Exerc.* 40(6):1039-1048.

Szivak, T.K., Hooper, D.R., Dunn-Lewis, C., Comstock, B.A., Kupchak, B.R., Apicella, J.M., Saenz, C., Maresh, C.M., Denegar, C.R., Kraemer, W.J. (2013). Adrenal cortical responses to high-intensity, short rest, resistance exercise in men and women. J. Strength Cond. Res. 27(3):748-760.

Tipton, K.D., Rasmussen, B.B., Miller, S.L., Wolf, S.E., Owens-Stovall, S.K., Petrini, B.E. (2001). Timing of amino acid carbohydrate ingestion alters response of muscle to resistance exercise. Am J Physiol Endocrinol Metab 281:E177-E206.

Vahnovan P., Iliin G., Lefter N., Manolachi V., Popușoi A. (2004). Natural-scientific and practical aspects of nutrition for athletes; Dietary lipids: functions, metabolism, bioenergy, prostaglandins, vitamins, plant sources. Dep. Youth and Sports Republic of Moldova. Scientific research of the NIFVIS laboratory. Athletics Chair , combat sports. Chisinău: Valinex. 134 p.

Veltman, A.L., Wiedeman, L., Veltman, J., Weldguis, I.D. (2008). Acute and chronic changes in growth hormone in response to aerobic exercise. In the book: Kremer W.J. and Rogol A.D., ed. Endocrine system, sports and physical activity. C.: Olympic literature. pp. 126-135.

Vingren, J.L., Kraemer, W.J., Ratamess, N.A., Anderson, J.M., Volek, J.S., Maresh, C.M. (2010). Testosterone physiology in resistance exercise and training: The up-stream regulatory elements. Sports Med. 40(12): 1037-1053.

Viru, A., Viru, M. (2008). Strength training and testosterone. In the book: Kremer W.J. and Rogol A.D., ed. Endocrine system, sports and physical activity. Kiev: Olympic literature. pp. 314-332.

Volek, J.S., Sharman, M.J. (2008). Diet and hormonal response: potential effects on body composition. In the book: Kremer

W.J. and Rogol A.D., ed. Endocrine system, sports and physical activity. Kiev: Olympic literature. pp. 417-434.

Westing, S.H., Seger, J.Y, Thorstensson, A. (1990). Effects of electrical stimulation on eccentric and concentric torque-velocity relationships during knee.

Wilmore, J.H., Costill, D., Kenney, W.L. (2009). Physiology of sport and exercise. 4th ed. Human Kinetics, 529 p.

Wilmore, J.H., Costill, D.L. (2004). Physiology of sport and exercise. Champaign, IL: Human Kinetics, p. 726.

Yudaev, N.A., Pivnitsky, K.K. (1983). 1982 Nobel Prize in Medicine - S. Bergström, B. Samuelsson, J. Wein. Nature, no. 1, pp. 96-99.

# Food Waste and its Impact on the Future of Mankind

**Dimitrie Stoica**[1], **Maricica Stoica**[2]

[1]Dunarea de Jos University of Galati, Romania

[2]Cross-Border Faculty, "Dunărea de Jos" University of Galati

stoica_dimitrie2008@yahoo.com, Maricica.Stoica@ugal.ro

## ABSTRACT

Loss and waste can appear at each phase of the food supply chain, from farm-level down to final consumption-level food. Food loss and waste are viewed as a dramatic global issue, with a negative impact not only on the sustainability of the food system but also on the future of humanity.

The terminology related to food loss and food waste is often confusing, their understanding being significant for the sustainability of the food system. This chapter presents food loss, food waste and Zero Waste terminology and also explores the economic consequences of food waste. Knowledge of food waste terminology and its consequences on the economic dimension can have a positive impact on the natural resource efficacy and existence of humanity in the future.

**Keywords:** *Food supply chain; Food loss and waste; Food security.*

# 1. INTRODUCTION

The food supply chain (FSC) defines the succession of food production and distribution from farmers to consumers [FAO, 2011, 2019; Nicastro and Carillo, 2021; Usmani et al. 2021; Wunderlich, 2021]. In rural societies, FSC may be short, while in the large urban zones, FSC is longer and consists of several interconnected phases that bring food from the farm to the final consumer (primary agricultural production, harvest; distribution; initial processing; industrial processing; retail; final consumption) [Abideen et al. 2021; BCFN, 2012; Chauhan et al. 2021; Dumitru et al. 2021; Ishangulyyev et al. 2019; Jungowska et al. 2021; Ojha et al. 2020; Perry, 2019; Santeramo, 2021; Socas-Rodríguez et al. 2021; Stoica et al. 2022, 2022a]. At every point in the FSC, from primary agricultural production down to final consumption, there are circumstances for food loss (FL) and food waste (FW) to occur [Bajzelj, 2019; BCFN, 2012; Dhir et al. 2020; FAO, 2011, 2019; Nicastro and Carillo, 2021; Pocol et al. 2020; Schanes et al. 2018; Usmani et al. 2021; Wang et al. 2021].

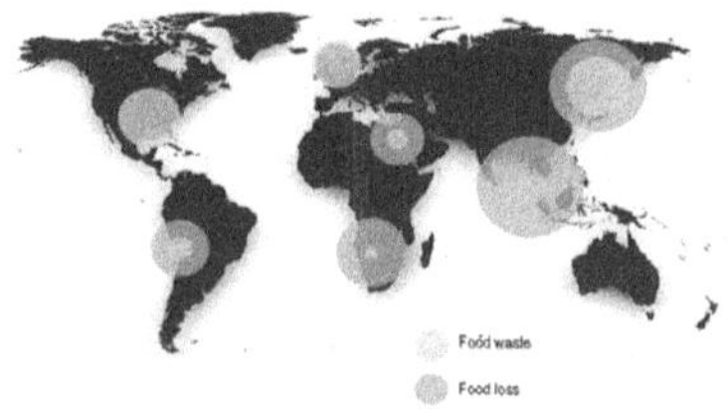



**Fig. 1** Low-income countries lose more food, while higher-income countries waste more food

Source: http://valuenetworkissues.blogspot.com/2014/11/reducing-food-loss-waste-to-feed-worlds.html

In low-income countries, the largest FL level occurs during primary agricultural production; conversely, in higher-income countries, the largest FW level occurs during final consumption [Dusoruth and Peterson, 2020; EFSA, 2021; Nicastro and Carillo, 2021; Przezbórska-Skobiej and Wiza, 2021; Schanes et al. 2018; Slusarczyk and Machowska, 2019; Stancu et al. 2019; Talwar et al. 2021] (Fig. 1).

The Food and Agriculture Organization (FAO) affirms that nearly one-third of the global annual food production for human consumption (about 1.3 billion tons each year) goes to loss and waste globally [FAO, 2011, 2015, 2019, 2020]. About 95% of FW goes to landfills or open areas (in the case of economically weaker nations) [Gayton, 2019; Usmani et al. 2021; World Bank, 2020]. In landfills (Fig. 2) or open areas, wasted (uneaten) foods break down and generate harmful greenhouse gases ($CO_2$ – carbon dioxide and $CH_4$ – methane; 3.3 billion tonnes of $CO_2$ emissions globally and more emissions in the form of $CH_4$) into the atmosphere [Grosh et al. 2016; Seberini, 2020; Usmani et al. 2021]. Moreover, the carbon footprint of FW is almost three times higher than that of plastic-based waste [Nguyen et al. 2020].

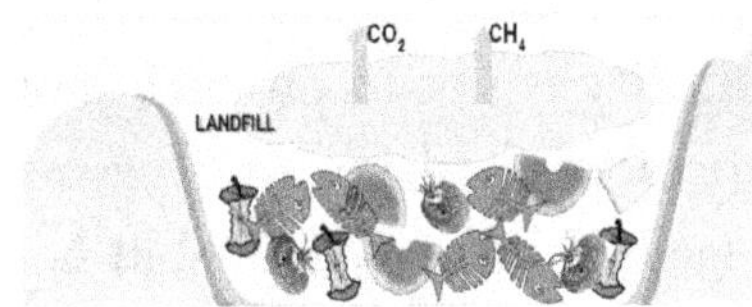


Fig. 2 FW - the largest producer of greenhouse gases. Wasted foods
rot and generate CO2 and CH4 gases.
Source: https://www.geoengineer.org/education/web-class-projects/
cee-549-geoenvironmental-engineering-fall-2015/assignments/monitor-
ing-landfill-gas-systems

This shows that the food system is far from perfect [WWF, 2017]. There is staggering evidence of the ineffectiveness and incongruities of the present food system, tremendous levels of the resources used in food production (capital, energy, water, etc.) being also wasted [FAO, 2011, 2015; Vizzoto et al. 2021; WWF, 2017]. This only further aggravates the food insecurity to which the world is already exposed. Many people still go hungry, food security being a significant concern in considerable areas of developing countries [FAO, 2011; WWF, 2017]. The world is now facing many challenges, including the population growing to nearly 10 billion by 2050 (10.9 billion in 2100) [Alexander et al. 2017; Babbitt et al. 2021; FAO, 2017; The Economist, 2011; UNDESA, 2019; WWF, 2017]. Such growing in world's population comes with both higher demand for food and an intensified competition for limited natural resources (land, water, energy) [Ahmad et al. 2021; Alexander et al. 2017; Babbitt et al. 2021; FAO, 2011, 2017; The Economist, 2011; To and Grafton, 2015; WWF, 2017]. The questions are: how could we answer a clear increased need for food *worldwide*, where we will find enough food for 10 billion people, how could we ensure that the world's needful humans are no longer hungry? The priority is not to produce more food; there is plenty of nutritious food for all. The question should not be how to feed 10 billion people but how to end FW and move towards Zero Food Waste (ZFW), to a more sustainable future for the generations to come. The shift to the reduction in FW or even to ZFW, requires radical modifications in the way food is produced along the

FSC. In addition, understanding terminology (FL, FW, ZFW), the interrelated drivers of FW (dietary transitions to more diversified and resource-intensive food, globalisation and global trade, large-scale urbanisation), and the consequences of FW are significant for a sustainable food system [WWF, 2017]. A lack of knowledge related to terminology, the drivers of FW and the consequences of FW can limit the ability to improve resource efficacy in the future of mankind [Luo et al. 2021]. In this chapter, emphasis will be laid on defining food loss, food waste and Zero Waste concepts. Special emphasis is given to food waste consequences on the economic dimension.

## 2. FL AND FW TERMINOLOGY

The problem is that the FL and FW terminology is confusing [Vizzoto et al. 2021]. FL and FW can appear at each phase of the FSC, from farm-level to consumption-level, but there is a fine difference between them. FL is the food wasted at the beginning of the FSC, while FW is the food lost at the end of the FSC [Dhir et al. 2020; FAO, 2011, 2019; Nicastro and Carillo, 2021; Usmani et al. 2021; Wang et al. 2021; WWF, 2017]. FL is a diminishing in the quantity/quality of edible food weight as a result of unfavourable climatic conditions, inefficient storage, poor handling, inappropriate infrastructure, and logistics, being generated especially at the farm level. FW is also a reduction in the quantity/quality of edible food weight, but which is generated especially at the consumption level (at-home settings: households-level; out-of-home-settings: restaurants distribution, retail) [Chauhan et al. 2021; Dumitru et al. 2021; Ishangulyyev et al. 2019; Jungowska et al. 2021; Lipinska et al. 2019; Ojha et al. 2020; Santeramo, 2021; Seberini, 2020; Socas-Rodríguez et al. 2021; Stoica et al. 2022, 2022a]. It is a consequence of consumer behaviour, retailer options, and economic instruments. Quantitative food loss and waste (FLW) refers to foods that leave the FSC, and qualitative FLW refers to a diminishing in the attributes of food that reduces its value in terms of intended use [Cattaneo et al. 2021]. In low-income countries with inappropriate infrastructure and logistics, FL occurs at the farm level, while in richer countries, FW occurs at the consumption level [Nicastro and Carillo, 2021]. The waste that appears at all levels of the FSC has enormous economic, environmental and social implications, being seen to be one of the principal contributors to food insecurity and reduced sustainability of our global food system [Beullens and Ghiami, 2021; Dora et al. 2020; Ishangulyyev et al. 2019; Li et al. 2022; Ojha et al. 2020; Santeramo, 2021; Seberini, 2020; Stoica et al. 2022, 2022a], food security being a significant concern in developing countries [FAO, 2011; WWF, 2017]. FL and FW represent a symptom of the ineffectiveness and unsustainability of FSC, their prevention or reduction being one of the most effective ways to achieve more sustainable and equitable food systems [Benyam et al. 2021; Fami et al. 2021]. The FW is part of the European Green Deal, as highlighted in recent action plans and strategies set out in recent action plans and strategies established in the European Union, such as the F2F (Farm to Fork strategy) and the new Circular Economy Action Plan [European Commission, 2020, 2020a].

## 3. ZERO WASTE CONCEPT

The emerging Zero Waste concept (a strategy to reduce the influence of waste on all individuals, human society, and the environment) was initiated by the United Nations in the early 21st century and has been widely sought after by numerous governments [Seberini, 2020; Zhang et al. 2021]. The Zero Waste (ZW) strategy is one of the most promising and clear ways to find an answer to waste management and recycling issues, inspiring reshaping the supply chain with the fact that entire products or by-products can be reused and recycled [Awasthi et al. 2021]. ZW focuses on maximising recycling and more reuse of waste, minimising waste generated and reducing consumption [Nguyen et al. 2020]. This strategy avoids the production of waste in today's humanity and directs the consumer to modify their lifestyle and their daily practices [Seberini, 2020]. The Food Waste Index Report 2021 assesses that around 931 million tons of FW were produced in 2019 (17% of entire global food production), the level of FW being expected to pick up owing to population growth and large-scale urbanisation and industrialisation [Sakcharoen et al. 2021; UNEP, 2021]. Urbanisation and industrialisation are closely linked not only to food insecurity, inequitable access to healthy food nutritional impacts and health consequences but also to the fact that megacities are vulnerable and more susceptible to natural and human-made disasters [Knorr et al. 2018], jeopardising our entire food system [FAO, 2021]. Zero Food Waste means capitalising on almost everything that exists in the kitchen as raw material and minimising the quantity of food sent to landfills by using as much of the product as possible [Vasiliu, 2021; Zhang et al. 2021]. Globally, many policies have been carried out on a large scale to minimise the environmental impact of waste (e.g., *Advancing Towards Zero Waste Declaration* of the C40 cities, the *Zero-Waste 2040 Strategic Plan* of Vancouver and the *European Green Deal*).

## 4. ECONOMIC IMPACT OF FW

The FW negatively impacts not only the environmental and social but also the economic dimensions [Friman and Hyytiä, 2022; Seberini, 2020; UNEP, 2021; Usmani et al. 2021; Vizzoto et al. 2021]. Both manufacturers and consumers are the protagonists of the complex economic system, consumer options being one of the crucial elements with a major influence on the behaviour of manufacturers. Consumers exert influence on which foods are produced and in what quantity [Seberini, 2020]. The use of resources (water, cropland, fertilizers, pesticides, labour, money, energy) is dependent on the manufacturing technology, storage, transport (distribution/redistribution), marketing, as well as the level of final consumption, which grows with the increasing of the world's population [Grosh et al. 2016; Seberini, 2020; Stoica et al. 2022, 2022a]. According to FAO, about one-third of foods (globally level, over a billion tons of foods annually; consisting of fruits, vegetables, cereals, oils, spices, roots, milk, and meat products) go to loss and waste, annually costing nearly $1trillion from resource costs [FAO, 2011, 2015, 2019, 2020; Gayton, 2019; Jayadevan, 2022; Starling, 2022; https://www.epa.gov/international-cooperation/international-efforts-wasted-food-recovery]. FW is one of the biggest problems mankind is facing today [Friman and Hyytiä, 2022; Starling, 2022]. As is shown in Introduction Section, there is a high amount of food in landfilling [Gayton, 2019; Usmani et al. 2021; World Bank, 2020]. In addition to the cost of purchasing food, food waste creates other problems, including other types of costs such as the cost of resources, environmental externalities, and social costs [Au, 2019; Gayton, 2019]. A lot of money is wasted on manufacturing foods which are never eaten. Additionally, the wasted labour, material resources, time and energy which go into food manufacturing must be considered. It is nearly impossible to evaluate the potential economic advantages from redirecting these resources [Gayton, 2019]. FW is economically unsustainable [Friman and Hyytiä, 2022], however, by 2030, reducing FW through investing in cost-effectiveness interventions (e.g., consumer education campaigns, standardised date labelling, spoilage prevention packaging, waste tracking and analytics) represents an economic opportunity [Read and Muth, 2021; https://www.epa.gov/international-cooperation/international-efforts-wasted-food-recovery]. In addition to wasted resources, there is also the environmental influence due to overuse of resources (soil erosion, water scarcity) and pollution. The environmental cost of FW is estimated at \$700 billion annually, considered by quantifying the costs of carbon, land and water and potential savings, which add to the semi-quantifiable cost factor of biodiversity. The surplus lost by the consumer as a result of FW increases the price of foods [Gayton, 2019]. This loss has a relatively higher influence on people with low incomes, who cannot afford to spend more money on foods and are most at risk. Consequently, higher prices and lower amount of foods invariably cause nutritional deficiencies for poorer people [Gayton, 2019; Seberini, 2020]. This, in turn, can lead to higher healthcare costs and lost productivity from people helpless to nutritional deficiencies and food insecurity, the social cost being estimated at about \$ 900 billion a year [Gayton, 2019].

# 6. CONCLUSIONS

The world population will grow to nearly 10 billion by 2050, which means that the pressure on natural resources (cropland, water, energy) will get larger, with accessibility to food being a major concern for all nations, primarily for underdeveloped or developing nations. The food system is far from perfect; nearly one-third of the annual food production for human consumption is lost or wasted globally. Understanding *food loss, food waste* (often confusing) and *Zero Waste* terminology is significant for a sustainable food system. Knowledge related to the consequences of food waste (a far-reaching concern) on the economic dimension can positively influence the resource efficacy and existence of mankind (already stressed) in the future. Unfortunately, food waste can result in food insecurity and an unsustainable global food system, which can generate world instability. Food security depends on all of us, both the people that work the croplands (stewards of the land), manufacture, store and handle foods, and consumers. Food security encourages national security, long-term stability and peace, the greatest triumphs of humanity.

# REFERENCES


Abideen, A.Z., Sundram, V.P.K., Pyeman, J., Othman, A.K., Sorooshian, S. 2021. Food Supply Chain Transformation through Technology and Future Research Directions – A Systematic Review. *Logistics*. 5(4), 83. https://doi.org/10.3390/logistics5040083.

Ahmad, S.H., Mansor, F., Yaacob, N.J.A., Kamaruddin, N.I., Ali, R. 2021. Household Food Waste: Exploring the Modern Throw-away Culture in Raub, Pahang, Malaysia. *International Journal of Academic Research in Business and Social Sciences*. 11(5), 1508-1524.

Alexander, P., Brown, C., Arneth, A., Finnigan, J., Moran, D., Rounsevell, M.D.A. 2017. Losses, inefficiencies and waste in the global food system. Agricultural Systems. 153, 190-200.

Au, I. 2019. Food Waste and Food Loss are Problems Worth Solving to Create a More Sustainable Food System. https://www.landandladle.com/food-waste-and-food-loss-are-problems-worth-solving-to-create-a-more-sustainable-food-system/ (accessed on 26 March, 2022).

Awasthi, A.K., Cheela, V.R.S., D'Adamo, I., Iacovidou, E., Islam, M.R., Johnson, M., Miller, T.R., Parajuly, K., Parchomenko, A., Radhakrishan, L., Zhao, M., Zhang, C., Li, J. 2021. Zero waste approach towards a sustainable waste management. *Resources, Environment and Sustainability*. 3. 100014. https://doi.org/10.1016/j.resenv.2021.100014.

Babbitt, C.W., Babbitt, G.A., Oehman, J.M. 2021. Behavioral impacts on residential food provisioning, use, and waste during the COVID-19 pandemic. *Sustainable Production and Consumption*. 28, 315-325.

Bajzelj, B. 2019. Food waste in primary production in the UK. https://wrap.org.uk/resources/report/food-waste-primary-production-uk (accessed on January 23, 2022).

BCFN, 2012. Food Waste: Causes, Impact and Proposals. Barilla Center for Food & Nutrition. People, Environment, Science, Economy. https://www.barillacfn.com/m/publications/food-waste-causes-impact-proposals.pdf (accessed on February 14, 2022).

Benyam, A.A., SomA, T., Fraser, E. 2021. Digital agricultural technologies for food loss and waste prevention and reduction: Global trends, adoption opportunities and barriers. *Journal of Cleaner Production*. 323. 129099. https://doi.org/10.1016/j.jclepro.2021.129099.

Beullens, P., Ghiami, Y. 2022. Waste reduction in the supply chain of a deteriorating food item – Impact of supply structure on retailer performance. *European Journal of Operational Research*. 300(3), 1017-1034.

Cattaneo, A., Sanchez, M.V., Torero, M., Vos, R. 2021. Reducing food loss and waste: Five challenges for policy and research. *Food Policy*. 98. 101974. https://doi.org/10.1016/j.foodpol.2020.101974.

Chauhan, C., Dhir, A., Akram, M.U.I., Salo, J. 2021. Food loss and waste in food supply chains. A systematic literature review and framework development approach. *Journal of Cleaner Production.* 295, 126438. https://doi.org/10.1016/j.jclepro.2021.126438.

Dhir, A., Talwar, S., Kaur, P., Malibari, A. 2020. Food waste in hospitality and food services: A systematic literature review and framework development approach. *Journal of Cleaner Production.* 270, 122861. https://doi.org/10.1016/j.jclepro.2020.122861.

Dora, M., Wesana, J., Gellynck, X., Seth, N., Dey, B., De Steur, H. 2020. Importance of sustainable operations in food loss: evidence from the Belgian food processing industry. *Annals of Operations Research.* 290, 47-72.

Dumitru, O.M., Iorga, C.S., Mustatea, G. 2021. Food Waste along the Food Chain in Romania: An Impact Analysis. *Foods.* 10(10), 2280. https://doi.org/10.3390/foods10102280.

Dusoruth, V., Peterson, H.H. 2020. Food waste tendencies: Behavioral response to cosmetic deterioration of food. *PLOS One.* 15(5), e0233287. https://doi.org/10.1371/journal.pone.0233287.

EFSA, 2021. Evidence-based decision-making to change social norms towards zero food waste. https://www.efsa.europa.eu/en/funding-calls/evidence-based-decision-making-change-social-norms-towards-zero-food-waste (accessed on December 30, 2021).

European Commission, 2020. Communication from the commission to the european parliament, the council, the european economic and social committee and the committee of the regions. A Farm to Fork Strategy for a fair, healthy and environmentally-friendly food system. (COM/2020/381 final). https://eur-lex.europa.eu/legal-content/EN/TXT/?uri=CELEX%3A52020DC0381&qid=1644854073318 (accessed on 20 March, 2022).

European Commission, 2020a. Communication from the commission to the european parliament, the council, the european economic and social committee and the committee of the regions. A new circular economy action plan for a cleaner and more competitive europe. (COM/2020/98final). https://eur-lex.europa.eu/legal content/EN/TX-T/?uri=CELEX%3A52020DC0098&qid=1644853900053 (accessed on 20 March, 2022).

Fami, H.S., Aramyan, L.H., Sijtsema, S.J., Alambaigi., A. 2021. The relationship between household food waste and food security in Tehran city: The role of urban women in household management. *Industrial Marketing Management.* 97, 71-83.

FAO, 2011. Global food losses and food waste. Extent, causes and prevention. https://www.fao.org/3/i2697e/i2697e.pdf (accessed on December 29, 2021).

FAO, 2015. Food Wastage Footprint and Climate Change. https://www.fao.org/3/bb144e/bb144e.pdf (accessed on December 29, 2021).

FAO, 2017. The future of food and agriculture Trends and challenges. https://www.fao.org/3/i6583e/i6583e.pdf (accessed on January 14, 2022).

FAO, 2019. The State of Food and Agriculture. Moving forward on Food Loss and Waste Reduction. https://www.fao.org/3/ca6030en/ca6030en.pdf (accessed on December 29, 2021).

FAO, 2020. Food Loss and Waste Must Be Reduced for Greater Food Security and Environmental Sustainability. http://www.fao.org/news/story/en/item/1310271/icode/ (accessed on January 15, 2022).

FAO, 2021. The impact of disasters and crises on agriculture and food security https://www.fao.org/documents/card/en/c/cb3673en (accessed on March 22, 2022).

Friman, A., Hyytiä, N. 2020. The Economic and Welfare Effects of Food Waste Reduction on a Food-Production-Driven Rural Region. *Sustainability.* 14, 3632. https://doi.org/10.3390/su14063632.

Gayton, C. 2019. Food Waste Economics. https://theeconreview.com/2019/01/29/food-waste-economics/ (accessed on March 26, 2022).

Ghosh, P.R., Fawcett, D., Sharma, S.B., Poinern, G.E.J. 2016. Progress towards Sustainable Utilisation and Management of Food Wastes in the Global Economy. *International Journal of Food Science.* 22. https://doi.org/10.1155/2016/3563478.

Ishangulyyev, R., Kim, S., Lee, S.H. 2019. Understanding Food Loss and Waste Why Are We Losing and Wasting Food?. Foods. 8(8), 297. https://doi: 10.3390/foods8080297.

Jayadevan C.M. 2022. Impacts of food wastage on economic growth. *World Food Policy.* 1-8. https://doi.org/10.1002/wfp2.12038.

Jungowska, J., Kulczynski, B., Sidor, A., Gramza-Michałowska, A. 2021. Assessment of Factors Affecting the Amount of Food Waste in Households Run by Polish Women Aware of Well-Being. *Sustainability.* 13(2), 976. https://doi.org/10.3390/su13020976.

Knorr, D., Khoo, C.S.H., Augustin, M.A. 2018. Food for an Urban Planet: Challenges and Research Opportunities. Frontiers in Nutrition, 19. https://doi.org/10.3389/fnut.2017.00073.

Li, C., Bremer, P., Harder, M.K., Lee, M.SW., Parker, K., Gaugler, E.C., Mirosa, M. 2022. A systematic review of food loss and waste in China: Quantity, impacts and mediators. *Journal of Environmental Management*, 303, 114092. https://doi.org/10.1016/j.jenvman.2021.114092.

Lipinska, M., Tomaszewska, M., Kołozyn-Krajewska, D. 2019. Identifying Factors Associated with Food Losses during

Transportation: Potentials for Social Purposes. *Sustainability*. 11(7), 2046. https://doi.org/10.3390/su11072046.

Luo, N., Olsen, T.L., Liu, Y. 2021. A Conceptual Framework to Analyze Food Loss and Waste within Food Supply Chains: An Operations Management Perspective. *Sustainability*. 13, 927. https://doi.org/10.3390/su13020927.

Nguyen, X.C., Tranc, T.P.Q., Nguyena, T.T.H, Lad, D.D., Nguyene, V.K., Nguyenf, T.P., Nguyeng, X.H., Changh, S.W., Balasubramanih, R., Chungh, W.J., Nguyenh, D.D. 2020. Call for planning policy and biotechnology solutions for food waste management and valorization in Vietnam. *Biotechnology Reports*. 28. e00529. https://doi.org/10.1016/j.btre.2020.e00529.

Nicastro, R., Carillo, P. 2021. Food Loss andWaste Prevention Strategies from Farm to Fork. *Sustainability*. 13, 5443. https://doi.org/10.3390/su13105443.

Ojha, S., Bußler, S., Schlüter, O.K. 2020. Food waste valorisation and circular economy concepts in insect production and processing. *Waste Management*. 118, 600-609.

Perry, G. 2019. What is Food Loss and Food Waste? And Why Does is It Matter for People and the Planet?. https://vine.press4.pagedesign.us/what-is-food-loss-and-food-waste-and-why-does-is-it-matter-for-people-and-the-planet/ (accessed on February 14, 2022).

Pocol, C.B., Pinoteau, M., Amuza, A., Burlea-Schiopoiu, A., Glogovetan, A.I. 2020. Food Waste Behavior among Romanian Consumers: A Cluster Analysis. *Sustainability*. 12(22), 9708. https://doi.org/10.3390/su12229708.

Przezbórska-Skobiej, L., Wiza, P.L. 2021. Food Waste in Households in Poland-Attitudes of Young and Older Consumers towards the Phenomenon of Food Waste as Demonstrated by Students and Lecturers of PULS. *Sustainability*. 13(7), 3601. https://doi.org/10.3390/su13073601.

Read, Q.D., Muth, M.K. 2021. Cost-effectiveness of four food waste interventions: Is food waste reduction a "win-win?. *Resources, Conservation and Recycling.* 168. 105448. https://doi.org/10.1016/j.resconrec.2021.105448.

Sakcharoen, T., Ratanatamskul, C., Chandrachai, A. 2021. Factors affecting technology selection, techno-economic and environmental sustainability assessment of a novel zero-waste system for food waste and wastewater management. *Journal of Cleaner Production.* 314, 128103. https://doi:10.1016/j.jclepro.2021.128103.

Santeramo, F.G. 2021. Exploring the link among food loss, waste and food security: what the research should focus on?. *Agriculture & Food Security.* 10(26). https://doi.org/10.1186/s40066-021-00302-z.

Schanes, K., Dobernig, K., Gözet, B. 2018. Food waste matters – A systematic review of household food waste practices and their policy implications. *Journal of Cleaner Production.* 182, 978-991.

Seberini, A. 2020. Economic, social and environmental world impacts of food waste on society and Zero waste as a global approach to their elimination. *SHS Web of Conferences.* 74, 03010. https://doi.org/10.1051/shsconf/20207403010.

Slusarczyk, B., Machowska, E. 2019. Food Waste in the World and in Poland. *Академіичный огляд.* 1, 91-99.

Socas-Rodríguez, B., Alvarez-Rivera, G., Valdés, A., Ibáñez, E., Cifuentes, A. 2021. Food by-products and food wastes: are they safe enough for their valorization?. *Trends in Food Science & Technology.* 114, 133-147.

Stancu, V., Haugaard, P., Lähteenmäki, L. 2016. Determinants of Consumer Food Waste Behaviour. Two Routes to Food Waste. *Appetite.* 96, 7-17.

Starling, M. 2022. Throwing money in the bin: the huge cost of food waste. https://www.theweek.co.uk/news/uk-news/955861/the-huge-cost-of-food-waste (accessed on March 26, 2022).

Stoica D., Micu A.E., Stoica M. 2022. Factors that influence the food losses at the primary production stage. *Across.* 5(3), 12-20.

Stoica D., Micu A.E., Stoica M. 2022a. Factors that influence the household food waste. *Across.* 5(3), 28-35.

Talwar, S., Kaur, P., Yadav, R., Sharma, R., Dhir, A. 2021. Food waste and out-of-home-dining: antecedents and consequents of the decision to take away leftovers after dining at restaurants. *Journal of Sustainable Tourism.* https://doi.org/10.1080/09669582.2021.1953512.

The Economist, 2011. The 9 billion-people question. A special report on feeding the world. https://www.economist.com/sites/default/files/special-reports-pdfs/18205243.pdf (accessed on December 30, 2021).

To, H., Grafton, R.Q. 2015. Oil prices, biofuels production and food security: past trends and future challenges. *Food Security.* 7(2), 323-336.

UNDESA, 2019. World Population Prospects 2019: Highlights. https://population.un.org/wpp/Publications/Files/WPP2019_Highlights.pdf (accessed on March 16, 2022).

UNEP, 2021. Food Waste Index Report 2021. https://www.unep.org/resources/report/unep-food-waste-index-report-2021 (accessed on December 30, 2021).

Usmani, Z., Sharma, M., Awasthi, A.K., Sharma, G.D., Cysneiros, D., Nayak, S.K., Thakur, V.K., Naidu, R., Pandey, A., Gupta, V.K. 2021. Minimizing hazardous impact of food waste in a circular economy – Advances in resource recovery through green strategies. *Journal of Hazardous Materials.* 416, 126154. https://doi.org/10.1016/j.jhazmat.2021.126154.

Vasiliu, O. 2021. Zero food waste: restaurantele românești care nu vor să creeze deșeuri (Zero food waste: Romanian restaurants that do not want to create waste). https://mindcraftstories.ro/societate/zero-food-waste-restaurantele-romanesti-care-nu-vor-sa-creeze-deseuri/N (accessed on December 30, 2021).

Vizzoto, F., Testa, F., Iraldo, F. 2021. Strategies to reduce food waste in the foodservices sector: A systematic review. *International Journal of Hospitality Management*. 95, 102933. https://doi.org/10.1016/j.ijhm.2021.102933.

Wang, Y., Yuan, Z., Tang, Y. 2021. Enhancing food security and environmental sustainability: A critical review of food loss and waste management. *Resources, Environment and Sustainability*. 4, 100023. https://doi.org/10.1016/j.resenv.2021.100023.

World Bank, 2020. What a waste 2.0 – Global Food Loss and Waste. https://datatopics. worldbank.org/what-a-waste/global_food_loss_and_waste.htm (accessed on March 15, 2022).

Wunderlich, S.M. 2021. Food supply chain during pandemic: changes in food production, food loss and waste. International *Journal of Environmental Impacts*. 4(2), 101-112.

WWF, 2017. Food Loss and Waste: Facts and Futures. https://wwfafrica.awsassets.panda.org/downloads/wwf_2017_food_loss_and_waste_facts_and_futures.pdf?21641/Food-Loss-and-Waste-Facts-and-Futures-Report (accessed on December 29, 2021).

Zhang, P., Xie, Y., Wang, Y., Li, B., Li, B., Jia, Q., Yang, Z., Cai, Y. 2021. Water-Energy-Food system in typical cities of the world and China under zero-waste: Commonalities and asynchronous experiences support sustainable development. *Ecological Indicators*. 132. 108221. https://doi.org/10.1016/j.ecolind.2021.108221.

http://valuenetworkissues.blogspot.com/2014/11/reducing-food-loss-waste-to-feed-worlds.html.

https://www.epa.gov/international-cooperation/international-efforts-wasted-food-recovery.

https://www.geoengineer.org/education/web-class-projects/cee-549-geoenvironmental-engineering-fall-2015/assignments/monitoring-landfill-gas-systems.

# Exercises for Improving the Life Quality of People with Disabilities

**Gheorghe BRANIȘTE**[1,2]**, Dumitru PRODAN**[1]*****,
**Viorel DORGAN**[1,2]

[1] Cross-Border Faculty, "Dunărea de Jos" University of Galati

[2] State University of Physical Education and Sport, Chișinău,
Republic of Moldova

* Corresponding author: dima_pda@mail.ru

## ABSTRACT

This paper provides information on the following
terms: disability and quality of life. In addition, it also de-
picts the components of quality of life. Physical education
plays an important role both in the life of an individual
and of society as a whole. Physical exercise contributes to
the harmonious development of the individual since it has
significant educational potential, maintains their physical
and mental health and contributes to the socialisation of
people of all ages.

In recent years, more and more attention has been
paid to inclusion, physical activity, and sports for people
with special needs. Therefore, we set out to research the
literature sources to elucidate the need for exercise and its
effects on the quality of life of people with disabilities.

Looking up the term disability, we found the following: DISABILITIES, disabilities, s. F. Physical, mental
or mental state which limits a person movement, activity, reception; handicap derived from English "disability"

[10]. Furthermore, we consulted the definition of the term "quality of life" on Wikipedia. World Health Organization defines the term "quality of life" as an individual's perception of their position in life in the context of the culture and value systems in which they live and in relation to their goals, expectations, standards, and concerns. In medicine, quality of life means the physical, mental, and social well-being, as well as the patients' ability to perform their usual tasks in their daily lives. In the British Encyclopedia, quality of life is defined as "the extent to which a person is healthy, comfortable, and able to participate in or enjoy life's events." [11].

The concept of quality of life has been actively used in the literature since the 1960s, and despite its long usage, this term is treated differently. Even at this time, there is no consensus on the term "quality of life". On the other hand, one of the opinions that everyone shares is that this social phenomenon is extremely complex. According to Shekotin E. V., there are two reasons for this position of the concept of quality of life. First of all, it is due to its interdisciplinary nature; in different scientific disciplines, the term "quality of life" is defined in different ways. Secondly, the quality of life itself is related to satisfactory living conditions, material well-being, standard of living, happiness, satisfaction, human potential, physical capacity and much more, which produces an even greater ambiguity about this concept. Therefore, a very important and urgent task in the study of quality of life is a conceptual and categorical analysis of the content of this concept. The author Shhekotin E. V. also mentions that usually the authors involved in the theoretical development of quality of life pay attention to the term "quality" and practically do not analyse the concept of "life", although, in the author's opinion, this is more important for interpreting the concept of quality of life [7].

One thing that is generally acknowledged is that physical education plays an important role in the life of both an individual and society as a whole. It contributes to the harmonious development of the individual, maintaining their physical and mental health. It also has significant educational potential since it contributes to the socialisation of people of any age. At the same time, one thing is for sure, the potential of physical culture and amateur sports has a positive effect on improving the society's quality of life, ensuring the economic security of the state and shaping a person's worldview. Through harmonious physical development of the population, direct action will be taken on the long-term socio-economic development of the state. In this respect, the development of social infrastructure improves the quality of the socio-economic space in the region and ensures a higher standard of living. Physical culture can also be represented as a social institution and, from this point of view, it shows that physical culture and amateur sports expand the boundaries of communication, create communities of interest, which contributes to the growth of human potential and leads to the formation of civil society. This perspective highlights the ability of physical culture to ensure the harmony of biological (bodily) and social (cultural) aspects of human life, which further leads to the idea of the interdependent existence of man, nature, and society.

It is obvious that the population's standard of living plays a huge role in determining the efficiency of the economic processes, the social and demographic policy of the state. Therefore, some of the most relevant indicators are economic ones, which include wages, purchasing power, consumer income structure, etc. In addition, indicators of personal status, along with employment, income, place of residence, marital status, etc., also include the category of health (physical, mental, emotional). Quality of life is determined not only by material and financial indicators but also by spiritual characteristics. The purpose of life, the fullness of the inner world, the identity, the maintenance of harmony between the physical and the spiritual are the components of the quality of life. The result is physical and mental health, emotional health and identity that largely determine a person's quality of life.

In this regard, we will analyse how physical culture affects the physiological, emotional, and spiritual sphere of human life. The positive influence of physical culture on the physiological sphere of life is the most studied. According to a number of physiologists, the physical culture of improving health occupies a leading position among the effective methods of preventing various diseases. The healing effect of physical activity on a person is due to the increase of their motor activity, the activation of metabolism and the strengthening of the musculoskeletal system. Lack of physical activity causes a violation of the regulation of the neuro-reflex of the body's physiological functions, which leads to dysfunctions of many systems such as the cardiovascular or the endocrine system, which triggers metabolic disorders and the development of many diseases [9].

Summarising the analysis of the conclusions of the article written by Zykov A.V. [9], we infer that physical culture has a huge impact on different spheres of life, namely it increases a person's satisfaction in the process of self-knowledge and self-realisation. The author mentions that physical training has a positive effect, namely: improving health indicators, increasing energy potential, and increasing life expectancy, which creates premises for improving the quality of life. Physical activity reduces stress levels and increases emotional stability. Moreover, the emotional stability developed in the process of physical activities prevents emotional exhaustion.

More and more often, there are articles and research which put forward the idea that for the rehabilitation and social insertion of people with special needs, their involvement in socially useful work, social and physical adaptation of the body of a person with disabilities musculoskeletal is achieved through the methods of physical culture and sports. Systematic physical activities increase the adaptability of people with disabilities by changing their functionality and contribute to the formation of co-ordination in the functioning of the musculoskeletal, cardiovascular, respiratory, digestive, and excretory systems. Thus, physical exercise has a good effect on living conditions, increase the mental level of people with disabilities and instil a sense of social utility, that is, they improve the quality of life [1].

Physical activity, in one way or another, encompasses all spheres of society and affects the main areas of life. Sport creates a modus vivendi for people as well as a professional side, which contributes to the formation of moral values and others. Physical education has become one of the most important difficulties in the politics of any state. The main reason for this is the decline in population health. In this sense, the main task is to find effective ways in order to implement physical education for the new generation. Physical activity can lead to a number of positive outcomes that significantly affect a person's life. These results include acquiring new motor skills, increasing the speed of learning new exercises and load changes, increasing physical work capacity, harmonious development of the body, developing personal qualities that positively affect a person's life, desire to live and be active, the ability to overcome physical and mental difficulties.

At present, no field of human life exists without sport. It is generally acknowledged that physical culture provides both material and spiritual value to society as a whole. Physical education is a good foundation for the formation of positive personality traits, leadership, overcoming oneself, the formation of competitive skills, the complete preparation for the encounter with various stressful situations. During sports activities, the volitional qualities necessary to achieve the goal are manifested, the person relying only on his own strength and acting effectively in stressful situations.

Throughout life, physical culture acts on the muscular system. Moreover, physical activity also stimulates brain activity and intellectual activity. Physical education is useful for any person, especially for people who lead a predominantly sedentary lifestyle, most of which often being people with special needs. A person with disabilities moves a little, which leads to deformity of the skeleton, spine, and muscle atrophy. Physical education is what will allow these people to strengthen their muscles. Thus, the interest in sports, fitness and a healthy lifestyle must bear relevance among these people.

Physical education and sports offer a number of opportunities for educating a multilaterally developed personality. The most important ones have moral, mental, physical, and aesthetic potential. It is noteworthy to emphasize that physical effort cannot be compensated or replaced. It is that part of human activity that has unique features that cannot be replaced by any other type of activity [6].

Adaptive physical culture through which the physical activity of people with special needs is performed is a type of physical culture whose purpose is to develop the maximum possible viability of a person with stable deviations in health by ensuring the optimal functioning of motor and spiritual characteristics, their harmonisation for maximum self-realisation as a significant social and individual subject. As Urivava N.A. and Nagaiţeva I.F. point out in their article [8], the general problems related to the use of adaptive physical culture for people with disabilities are addressed in the scientific papers of a number of authors like A. A. Dyskin, S. N. Konokin, D. I. Lavrova,

A. M. Osadchikh, O. N. Pisareva, L. N Smirnova, V. B. Smychek, L. M. Shipitsina and many others. The authors also cite other significant scientists who have contributed to the development of adaptive physical culture, such as I. V. Muratova, A. V. Lupandina, A. I. Bakshina, V. U. Ageevts, T. V. Sastamoinen, A. S. Solodkov, E. G. Milner, V. M. Vydrin, A. D. Dzhumaev and others (Urevava N.A. and Nagaiṭeva I.F. 2018).

Currently, among the means proposed by the adaptive physical culture, we can mention:

1. Massage – a local and general effect (humoral and reflex) on the body; there is a release of biologically active substances – histamine, acetylcholine, etc., which is accompanied by the activation of physiological processes.

2. Reflexology – a set of methodological techniques based on the use for therapeutic purposes of various physical factors, mainly non-medicinal that activate certain specific areas of the body surface (acupuncture points).

3. Physical exercises (gymnastics, sports, applications, etc.).

4. Outdoor games – based on various types of vital movements and the fact that these movements are performed in a wide variety of conditions; with fast movements during the game, the breathing process improves, resulting in a faster saturation of blood oxygenation, accelerated metabolism, increased blood circulation and more [8].

As for the people with special needs, the issue of creating the conditions for improving their physical and personal development, re-establishing contact with the outside world and socializing with full rights is of particular relevance. The solution to this problem is to increase the effectiveness of rehabilitation measures by increasing physical activity as a natural means of developing and forming a healthy body. Physical activity can be done through the use of physical culture in a large volume as a factor that contributes to lowering the level of disability, but its role is currently underestimated, especially among specialists involved in motor rehabilitation problems of people with disabilities. It is necessary to enrich the information support and activate the role of the family in understanding the importance of physical culture in solving the health problems of a person with disabilities. Few family members can appreciate the importance of physical exercise in improving the condition of a person with a disability. Children with locomotor disabilities, including those with cerebral palsy, usually lead a sedentary lifestyle which leads to a delay in physical and functional development, difficulties in communication, learning and the development of professional skills. Insufficient understanding of the need to expand motor activity and stimulate the movement of a child with disabilities by physicians and rehabilitation specialists delays the realization of their motor potential. At the same time, well-organized regular training that makes it possible for children with disabilities to be involved in physical activity contributes to the effective development of motor skills, stimulates them to exercise independently and improves their quality of life. Relevant findings confirm the positive effect of exercise on the development of motor skills of children with disabilities, but the methodology of such training has not yet been sufficiently developed [3].

Analysing the article written by Kremneva V. N. [4] we grasped the following: 1. People with disabilities really appreciate the role of healthy lifestyle factors; 2. Only half of the people with disabilities practice physical activity in order to maintain their health; 3. The most common way to maintain health among people with disabilities is to use time to rest and avoid harmful habits; 4. In general, people with disabilities have a positive attitude towards physical activity but do not have enough motivation to practice these activities; 5. A negative factor in the process of practising physical activities for people with disabilities is that they cause physical discomfort. It seems that people encounter discomfort in front of other people when they are engaged in such activities; some do not see the purpose of such activities. Another obstacle is the negative experience of the training sessions and the lack of information about the intensity and the sets of exercises that are suitable for them; 6. Half of the people with disabilities show negative emotions related to physical activity, which is even more obvious if they have an unfavourable emotional balance; 7. People with disabilities are generally positive about the implementation of individual exercise programs. They believe that such programs would improve their well-being and health and will have a positive change in the field of leisure. 8. Variables of subjective happiness such as self-efficacy, subjective happiness, life satisfaction, adaptability to the educational process are positively associated with the factors of a healthy lifestyle and the positive effects of physical education.

Thus, we may conclude that the attitude of people with disabilities towards a healthy lifestyle and physical education demonstrates the need to improve physical education and work in order to achieve health for this category of people and provide social and psychological support for their involvement in daily life. In order to increase the effectiveness of physical education and health work programs for people with disabilities, it is recommendable to use the key provisions of theories of healthy behaviour formation. Behavioural changes based on these provisions have a significant impact on changing healthy behaviour. It is therefore a list of the main components of intervention programs based on socio-cognitive theory: – information to assess the risks and benefits associated with a particular behaviour; – teaching social and cognitive skills that can be used to initiate behavioural change; - defining self-efficacy criteria for maintaining and strengthening healthy behaviour; – social support to sustain and consolidate change.

In this regard, any participant in the physical education program for recreation and rehabilitation must meet certain requirements: 1. To express a desire (motivation) or pronounced predisposition to participate in the program. 2. To possess a minimum of information, logistical, social, and environmental possibilities in order to implement the health-strengthening behaviour inside and outside the program. 3. To hold the belief that they have the necessary external and internal resources to strengthen and maintain a healthy lifestyle. 4. To consider that participation in the program will strengthen their health. 5. Participation in physical activity is voluntary, and there are no penalties for lack of activity. 6. Acquiring positive emotions in connection with participation in physical activity. 7. For a fuller involvement of people with disabilities in physical activities, along with information support, explanatory works, and psychological support is also needed to form an internal motivation for attending these activities [4].

At present, social rehabilitation and disability have been considered as a complex socio-medical problem, including multiple aspects such as: medical, physical (physiological), economic. In order to fulfil the normal psychological, professional, and social recovery of the vital activity of a person with disabilities, it is necessary to carry out social rehabilitation with the following aspects: maximum restoration and rehabilitation of disturbed physical (physiological) functions of the body and if this cannot be done, to resort to the development of compensatory and replacement functions.

Thus, the social rehabilitation of people with disabilities is a multilateral process of social rehabilitation of their health and social environment. All types of social rehabilitation must be considered as being interconnected. Physical (physiological) rehabilitation includes medical, social, and professional rehabilitation, which is the recovery or physical compensation of the body through the means and methods of physical culture and a system of measures to increase intellectual capacity and abilities, increase body function, improve physical qualities, mental stability, emotional and adaptive reserves of the body by practising sports training. Physical culture is a special component of culture that fulfils the functions of social rehabilitation and recovery through the development of work capacity, the musculoskeletal system, increased communication needs, restoring the satisfaction of the psychological state and others.

The main role in social rehabilitation and recovery of physical and psychological strength, of abilities of people with disabilities, recovery, transition from one type of activity to another, maintaining physical strength, vitality is played by motor psychological rehabilitation, which has the following objectives: support and development of physical qualities and functional requirements; development of motor skills; improving basic motor skills and abilities; consolidating and deepening knowledge on physical culture issues; developing a positive attitude towards active forms of recreation by strengthening the habit of exercising systematic physical activity; strengthening the body, training hygiene skills, ability and desire to lead a healthy lifestyle.

It is necessary to use all types of physical activity in physical activities for people with disabilities. It is also important that they are developed in strict accordance with the corrective and compensatory tasks and applied separately for each group of people with disabilities. Various exercises are attributed to the means and methods of physical culture for people with disabilities, in which the main physical qualities are manifested as strength, speed, strength-speed, for the development of general and special endurance, for the development of flexibility, and others. Due to the character of the motor activity, physical exercises of a cyclical nature or acyclic nature include mixed motor physical actions. The main forms of physical education for people with disabilities are independent activities, group and sectional physical activities and sports, independent exercises at home, morning exercises performed daily, regardless of person and type of disability (home, hospital, sanatorium, rehabilitation centre), walking, hiking and use of specific equipment and devices; special corrective courses, preventive measures (gymnastics, massage, posture correction), as well as orthopedic appliances and training exercises that contribute to the total or partial elimination of musculoskeletal insufficiency for which no special training is required, including a multifunctional apparatus.

Because the person with disabilities gets tired quickly, movement disorders, muscle imbalance, muscle hypertonicity and, therefore, injuries and diseases set in faster. The use of physical education elements for the psychological, social, and physical rehabilitation of people with disabilities has long been used by specialists. Group games with people with disabilities have a positive effect on their psychological, emotional, and physiological spheres. Injuries and diseases of the nervous system, etc. lead to structural (morphological) changes in motor functions, in the musculoskeletal system, etc. However, regardless of the effect such diseases have on the capacity to undergo physical training and sports activities, they still result in psychological, emotional and social satisfaction.

Disability does not allow these people to perform a certain thing or movement correctly, or exercise. In this sense, technically incorrect movements can be developed with other repeated diseases of the musculoskeletal system (per arthritis, periostitis, myositis, abrasions, etc.). Therefore, it is very important to select the types of exercises, taking into account the pathology characteristics. In addition, there may be a degree of recovery of motor function. Recovery physical culture has a positive effect on the health and general mental and physical condition of people with disabilities and effectively solves the problem of their socialization.

Recovery physical education helps people with disabilities to solve many problems, such as: eliminating or reducing the side effects of urban overload, achieving the hypokinesia of life, in particular excessive, irrational neuro-emotional eating, increasing work capacity; ensures the necessary physical activity increases a person's natural immunity; offers a person the opportunity to move from everyday, monotonous and boring living conditions to new objects of the social environment, distracts them from the tiring and negative effects of everyday life; stimulates a sense of desire to overcome obstacles and other valuable moral and volitional qualities that play an important role in preventing both physical illness and deviant neuropsychic manifestations in behaviour; ensures an increase in the level of metabolic processes, endocrine activity and tissue immunity, helps to reduce harmful outbreaks [2].

In order to implement various high-quality physical activities for people with disabilities in the field of physical culture, of course, extensive systemic measures are needed. Firstly, measures related to the regulation of legislation and the regulation of activities in the field of inclusive education in general. In addition, it is necessary to generally retrain the people who will lead this process (physical education teachers, coaches, etc.). And, of course, the creation of the educational, managerial, scientific, and informational conditions and the organizational, material and technical methodological ones for the full implementation of the general adaptive curricula at all levels of the education system [5].

# REFERENCES

Andreev I. I., Rubcova N. O., Rubcov A. V. Vlijanie povysh-enija urovnja koordinacionnyh sposobnostej na kachestvo zhizni detej 10-12 let s porazheniem oporno-dvigatel'nogo apparata v processe zanjatij basketbolom na koljaskah. Mezhdunarod. Nauch. Kongress. «Dvadcatipjatiletnij put' razvitija adaptivnoj fizicheskoj kul'tury». Nacional'nyj gosudarstvennyj universitet fizicheskoj kul'tury, sporta i zdorov'ja imeni P.F. Lesgafta. Sankt-Peterburg. 2020. 18-27.

Chufarova L. I., Kuz'mina A. P. Zanjatija lfk kak metod social'noj reabilitacii i vosstanovlenija dvigatel'nyh funkcij invalidov. Nauka-2020: Fizicheskaja kul'tura, sport, turizm: problemy i perspektivy 2019. # 1(26). 51-57.

Gross N. A., Sharova T. L., Molokanov A. V. Vlijanie aktivnyh fizicheskih uprazhnenij na razvitie dvigatel'nyh navykov detej-invalidov. Uchenye zapiski universiteta imeni P.F. Lesgafta. 2021. # 3 (193). 86-93. DOI: 10.34835/issn.2308-1961.2021.3.p86-93

Kremneva V. N. Otnoshenie studentov s ogranichennymi vozmozhnostjami zdorov'ja k zdorovomu obrazu zhizni. Nepreryvnoe obrazovanie: XXI vek. 2021. Vyp. 2 (34).DOI: 10.15393/j5.art.2021.6928.

Pevicyna L. M. Podgotovka uchitelej fizicheskoj kul'tury k realizacii adaptivnyh obrazovatel'nyh programm. Mezhdunarod. Nauch. Kongress. «Dvadcatipjatiletnij put' razvitija adaptivnoj fizicheskoj kul'tury». Nacional'nyj gosudarstvennyj universitet fizicheskoj kul'tury, sporta i zdorov'ja imeni P.F. Lesgafta. Sankt-Peterburg. 2020. 303-308.

Polovodov I.V., Kozinskaja E. E. Vazhnost' zanjatij fizicheskoj kul'tury v stanovlenii lichnosti cheloveka. Nauka-2020: Fizicheskaja kul'tura i sport: nauka, praktika, obrazovanie, 2019 # 6(31). 124-128.

Shhekotin E. V. Koncept «zhizn'» v issledovanijah kachestva zhizni. Logos et Rraxis. 2020. Vol. 19. No. 3. 47-57. DOI: https://doi.org/10.15688/lp.jvolsu.2020.3.5

Uryvaeva N. A., Nagajceva I. F. Primenenie sredstv adaptivnoj fizicheskoj kul'tury dlja zanjatij s det'mi doshkol'nogo vozrasta s ogranichennymi vozmozhnostjami zdorov'ja. Nauka-2020: Fizicheskaja kul'tura i sport: nauka, praktika, obrazovanie, 2018 # 1-2(17).118-121.

Zykov A.V. Vlijanie fizicheskoj kul'tury na kachestvo zhizni. Pedagogicheskij zhurnal Bashkortostana. 2021. # 2(92). 86-95.

https://dexonline.ro/definitie/dizabilitate, acesat 20.03.2022

https://ro.wikipedia.org/wiki/Calitatea_vie%C8%9Bii

# Intercultural Communication Competence and its Implications on the Integration of Foreign Students

**Georgiana CIOBOTARU,** Lecturer, Cross-Border Faculty,
"Dunărea de Jos" University of Galati,
georgiana.ciobotaru@ugal.ro

## 1. INTRODUCTION

Romanian as a foreign language taught in the academic program *The preparatory year for the formation and development of linguistic skills of oral and written expression* relies on the coexistence of an ethnocultural diversity distinct from that of the local environment. A multitude of cultural factors is involved in the entire social communication as well as the didactic one, modifying not only the individual's behaviour but also the communication itself. Foreign students who learn the Romanian language relate to it from the perspective of their mother tongue, thus scaffolding a mental construct and defining themselves in contact with the Other, which mirrors a different religion, a different culture, a different ethnicity. That is why the reception and understanding of the message are conditioned by the range of cultural contexts with which man intersects their existence and within which they lead their life for at least a certain period of time. The preparatory year intended to teach Romanian as a foreign language involves linguistic, discursive acquisitions, a relevant factor being the interaction with the entire host culture in which the student undergoes his professional development. Learning a foreign language online is even more challenging, as students do not have the opportunity to interact frequently with the language they are studying and have to rely heavily on technology-mediated didactic communication for a short period of time limited to class attendance, then re-entering their living environment and interacting with peers.

## 2. LIFE QUALITY AND CULTURAL DIVERSITY WITHIN EDUCATIONAL CONTEXTS

Foreign students' life quality is closely related to this broadly defined notion, but to all the aspects previously mentioned, we can add the fact that they change their native environment with another, sometimes completely different and have to quickly adapt to a community other than their native one. Consequently, they have to take into account the new socio-economic context and why not the political one as well. The multicultural educational communities they enter make them redefine their relationships with people who are driven by different mentality and customs. Thus, on the one hand, foreigners interact with Romanians. On the other hand, they can seldom interact with their compatriots or with other citizens from different parts of the globe who have come to study in Romania. Everyday life somehow follows the same patterns only that they are applied to another country with its own social and educational system, its own customs and traditions with which foreign students must get acquainted.

In addition, foreign citizens who arrived in Romania to continue their studies sometimes settle here to practise, especially after completing university and postgraduate studies must define their existence by reference to the field of activity they study or in which they will later crystallize their profession. Relations with the authorities that regulate the possibility of living in a foreign country in legal conditions are also defining for the cultural shock that foreign students face and that they must overcome quickly for an active integration in the new society and the academic environment.

A relevant component of what we call life quality refers to each individual's lifestyle, the one linked to their native country and the one they must adopt as soon as they arrive in another geographical-political area. People often experience contradictory states throughout their existence, especially in a context other than the natural one. They may feel an increased level of satisfaction or dissatisfaction, happiness or anxiety, fulfilment or failure, stress or deep frustration. They need to know how to manage these strengths, re-evaluate their behaviour in order to get feedback on their own person in order to have an optimal behaviour in the future. Proper management of one's own condition is an important factor for easy integration into new living environments. Both personal and communal lifestyles, as well as the degree of attraction society offers, are necessary conditions for newcomers to adapt to the country.

When it comes to the students' life quality, in general, and that of foreign students, in particular, the concept of the student's status as a whole must be taken into account, so the higher educational institution, faculty or university in which they come to study is supposed to provide them with a level of subsistence by making use of the living conditions and the means that are available at that moment. If these institutions are meant to offer the Romanian students facilities to ensure high professional standards, the same entities must do the same for foreign students in order to create contexts both to raise their academic standards and ensure adequate professional training. Needless to say that it is even more important to create an area of comfort, integration, communication, and optimal interrelationship with those around, so that the two necessary conditions mentioned before are met.

The academic, didactic and research environment is also responsible for an adequate quality life, the way foreign students interact with teachers, the way the latter give them feedback or facilitate their learning of the Romanian language, which is so necessary for daily survival and optimal interaction with the natives or with other colleagues with whom they could not interact. Learning, teaching, assessment activities, materials and methods used, attractive seminars and courses, integration of technology in optimal teaching, especially in a pandemic context, open discussions on current topics, support for overcoming bureaucratic constraints, all these are defining premises for an appropriate active integration in the host community.

Cultural diversity within an educational context means evolution, innovation in terms of methods, teaching procedures, teaching-learning-assessment tools as well as in terms of interaction and didactic communication. Cultural factors are fundamental in learning RFL as well as other foreign languages, all of which entail the development of intercultural competence. Thus, the development of language skills is doubled in this context by the formation and development of intercultural competence, which is constantly monitored, the way the messages are understood in a cultural context other than the native one. The cultural variety in the field of education stimulates each other's learning, enriching both the native and host language, as well as that of the foreign student, generating a metamorphosis of their cultural identity which is, in fact, in a perpetual change. Foreign students do not only come from spheres different from those of the Romanian language and culture but also present themselves, at an individual level, as a cultural variation, often having multiple identities and expressing their belonging to different cultures. Students often refer to distinct cultures, religions, and idioms because they often belong to several spheres at the same time, their families being heterogeneous. In this context, their cultural identity is multiple, and the teaching of the Romanian language appears as a challenge, as it is another foreign idiom whose patterns are based on the pre-existing ones, which, moreover, are extremely different. Thus, the whole didactic approach must be multilingual, inclusive, and innovative. Teaching Romanian as a foreign language is not an approach with a long tradition, so it is worth considering "the personal experience of each author both in the field of teaching Romanian as a foreign language and in the field of teach-

ing materials needed for teaching (textbooks, grammar)."
(Strasbourg: Consiliul Europei, p. 12)

To approach the instructive-educational process from an intercultural perspective means to identify both the differences and similarities so that we are able to counteract the imminent blockages that could appear in the didactic communication, from the most banal inadvertences to aspects related to discrimination. Education, in all its forms, also entails cultural diversity which highlights the capitalisation of the elements between cultures and the phenomenon of mutual influence. Romanian as a foreign language means shifting the emphasis from the communication model specific to the native speaker to that of the intercultural speaker because the communicational situations thus relate to two or more cultural spheres, that of the student learning the Romanian language and that of his interlocutor. Therefore, a series of metamorphoses of identities take place, and intercultural communication can be studied from the perspective of a process in a perpetual evolution. Intercultural reporting to education means establishing an analogy between the local culture and the one to be assimilated. The student can relate critically to both their own cultural background and the learned culture, thus developing his intercultural competence. The person who becomes an intercultural speaker will be able to easily adapt to the new contexts in which they find themselves and define their identity through interculturality.

Didactic communication regarding the teaching of Romanian as a foreign language also means an interaction between two or more speakers, a complex process of encoding and decoding messages, the verbal intertwining with the nonverbal and the paraverbal, often generating critical attitudes from the interlocutors. The efficiency of the didactic communication is supported by optimal knowledge of all the peculiarities of the working group, the foreign students having their own learning needs and their own expectations regarding the host language and culture. In the learning process, they will also be influenced by pre-existing aspects in their mind depending on the country they come from or the mother tongue they speak. Didactic communication takes place; therefore, both between teacher and student and between students, intercultural education is optimally developed through those methods and tools that facilitate the combination of verbal, paraverbal and nonverbal, and those that support collaborative learning. Collaborating in the learning process means cooperating, supporting, and encouraging the oral and written expression of the foreign language learner. Optimal interaction between colleagues, motivation, encouragement, suitable exploitation of interventions, and learning in various social contexts contribute to the development of specific language skills as well as the crystallization of values and attitudes related to tolerance, acceptance, non-discrimination, and diversity. Like any didactic approach, the process of teaching-learning a foreign language from an intercultural perspective relies, in fact, on a series of methods and tools meant to develop those skills that are necessary for communication in a foreign language such as problematisation, project work, portfolios, games roles, dramatizations, storytelling. Thus, for learning RFL, methods based on the indirect exploration of reality should be combined with oral teaching methods – debates/ conversations, individual and pair work methods, the use of equipment, especially online, methods based on real interaction in a particular field of activity, interaction with native speakers, limited methods, if, learning is not face to face, but only mediated by computer/ laptop/ tablet. Returning to one of the methods mentioned before, namely the role-play, the foreign student has in this way the opportunity to step in the shoes of a native speaker, to empathise with him by getting involved in the communication situation as an actor from this perspective and develops intercultural communication, because it faces unique situations of life, of expression, having to deal with blockages, but also cultural and religious prejudices because everyone has some pre-existing communication patterns. When the student learns the Romanian language in Romania and moves, at least for a while, to another country to study, there is also a cultural and linguistic shock that can only be overcome through adaptation, collaboration, communication, acceptance of diversity, contact with the other, with otherness, being defining. Face-to-face learning allows the use of several methods based on direct contact with immediate reality, and often students take responsibility for their learning process, capitalising on concrete life experiences. Every learning activity has also a stage of reflection, at which point it is necessary to make an analysis of the process, analysis that will later lead to a real-world application of the experiences gained. RFL courses must be accompanied by those of Romanian culture and civilization because only in this way all those skills of an intercultural speaker can be developed. Of course, in order to access the essence of a culture, the foreign student must have some basic language skills, but teaching the elements of culture is a necessity. However, it depends a lot on the category to which the student belongs, namely: if they come to Romania through a cooperation stage, etc." (Pricope, 2018, p. 110).

Oral and written skills as well as receptive skills and the acquisition of vocabulary elements, ranging from the elementary ones to the most complex ones, such as phraseologies are developed within the RFL courses depending on the language level addressed. All the aspects mentioned above have a strong intercultural impact since the contents can be selected, so as to develop the foreign students' multicultural communication competence. Also, the intercultural learning dimension can be exploited in so far as the learners listen to, observe recorded or filmed materials, materials that can illustrate either barriers in communication or dissensions, controversies, and disputes. They are asked to express their opinion in order to solve blockages of any kind while practising their oral expression competence and pinpointing an intercultural approach to the learning process. The contexts proposed for the analysis also involve critical thinking, as, most of the time, the obstacles are generated by different mentalities, misperceptions, or cultural prejudices that man brings in when they arrive in a foreign country to study.

Comparative studies are, therefore, the most appropriate in these situations because they call for the identification of alternatives to address the problems, proposing optimal solutions to conflicts and revealing the causes that led to those dissensions.

Both face-to-face learning and the current context of online learning allow the selection of methods, tools and procedures that stimulate cooperation, collaboration, and multicultural communication. Cultures have their own peculiarity, customs, traditions, and rituals which vary from one area to another, especially if people belong to other continents. Thus, feelings, refusals or approvals are expressed in a distinct way from one culture to another, and the distinctive note can be noticed only through dramatizations when students can directly observe the different ways of communication and action as well as how verbal elements mingle with paraverbal and nonverbal ones. Also, with a view to providing an intercultural education, the RFL study could involve the creation of interviews with native speakers, the foreign student being able to be both an interviewer and an interviewee, facing authentic life situations. When we talk about culture, we highlight that set of features of a community: "Culture generally refers to a set of characteristics of a community, according to which a person feels that they belong to that community (Rus, Neștian-Sandu, Bajka, 2019). Thus, each constructs their identity, both in relation to themselves – "self-definition" and in relation to the others – "hetero definition" (Rus, Neștian-Sandu, Bajka, 2019).

Intercultural learning can also take place by studying the literature of the people whose language is acquired. Certainly, the texts must be carefully selected so that they are accessible, illustrative of the local colour of times or places, but relevant enough from the perspective of the language used, from the perspective of the vocabulary, the words encountered should have a certain frequency and in use. Foreign students learning Romanian can produce messages that suit various cultural, secular, or religious events to present to native speakers or even exchange them so that they can observe each other's way of expressing themselves, but to report those texts and those of the Romanians. These messages can be a subject of analysis, of reflection in the courses, observing the information, but also the attitudes, the values, the feelings transmitted, the unique and different ways of constructing the texts.

The groups of students taking Romanian language courses as a foreign language during the Preparatory Year are heterogeneous, and cultural, ethnic, religious diversity is often a challenge, so the activities must be complex and relate to the multi-ethnic sphere involved in the interactions between members of those classes.

The intercultural approach in teaching Romanian as a foreign language is absolutely necessary, especially in the current context of academic mobility and due to partnership projects aimed at developing multicultural communication skills as well. Language acquisitions are much better acquired when students move to the local area and interact directly with native people, so foreign students could even attend courses in the Romanian language or

Romanian history and civilization, which would enhance the cultural impact. The methods, teaching practices, procedures, and tools used in the academic context are not entirely new, but the approach is different, focusing on interculturality, multiculturalism and multilingualism. A language has a number of meanings from a cultural point of view, and therefore, the ability to communicate interculturalism is an end in itself, especially when it comes to teaching a modern language. Starting from the idea of the cultural meanings that a language has and extrapolating the phenomenon of teaching a foreign language, in this case the Romanian language, it can be noticed that in this context the intercultural component of communication is defining and essential for an open and dynamic contemporary society, constantly based on the idea of mobility for personal and professional development, students moving both from one university centre to another and from one country to another to study, to broaden their knowledge, and language is extremely relevant in this respect.

Given the current pandemic period, online learning has become a necessity. Consequently, foreign language learning, including Romanian, takes place exclusively in the virtual space, which is both generous due to the means and platforms provided and restrictive from other points of view because it limits the degree of interaction between students. Sometimes if the students do not leave their native country, from a linguistic and cultural perspective, they are unable to step out of their comfort zone and that is why the didactic activity mediated by technology becomes more difficult. However, there are a number of applications that support collaborative learning and facilitate an intercultural approach even at a distance. Take, for instance, Padlet, which is a useful application for language and cultural acquisitions, the result being a collective one and providing an overview of the group of students, as well as their dynamics. Under the sign of anonymity, all students can express themselves without bearing fear of making mistakes, without feeling ashamed, a natural state which always intervenes when a student is introduced to the secrets of a language. Each student presents a series of individual peculiarities but also information related to the country they come from. Allowing free expression, Padlet is an excellent tool for collaborative learning, an extremely useful source for knowledge systematisation courses, for recycling information/concepts, for effective and relevant preparation in order to take the final Romanian language exams.

## 3. INTERCULTURAL ACTIVITIES AND ONSITE QUALITY LEARNING

The host academic environment is responsible for the integration of foreign students in the socio-cultural space in which they participated for a short period of time or forever, in some cases. Curricular activities and extracurricular activities, in particular, are those that provide a comfort zone for foreign students. Thus, due to the fact that non-formal activities also have well-defined learning objectives, they can be used successfully in smoothing the culture shock and overcoming any linguistic, religious, and customary barriers. The 60 students from the Romanian Language Preparatory Year for the 2020-2021 academic year were involved in the following activities: The Intercultural Evening, The Gastronomy Week, Visits to the Dramatic Theatre, The Living Library. These special events were held during the ten weeks of the second semester, and they made them feel socially and culturally integrated and appreciated, their identity being able to be thus expressed by reference to the native country and also to the adoptive one.

"The Intercultural Evening" required that the 60 students be split into mixed teams consisting of individuals from several countries in order to present an attractive cultural element, discovered in Romania. The challenge was, first of all, for the team members to agree on the cultural aspect to highlight. Secondly, they had to use only the Romanian language to establish the role of each individual at the group level and to present the product of their activity. The most frequent Romanian cultural elements were those related to traditions, religious, and secular holidays that they witnessed during their stay in Romania. It was interesting to see the authentic perspective of depicting the Other, the native Romanian, from the foreigner's point of view. The fact that mixed groups were involved also led to original presentations on the life of Romanians. Another event included in the intercultural evening was meant to group teams consisting of individuals belonging to the same countries or ethnically related: Slavic, Muslim and Asian. This part of the non-formal activity, whose main objective was that of highlighting one's own cultural identity and accepting otherness, conjured up some cultural, religious, and economic elements of the countries they come from and the peculiarity of the native continents. Both stages of "The Intercultural Evening" aimed at shaping a defining profile for the foreign student in order to help them adapt and get integrated in the new linguistic, socio-cultural environment.

"The Gastronomic Week" is another impactful extracurricular activity carried out in partnership with an educational institution meant for native learners. Thus, every day of the week, during the five days of the course, the native teams had to bring a Romanian dish and present it in a creative way. The native teams made their choices, cooked the dishes, brought them to the foreigners and also presented the recipes. The students enjoyed the presentations and tasted the culinary creations made by the native students. In their turn, the 60 foreign students formed 10 teams, and 2 teams per day presented food specific to their native area. The teams were also formed taking into account the criteria of their geographical neighbourhood, religious affiliation, nationality so that they could find culinary elements.

Foreign students practised the Romanian language in a non-formal context, interacted with the 20 native speakers and were able to notice common culinary aspects during their presentations. Furthermore, there were also other benefits related to observing the difference between literary language frequently assimilated to RFL courses and the colloquial one because the activities took place outdoors, a space which also allowed a less standardized communication.

The last activity included in the series of non-formal events carried out onsite, but not in a typical classroom, was "The Visit to the Theatre". The students were guided by the teachers to go to a show that was accessible to them as far as the language level was concerned, to listen to the Romanian language spoken in the performance hall, also being able to interact with the other spectators, but especially at the end of the theatrical performance. Also, they could ask questions to the actors to find out information about the play, the staged opera, or curiosities about the acting profession. Most of the questions were related to the national and local dramatic art and the Romanian authors who performed on the stage.

All these extracurricular activities represented the premise of the foreign student integration since they began to have a different perspective on life, gastronomy, culture, or religion, redefining their existence in another country by keeping in touch not only with the natives but also with other people like them from other parts of the world.

## 4. INTERCULTURAL ACTIVITIES AND ONLINE LEARNING

Owing to the fact that the life of the entire planet has changed since 2020 because of the recent pandemic outbreak, the concept of life quality has also changed, the perception of the whole reality undergoing multiple metamorphoses, and that is why for a long time, education has been eminently accomplished online. Thus, the didactic approaches were rethought and acquired another dimension. Efforts to teach a foreign language have required rethinking the entire methodological paradigm. Even the cultural paradigm has undergone a change, with the emphasis shifting to open culture, that of an extremely generous internet that can now, more than ever, be used to its full potential due to the open educational resources it provides.

During the online activities, the 60 students were divided into two groups, and the didactic approaches also aimed at their cultural immersion and integration even before arriving in our country. The limitations of online learning have also meant difficulties in reaching students in our country at an optimal time, the Romanian language being thus assimilated in front of the computer through an interaction mediated by equipment, without direct contact with colleagues or teachers.

Among the activities initiated in the virtual space, beyond the thematic areas of the curricular contents, we included virtual tours of museums, virtual visits, and presentations of the Romanian cultural space. The students therefore became familiar with the city, the country they were going to arrive in because the pandemic context was going to be restrictive anyway, and human interactions were going to be limited, even during the onsite learning that alternated with the hybrid one, but also with the online one. The computer enabled students to get to know each other, even through this type of interaction mediated by a virtual space tool.

The virtual visits to museums and memorial houses meant the practise of the Romanian language through question-and-answer forms, but also the familiarisation with an audio and video presentation made by qualified people so that further lessons could be discussed with the Romanian language teacher.

The last part of these activities was the formulation of invitations from foreign students to present and create a virtual tour of a museum, building, city in their native country to get colleagues accustomed to the unity and diversity that countries, continents can possess. Beyond diversity, uniqueness and national identity, there is also a multicultural intersection point that helps us to dialogue, convince, accept each other, treat the Other with tolerance, and understand otherness. This aspect requires an intercultural approach, which is a complex process: "The intercultural approach and the action perspective can and must be combined, because in today's society there is a lot of emphasis on teamwork, especially if it is a multicultural team." (Pricope, 2018, p. 61).

# 5. RESEARCH METHODOLOGY

## *5.1 Case Study – Quality of Life and its Implications in the Integration of Foreign Students*

The case study dealing with the life quality of foreign students involved 60 students of the Romanian Language Preparatory Year, class 2020-2021, and followed some indicators on the degree of their insertion in the social and academic community of the host country, Romania.

The established indicators aimed at:
- quality and attractiveness of teaching activities;
- relations with state institutions;
- the services offered by the academic environment;
- the degree of interaction with the natives;
- attractions from the local and national area – cultural impact.

Thus, in the substantiation of the case study, a questionnaire was developed, which was given to students at the beginning of the academic year after a minimal interaction with the country, the place where they were meant to study, and at the end of the study period to assimilate the linguistic elements necessary for their social and professional integration, continuing their specialisation at the University of Galați. The administered questionnaire was anonymous, the students having to mention only their nationality in order that we could make a comparative study and notice the differences of integration, adaptation, any difficulties the students encountered depending on the area they come from. The teachable were willing to complete the questionnaire both at the beginning and at the end of the course, eager to mention the challenges they faced in a foreign country, how the "foreigners" treated them (namely the inhabitants, foreigners for them), the degree of satisfaction or dissatisfaction with the services, the compatibility or incompatibility with the way in which the state institutions react when they are asked for help by foreign citizens.

### 5.2 Questionnaire Administered to Foreign Students Regarding Life Quality During the Studies in Romania, in Galati

1. Name 3 of the teacher's qualities that helped you feel comfortable when studying abroad. / Menționați 3 calități ale profesorului care vă ajută să vă simțiți în zona de confort la studii în străinătate.

.............................................................................

2. Name 3 didactic activities that you consider useful for your cultural integration. / Precizați 3 activități didactice pe care le considerați utile pentru integrarea voastră culturală.

.............................................................................

3. Mention 3 difficulties you faced when you came to Romania. / Evidențiați 3 dificultăți cu care v-ați confruntat când ați venit în România.

.............................................................................

4. What are the 3 essential services that you consider the new academic environment must offer you? / Care sunt cele 3 servicii pe care le considerați foarte utile pe care noul mediu academic trebuie să vi le ofere?

.............................................................................

5. What activities are you passionate about? Do you think they resemble with the native students' hobbies so that you can interact optimally with them? Mention 3 of them. / Ce activități vă pasionează și credeți că sunt comune cu

cele ale nativilor pentru a putea interacţiona optim cu aceştia? Menţionaţi 3 dintre acestea.

.............................................................................................

6. Taking into account your hobbies, what are the areas of cultural attraction of a country that appeal to you? / Care sunt zonele de atracţie culturală ale unei ţări care vă atrag în funcţie de hobby-urile pe care le aveţi?

.............................................................................................

7. What activities would you like to do in your free time? Mention 3 of them. / Ce activităţi v-ar plăcea să faceţi în timpul liber, menţionaţi 3 dintre acestea.

.............................................................................................

8. What qualities do you value in your peers, compatriots or foreigners? / Ce calităţi apreciaţi la semenii voştri, conaţionali sau străini?

.............................................................................................

9. Mention an indispensable aspect that you would not be able to do without in the host country. / Menţionaţi un aspect indispensabil fără de care nu v-aţi descurca în ţara gazdă.

.............................................................................................

10. Write 5-6 lines describing how you felt upon your arrival in Romania in order to continue your studies/at the end of the Romanian language courses as a foreign language (as the case may be). / Prezentaţi, 5-6 rânduri, impactul privind interacţiunea cu noua ţară în care aţi ajuns pentru continuarea studiilor la venirea în România/ la sfârşitul cursurilor de limbă română ca limbă străină(după caz).

# 6. RESULTS

The questionnaire was administered twice: in the initial stage after the students' arrival in Galați, Romania and at the end of the academic Romanian language preparatory year.

As far as the first question is concerned, they initially answered that the teacher's main qualities that make them better integrated in the academic community would be the following, in the order listed, in terms of frequency: empathy, tolerance, openness, altruism, and the proactive attitude. Equally, they all appreciated the need for a multitude of mixed activities which involved both foreign and local citizens in order to feel more accepted and integrated in the social community. Therefore, the most preferred didactic activities would be the non-formal ones, held outdoors: intercultural evenings, gastronomy weeks, theatre evenings, karaoke evenings. Top three difficulties that foreigners faced when coming to our country would be the linguistic element, some of them not knowing any language of international circulation, bureaucracy - students appreciate that in Romania they face a series of bureaucratic actions different from those in their home country, the lack of adaptation to the environment, the climate, as at least two students come from areas where there are no four seasons and have difficulties adapting in this regard.

Due to the fact that the academic environment is thought to represent the main factor enabling foreign students to integrate in the society they adopt, they consider the hostel living conditions as being a priority, the existence of leisure areas where they are given the opportunity to spend their free time with other foreign students from higher years as well as local students so that they would adapt more easily to the new lifestyle. Foreign students reckon that non-formal, cultural and sports activities are the most relevant types of interactions that help them overcome the cultural shock. The most appealing cultural areas are the theatres, the museums, the Botanical Garden, V. A Urechia, and the Musical Theatre.

Leisure is extremely valuable for foreigners, so they expect to have a range of cultural and sports events in weekends or during holidays. Therefore, they believe that representatives from universities ought to make some flyers in order to promote such events, as sometimes it is quite difficult for them to find common interests if they do not find support from the native people.

From the foreign students' point of view, the defining character traits displayed by Romanians are empathy, open-mindedness and linguistic skills - most are speakers of two or three foreign languages, which makes those who, in turn, know an idiom of international circulation feel better or more self-confident.

The 21st century is obviously dominated by technology, and the foreign students unanimously emphasised that the Internet and the mobile phone are two indispensable tools used in any country not only for orientation, communication but also for education, especially during the pandemic period.

As for the last question, about the impact on the interaction with the new society, their testimonies reflected the fact that they were afraid at first as they did not know what to expect, they were annoyed by the administrative regulations while some of them even felt unwilling to comply with the new society and its culture. They also point out that all academic and extracurricular activities helped them to overcome all barriers and gradually integrate into the new community. Intercultural communication is very important when we talk about an environment where there are both native speakers and speakers of several countries around the world because foreign students who come to our country go through a double process of adaptation, on the one hand in the adoptive country with all its inhabitants, and on the other hand, they must interact optimally with others like them, similar in the status of foreign student but extremely different in culture, religion, traditions.

## 7 CONCLUSIONS

The quality of life of foreign students is important for their future development, their academic performance, how they evolve professionally and personally also depend on this, as they stay in Romania for a shorter or longer period of time, transforming how they are as people, becoming others, richer culturally, linguistically, people of modern, open democratic societies, able to adapt anywhere and interact with a different Other.

# REFERENCES

Nivel prag. (2001). Strasbourg: Consiliul Europei, p. 12: https://www.ilr.ro/wp-content/uploads/nivel_prag.pdf;

Pricope, Mihaela. (2018). Dezvoltarea competenței de comunicare interculturală a studenților străini – Factor al comunicării eficiente în mediul educațional, București: Editura Universitară, p. 110;

Rus, Călin, Neștian-Sandu, Oana, Oana Bajka.(2019). Timișoara: Institutul Intercultural Timișoara, p. 6, https://www.intercultural.ro/wp-content/uploads/2020/02/Ghid-Educatie-Interculturala-web.pdf

Ibidem, p. 7;

Pricope, Mihaela, op. cit., p. 61.

# BIBLIOGRAPHY

Pricope, Mihaela. ( 2018). Dezvoltarea competenței de comunicare interculturală a studenților străini – Factor al comunicării eficiente în mediul educațional, București: Editura Universitară;

Pretceille Abdallah, Martin. (2011). L education interculturelle, Ediția a 3-a, Paris: Pressses Universitaires de France;

Samovar, Larry and Richard Porter. (2003). Intercultural Communication. A Reader. Belmont, California: Wadsworth Publishing Inc.;

Scheidel, Thomas. (1972). Speech Communication and Human Interaction. New York: Scott, Faoressman;

Todorov, Tvetan. (1999). Omul dezrădăcinat. Iași: Institutul European;

# WEBOGRAPHY

Nivel prag. (2001). Strasbourg: Consiliul Europei: https://www.ilr.ro/wp-content/uploads/nivel_prag.pdf;

Rus, Călin, Neștian-Sandu, Oana, Oana Bajka.(2019). Timișoara: Institutul Intercultural Timișoara https://www.intercultural.ro/wp-content/uploads/2020/02/Ghid-Educatie-Interculturala-web

# The Pragmatics of Facebook Interactions in Romania and the Republic of Moldova

**Alexandra-Monica TOMA,** Cross-Border Faculty, "Dunarea de Jos" University of Galati

## ABSTRACT

The rise of social media determined a fast-paced and ground-breaking change in communication patterns. New linguistic conventions aiming to compensate the lack of nonverbal and paraverbal cues and multimodal tools (emojis, GIFs, memes) have developed with amazing speed in order to add nuance and depth to meaning in virtual communication.

This paper presents the results of a survey conducted on a corpus of Facebook posts and compares patterns of online interaction through this social media platform in Romania and the Republic of Moldova, with an emphasis on linguistic methods of expressivity and the pragmatics of communicative exchanges. Moreover, the paper will corroborate the discoveries of the surveys with cultural elements (common and distinct) in order to reveal the way culture is mirrored in communication through Facebook.

**Keywords:** *computer-mediated communication, emoji, pragmatic markers, speech acts*

## 1. INTRODUCTION

The new technological advancements offered by social media give users the opportunity to employ a wide range of multimodal resources to express their identities and ideas. The methods of communication are not restricted to the written word but also include various combinations of pictures and videos, with different degrees of complexity. Creativity and dynamism, key features of the language, are also characteristic of interactions in the virtual environment.

Social media is a form of virtual communication that enables users to share text, images, videos, and other types of information. As defined by Kaplan and Maenlein, "social media is a group of internet-based applications that build on the ideological and technology of Web 2.0, and that allow the creation and exchange of User Generated Content (Kaplan & Maenlein, 2010: 61). Starting from the ambitious goal of bringing people together, reinforcing friendships or creating new ones, regardless of physical boundaries, it constitutes „...a cocoon-like zone of intimacy" (Rainie and Wellman, 2012) where users express themselves freely, document their memories, and reach out to the world, while carefully building their virtual identity.

Beyond the simple definition, the use of social media poses various issues and comes with its own advantages and shortcomings. Research has acclaimed its positive role in bringing people together and creating communication opportunities that go beyond geographical limits while also fretting about the lack of face-to-face interaction, which hinders socialization in its truest form and severely affects human bonds. "Mobile Social Media does not come without a price. Some would argue that while it enables the detailed following of friends half-way across the world, it can foster a society where we don't know the names of our own next-door neighbours. Be that as it may, and independent of whether or not one approves of such an evolution, it seems undisputable that (Mobile) Social Media will be the locomotive via which the World Wide Web evolves." (Kaplan & Maenlein, 2010: 67 - 68).

For the purposes of this paper, we shall also touch on the influence of social media on language. Concerns related to language alteration were advanced since the apparition of one of the first studies focusing on CMC language and dismissed by researchers like David Crystal (2004) and John McWhorter (2014), who stressed that the modification of language in computer-mediated communication is a natural sign of linguistic adaptation, without drastic effects.

Related to the effects of virtual interactions on language, Baldwin considers that communication through social media leads to "spelling inconsistencies, the free-form adoption of new terms, and regular violations of English grammar norms" (Baldwin, 2012: 58), an approach consistent with the idea of natural linguistic adaptation to the environment.

The survey conducted in 2015 by Thurairaj et al. also comes to dissuade concerns related to the negative effects of computer-mediated communication on language, as it reveals, based on statistical analysis, that social media language, however inconsistent with language norms, does not affect language proficiency, because of the participations' awareness of the difference of register between informal online interaction and formal language (Thurairaj, Hoon, Roy, Fong 2015).

However, some researchers support the idea that the paradigm switch triggered by computer-mediated communication in language is more dramatic than it might seem at first glance, given that the bewildering expansion of social media determined the creation of a specific language system aimed to support rapid communication. Danesi goes even further as he ponders the idea that we are probably witnessing a severe change of the human mind, generated by the emergence of a hybrid language that combines text with imagine, marking a shift from a linear language processing to an integrative one (Danesi, 2017: 13).

## FACEBOOK DATA COLLECTION

The history of social media traces back to 1979, when Tom Truscott and Jim Ellis created Usenet a global communication system that gave the opportunity to internet users to post messages. However, the turning point for social media came approximately 20 years ago, when the first "weblog" was used. Since then, the increase in internet quality and the expansion of cyberspace generated a true communication revolution, leading to the apparition of the first networking sites, MySpace and Facebook (2004), and to the coining of the term "social media" (Kaplan & Maenlein 2010: 60). It is almost a modern myth now how Mark Zuckerberg, in his dorm room at Harvard University (Markoff 2007), created what he then called "Thefacebook", and, within a month since launching, had half of the Harvard student population subscribing to it (Phillips 2007). Facebook has come a long way since then, undergoing a massive expansion, and it still is widely popular among users around the world, despite fierce competition from other applications (Instagram, Twitter, Tik Tok etc.), managing to maintain a leading place in social media statistics, with 2,910 million users (Statista, 2022).

This paper investigates Facebook interactions between users from Romania and the Republic of Moldova, placing emphasis on sociolinguistics and pragmatics and aiming to establish a connection between language, culture, and social media patterns. In order to examine the main features of online interaction, this study followed one hundred Facebook posts made by students and teachers from Romania and the Republic of Moldova throughout a one-week period, in January 2022. In order to have a fair amount of data to analyse, the users included in the study were those with intense online activity. The corpus was then analysed from a quantitative and qualitative perspective. The data collection and processing had in view the following objectives: classification of the posts, analysis of multimodal tools (Facebook reactions, emojis, GIFs), interpretation of occurrences, and linguistic and stylistic patterns.

The first step of this study was to divide posts by category, an approach which would subsequently become useful for the assessment of the interaction patterns. 25% of posts shared articles, events, funny or motivational pictures or videos, with no comment from the authors. The lack of a description or opinion reveals that such posts had two main purposes: information and entertainment. We discovered that teachers were mostly focused on sharing pieces of news, scientific articles and events related to their field of activity, while students aimed to amuse their Facebook friends with materials pertaining more to amusement. This observation is consistent with our expectations, as more mature Facebook users are more likely to approach serious topics.

The second category of content consists of posts accompanied by a comment that also shows the author's attitude or opinion towards the content (12 %). The purposes of such posts again include information sharing and entertainment, but this time, there is a stronger personal involvement. Teachers shared achievements of the institutions where they are employed accompanied by a description, promoted causes they believed in or insightful opinions about political, cultural, and social events. Students, on the other hand, chose to mostly share funny comments.

Personal posts constitute the majority of our corpus, with a weight of 63% of the total. These have a high emotional involvement from the author and refer to anniversaries, family events, personal achievements, and trips. Sometimes, they are simply anecdotal descriptions of life events or conversations and might be perceived as a hybrid between opinion and personal information. Most such posts are accompanied by photographs and include tags of other family members or friends involved in or related to the event.

## MULTIMODAL TOOLS

It is common knowledge in our world that there are linguistic conventions specific to cyber-communication that modify or simplify language to achieve maximum expressivity with minimal means by combining image and text in various forms. This paper focuses on the highly standardised emojis or the less conventionalised GIFs.

The roles of these multimodal tools, as we chose to call them, have been heavily debated in the literature. Although emojis originate in the need to reproduce nonverbal facial expressions, they cannot be construed as actual nonverbal language, as they are used voluntarily and according to a communicative strategy built in line with the goal each person follows in linguistic exchanges. Consensus has mainly been reached in terms of emoji functions, which have been the core of CMC debates: to provide extralingustic information, to express emotion, intimacy, closeness, to regulate interaction (Derks et al. 2007, Yus 2014, Dresner & Herring 2010, Vandergriff 2013).

For Facebook, it is very important to mention a special category of multimodal tools that are extensions of the Like button: the six reactions that have become criteria for feedback classification (Like, Love, Care, Haha, Wow, Sad and Angry). Originating in emojis, these options allow internet users to express a nuanced response to posts with the simple touch of a button. In terms of reactions' popularity, a study conducted in 2017 analysed 21,000 posts and found that, as expected, the default reaction "like" is the most frequent (78.9%), followed by "love", "angry", "sad", the less frequent being "wow". The conclusion was that the reactions accurately reflect the readers' overall sentiment related to the posts, noting that "people are more likely to share a post when the reaction is something other than "like", suggesting that stronger emotional attitude leads to more post sharing" (Molimpakis et al., 2017: 13). Moreover, the same team of researchers reached the conclusion that "Facebook reactions and comments are a good data source for investigating indicators of user emotional attitudes" (Molimpakis et al., 2017: 15).

The latest statistical data on social media show that 20,7% of all posts on Facebook, Instagram and Twitter use emojis in the caption, which leads to a higher engagement in comparison with posts that do not include emojis. The so-called "perfect posts" include over 20 emojis, short captions or videos, which are reflected in high engagement rates. (Lozan, 2019).

Reaction GIFs have known a recent surge in interest, consideration supported by a 2016 study that found they are liked more frequently than text, images, or video posts. Another important finding is that GIFs featuring faces generate more engagement and are more likely to trigger a response from the addressee (Bakhshi et al., 2016). Their dynamic nature and the use of animation to express attitudes and reactions definitely make them more appealing, attention-grabbing, and emotionally intense than static emojis, as researchers have already concluded (Tolins and Samermit, 2016: 83, Miltner and Highfield, 2017: 4, Veszelszki 2015: 139-140). Bakhshi et al.'s study also concluded that users prefer them in lieu of gestures or facial expressions and perceive them as more likely to trigger the desired communicative reaction when they stand for a personal reaction (Bakhshi et al., 2016: 583). The immediacy of communication and their ability to soundlessly tell a brief story are features that explain their popularity.

Reaction GIFs perform "an act of showing" and "an ostensive act", as the use of such multimodal tools requires interpretation that is based upon the addressee's pragmatic processing skills (Scott, 2022). The inference will lead to a set of weakly communicated (or even non-propositional) assumptions that generate attitudes and impressions.

Turning our attention to the corpus, we shall first tackle the issue of the author's choice of multimodal tools and then the issue of the user feedback. The first observation, which confirms both previous research and our assumptions, would be that personal posts, as opposed to opinion and information posts, use a higher number of emojis, given that they are perceived as intimate, informal, and more emotionally charged.

As a case in point, at the top of the emoji use hierarchy, there is a post made by a teacher from the Republic of Moldova to say happy anniversary to her niece. This is expressed by using 33 emojis (7 unique ones: smiling face with three hearts, smiling face with stars in their eye, dragonfly emojis, thumbs-up emoji, smile emoji, embrace emoji and anniversary emoji). The enthusiastic pictogram-marked discourse is also rich in exclamation marks and diminutives. The text of the post, introducing a set of pictures from the event, makes extensive use of metaphors, similes, and epithets, thus being a display of strong emotion and enthusiasm. An analysis of other posts made by the same user reveals that there is a pattern in emoji use, this being a constant feature of the user's virtual personality.

The feedback to the post consists of 33 comments, mostly theme-centred GIFs displaying birthday cakes, angels, flowers, balloons, etc. The congratulatory texts contain, as the text of the post itself, an impressive number of emojis, some meant to mirror the emotional state of the author, others displaying symbols typical for birthdays (cakes, flower bouquets, confetti etc.).

The reactions to the post were 100 likes, 19 love, and 3 care. It is somehow surprising that most friends used the default reaction, and there is a contrast between the highly emotionally marked comments using many GIFs and the reactions.

The second post that stands out from the point of view of multimodal tools is from a student from the Republic of Moldova sharing pictures of her cat, accompanied by a brief description and 14 emojis (3 unique: the cat symbol, the heart, and the smiling face with floating hearts). The reactions to the post were enthusiastic (51 likes, 57 love, 16 care). The friends' feedback consisted almost entirely of GIFs and very few emojis (all completing a text).

On the other side of the spectrum in terms of number of emojis use stand information and opinion posts, which use a small number of emojis, if any. Three information posts use the heart symbol instead of text to show the attitude towards the article or video shared, while some employ the blinking eye smiling face accompanied by a brief comment "Nice, ha?" (introducing news about the difficulty of passing a law in the Romanian Parliament).

The pragmatics of such contexts is intriguing, especially in the case of the blinking eye emoji, given that this face usually expresses attitudes ranging from mischief to irony and sarcasm. In this case, the meaning of the text is in opposition to the actual attitude of the user, and irony is clarified through the emoji use.

Given the analysis of the posts, beyond the hierarchy in terms of emojis, a few things stand out. The first is related to emoji repetition, which is perceived by the users as an indicator of emotional intensity. The posts that contain emojis are usually reflecting an emotionally intense state of mind and generate feedback that mirrors the feelings of the post's author. This observation is proven consistently throughout the corpus: emojis in the post are related to the use of more emojis and GIFs in the comments.

Moreover, the posts analysed in this survey show that emojis are mostly felt eloquent only when accompanied by text, used for three main functions: clarify ambiguity, generate irony (as in the blinking eye face example), and show depth and intensity of response. As opposed to emojis, GIFs are perceived as able to stand for themselves, given that many comments contain only reaction GIFs.

The reasons for this rise of GIFs in Facebook comments might be connected to the fact that they are less conventionalised than emojis, more dynamic and provide a wider range of options. Moreover, animation conveys a more elaborate combination of gesture and emotion, sometimes adding an intertextual trait into the mixture.

Following the analysis of GIFs used in the corpus, we discovered some patterns shown consistently. The first finding consists of the fact that there are no stand-alone GIFs posted by authors. GIFs are a feature of feedback, and, albeit more than able to express attitude and reaction without the support of textual information, they are never included in the posts that initiate communication. The reason behind this pattern is inherent in the name of these tools: they are used to react but not to start virtual interaction.

By making an inventory of reaction GIFs employed, we distinguished some specific categories. Referring to the general connotation of these animated tools, we found two types were consistently used: positive GIFs (that express approval, encouragement, consent, invitations) and negative GIFs (suggesting disapproval, disappointment, dissatisfaction). It is of course difficult to split all GIFs into these two very generic categories, as those used to show irony and sarcasm are hybrid types where humour is bitter-sweet, and it does not fit the positive/negative pattern. Moreover, depending on the context, the polarity might change, and unexpected transfers between these two categories might occur.

The corpus also provides eloquent data to identify two other categories: intertextual and non-intertextual GIFs. Feedback to many personal posts that evoke family events consists of animated GIFs that do not imply knowledge of pop culture or connections to movies, music, and the entertainment business. However, those GIFs that feature renowned artists and recognisable moments from movies, public events etc. hint to what Anna Everett called digitextuality, namely an entanglement between convergence culture, intertextuality and remixing strategies in a virtual environment, suggesting "a more precise or utilitarian trope capable at once of describing and deconstruction a sense-making function for digital technology's newer interactive protocols, aesthetic features, transmedia interfaces and end-user subject positions, in the context of traditional media antecedents" (Everett, 2003: 1-2). The posts under survey provide ample proof of digitextuality: Leonardo di Caprio raising his glass in an equally congratulatory and condescending fashion, the sloth from Zootropolis cracking a painfully slow and brilliant smile, Michael Jackson eating popcorn while enjoying a show with detachment, etc.

One last finding about GIF types resulted from the data collection refers to their role in achieving a specific communicative goal. From this point of view, we identified many decorative reaction GIFs, with no text added and low digitextuality degree, that could be portrayed as visually appealing moving images that convey positivity, inclusion, and intimacy, with an impressive amount of cliché symbols in the mixture. Teddy bears, hearts, rainbows, birthday cakes, rainbows, with sparkles around them, all glossy and vividly coloured, are kitsch and ornamental ways of expressing emotion to personal posts.

Far more intriguing are the intertextual reaction GIFs, where animation is sometimes combined with text and interpretation of meaning must consider several layers: the virtual communication context, the quoted situation and the text that supports the interpretation of the GIF (optional), all converging in order to guide the decoding of the message. This puzzle can be reconstructed in many ways, depending on the sociocultural, psychological, and linguistic context. The roles of these tools, as identified in the corpus, are to express a nuanced attitude to the post, to give ironic feedback, and to appeal to common knowledge with the aim of regulating interaction (positive politeness).

Unlike decorative GIFs, reaction GIFs that draw upon the power of previous stories are a peculiar combination of photography and film, undergoing subsequent stages of decontextualization and re-contextualization, and strongly rely on repetitiveness, circularity, and brevity to build content (Farinacci, 2019).

GIFs that feature famous actors and movie scenes are mostly used in opinion and information posts, while personal posts consist almost exclusively of positive decorative GIFs without intertextual references. A possible explanation that needs further investigation would be that ornamental use of multimodal tools is favoured in contexts where no ambiguity is desired with regard to feelings and attitudes.

# SOCIOCULTURAL PATTERNS

One of the goals of the study was to also identify some key elements associated with the sociocultural context of the users, which determined a data selection consisting of posts from Romania and the Republic of Moldova. Although the two countries share a common language, a common history, and strong emotional and cultural connection, there are some patterns of interaction that distinguish two different paradigms of approaching virtual communication and using multimodal tools to attain communicative goals.

The first finding refers to the use of figures of speech in social media discourse. 45% of the posts written by users from the Republic of Moldova contain tropes, whereas only 10% of Romanian Facebook authors make use of such means of expressivity. Furthermore, emojis are used in 67% of the Moldovan posts, mostly in series and displaying impressive diversity, as opposed to 34% of the Romanian ones, which seldom use emojis.

In terms of feedback, Moldovan users seem to prefer to use emojis and decorative GIFs, while Romanians have a preference for intertextual GIFs. The Romanian preference for intertextual GIFs might be construed as proof of higher enthusiasm for pop culture. As Romanian are more likely to be acquainted with mainstream TV shows, actors, singers etc., given their higher exposure to mainstream media coming from the west, they are also more likely to draw upon the expressivity of GIFs' intertextual dialogue. The extensive use of emojis and decorative GIFs by Moldovan users is also consistent with their employment of tropes and with the higher degree of emotional intensity expressed through the posts.

When analysing the pragmatic uses of emojis and GIFs in the corpus, we also focused on the occurrences when the image is in contradiction with the text or intention, thus leading to irony and sarcasm. It is obvious that such attitudes are often found in posts by Romanian users. Meanwhile, Moldovans choose not to generate meaning through such devices. A possible explanation would be the different ways these nationalities choose to define politeness norms, even among close friends. It is our intuition that Moldovans perceive the virtual use of irony and sarcasm as a sign of impolite behaviour and avoid such social strategies. In opposition, Romanians frequently use emojis and GIFs, where humour results from contradiction.

We also believe that the extensive use of tropes and multimodal tools by Moldovan users might be connected to the perception of the degree of formality of the environment and to their sociocultural background. While Occidental practice is to also use social media for more formal relations and for pitching products into the market, a strategy to which Romania adheres given its higher opening to the Occidental approaches, Moldovans perceive Facebook as a tool that enables informal communication with family, friends, and acquaintances. Given this perspective, the posts from the Republic of Moldova show a wide range of positive etiquette strategies, with high emotional charge, in accordance with the general politeness norms of their culture. However, these findings should be put to the test by extending the corpus to confirm the results.

## CONCLUSIONS

By using a corpus of Facebook posts shared by Romanian and Moldovan users, this paper sheds light on the social media communication patterns, considering the functions and impact of emojis and GIFs and the importance of the sociocultural background in virtual interactions.

The results of the study show that cultural identity consistently and significantly influences the use of tropes and multimodal tools. Romanian users show a tendency towards brevity and emotional detachment, preferring minimal comment and moderate use of emojis. In opposition, posts written by users from the Republic of Moldova are vividly expressive, with metaphors and similes, symbolic and facial emojis (with extensive repetitions) and many decorative reaction GIFs in feedback. This could be a point of departure for a more extensive study on how cultural and national identity is mirrored in social media behaviour.

## REFERENCES

Bakhshi, S., Shamma, D. A., Kennedy, L., Song, Y., de Juan, P., Kaye, J. (2016). Fast, cheap and good: Why animated GIFS engage us. *CHI '16: Proceedings of the 2016 CHI Conference of Human Factors in Computing Systems*, 575 – 586.

Baldwin, T. (2012). Social media: Friend or foe of natural language processing? *26th Pacific Asia Conference on Language, Information and Computation*, 58-59. Retrieved from https://www.aclweb.org/anthology/Y12-1005.pdf.

Brown, P., & Levinson, S. (1987). *Politeness: Some universals in language usage*. Cambridge, U.K.: Cambridge University Press.

Crystal, David (2004). *Language and the Internet*, Cambridge: Cambridge University Press.

Danesi, Marcel (2017). *The Semiotics of Emoji: The Rise of Visual Language in the Age of Internet*, Bloomsbury Advances in Semiotics.

Derks, Daantje, Agneta E.R. Bos, von Grumbkow, Jasper (2007). Emoticons and social interaction on the Internet: the importance of social context. *Computers in Human Behavior*, 23(1), 842-849.

Dresner, Eli, Herring, Susan (2010). Functions of the Nonverbal in CMC: Emotions and Illocutionary Force, in *Communication Theory*, 20(3), 249-268, doi: 10.1111/j.1468-2885.2010.01362.x

Everett, A. (2003). Digitextuality and Click Theory: Theses on Convergence Media in the Digital Age. In Everett, Caldwell (eds.), *New Media Theories and Practicies of Digitextuality*, New York, NY: Routledge.

*Farinacci, E.* (2020). "GIF's Anatomy". Explaining the Instrinsic Communicative Power of GIFs. Global Cremit. Retrieved from *https://www.cremit.it/global-cremit-GIFs-anatomy-explaining-the-intrinsic-communicative-power-of-GIFs/*

Kaplan, A., Haenlein, M. (2010). Users of the World, Unite! The Challengees and Opportunities of Social Media. Business Horizons, 53(1), 59-68, doi: 10.1016/j.bushor.2009.09.003.

Lozan, Teodora (2019), *[Study]*: 101,421,493 *Posts to Show How to Write the Best Content on Facebook vs. Instagram vs. Twitter in 2020*. Retrieved from https://www.socialinsider.io/blog/social-media-content-research/

Markoff, J. (2007). The tangled history of Facebook. *New York Times*. Retrieved from http://www.nytimes.com/2007/08/31/business/worldbusiness/31iht-facebook.5.7340806.html

McWhorter, J. (2014). The Language Hoax: *Why the World Looks the Same in Any Language*. Oxford: Oxford University Press.

Miltner, K., Highfield, T. (2017). Never Gonna GIF You Up: Analyzing the Cultural Significance of the Animated GIF. *Social Media + Society*, 3(3), doi: 10.1177/2056305117725223

Molimpakis, Emilia, Tian, Ye, Galery, Thiago, Dulcinati, Giulio (2017). Facebook Sentiment: Reactions and Emojis, in *Proceedings of the Fifth International Workshop on Natural Language Processing for Social Media*, 11-16. Retrieved from https://www.researchgate.net/publication/318740552_Facebook_sentiment_Reactions_and_Emojis.

Phillips, S. (2007, July 25). A brief history of Facebook. *Guardian*. Retrieved from www.guardian.co.uk/technology/2007/jul/25/media.newmedia

Rainie, L., Wellman, B. (2012). *Networked- The New Social Operating System*, Cambridge: Massachusetts Institute of Technology.

Scott, Kate (2022). *Language and Digital Media. Pragmatics Online*, New York: Routledge.

Statista (2022). *Most popular social networks worldwide as of January 2022, ranked by number of monthly active users*. Retrieved from https://www.statista.com/statistics/272014/global-social-networks-ranked-by-number-of-users/

Thurairaj S., Hoon, E. P., Roy, S. S. & Fong, P. K. (2015). Reflections of students' language usage in social networking sites: Making or marring academic English. *The Electronic Journal of e-Learning*, 13(4), 302-316.

Tolins, J., Samermit, P. (2016). GIFs as Embodied Enactments in Text-Mediated Conversation. *Research on Language and Social Interaction*, 49:2, 75-91, doi: 10.1080/08351813.2016.1164391.

Vandergriff, Ilona (2013). Emotive communication online: A contextual analysis of computer-mediated communication (CMC) cues. *Journal of Pragmatics*, 15, 1-12.

Veszelszki, Agnes (2015). Emoticons vs. Reaction-GIFs Non-verbal Communication on the Internet from the Aspects of Visuality, Verbality and Time. In Benedek, Andras, Nyiri, Kristof (eds). *Beyond Words. Pictures, Parables, Paradoxes*. Frankfurt: Peter Lang.

Yus, Francisco (2014). Not All Emoticons Are Created Equal. *Linguagem em (Dis)curso*, 14(3), 511-529, DOI:10.1590/1982-4017-140304-041

# Materials for a Better Life - Trends and Perspectives

**Podaru Geanina Marcela** Cross-Border Faculty, "Dunărea de Jos" University of Galati, geanina.podaru@ugal.ro

## 1. INTRODUCTION

Materials science deals with interdisciplinary issues involving the properties of matter and its applications in various fields of technology, and it is using knowledge of applied physics, chemistry, mechanical, and electrical engineering. After the emergence, in recent years, of nanosciences and nanotechnologies, materials science has been propelled to the forefront of many prestigious Universities around the world [Bolundut, I.L. – *Materials science and engineering*, Junimea Publishing, Iasi, 2010; Suciu, V., Suciu, M.V. – Study of materials, FAIR PARTNERS Publishing, Bucuresti, 2008; Serban, V.A., Raduta, A. – Materials science and engineering, Politehnica Publishing, Timisoara, 2010].

People's knowledge of materials began with pottery, developing from the Stone Age to the Bronze Age and then the Steel Age. The science of modern materials has developed from metallurgy and metallurgy (iron casting) has developed from mining. If at the beginning of the twentieth century it dealt only with metals, starting with the middle of this century it has also included plastics and ceramics, and more recently composites [Bolundut, I.L. – *Plastics and composites technology*, Junimea Publishing,

Iasi, 2010; Callister, W.D.Jr. – *Materials Science and Engineering – An Introduction*, Ed. John Wiley & Sons (5 th edition), New York, 2000; Colan, H., Tudoran, P., Ailincai, Gh., Marcu, M., Drugescu, E. – *Study of metals*, Didactic and Pedagogical Publishing, Bucuresti, 1983; Murray, G.T. – *Introduction to Engineering Materials*, Library Publishing Company, New York, 1992 ].

Materials have been the basis of all industrial conquests: steel for railways, copper for electricity, aluminium for aviation, plastics for post-war consumer goods, and silicon for computing. The separation of traditional materials (metals and alloys, ceramics, and polymers) from advanced ones is increasingly difficult to do because a material considered advanced today may fall into the category of traditional ones tomorrow [Ashby, F.M., Jones, R.H.D. – *Engineering Materials 1. An Introduction to Properties, Applications and Design* (fourth edition), Cambridge, 2009; Cojocaru-Filipiuc, V. – *Irons. Obtaining,* Samia Publishing, Iasi, 2002; Gladcov, P., Petrovici, A., Alexandrescu, V., Cosmulescu, D. – Materials technology (vol. I, II), PROINVENT Foundation of the "Politehnica" University of Bucharest, 1998]. The use of new materials is done according to a classic scenario: as their price decreases, they move from the top industries to the usual ones. Thus, the materials initially used in the armament or aerospace industries, are taken over by car manufacturers and end up being consumer goods. For example, composites have conquered the aerospace industry, to the detriment of aluminium alloys, which replace steel in car construction. At the same time, some of these materials are either very fragile or extra-hard or very thin and can only be processed by unconventional processes [Miravete, A. – *Materiales Compuestos*, Editorial Reverté S.A., Barcelona, 2007; Nocivin, A. – Advanced materials: composite materials; metallic materials with special properties, „Ovidius" University Press, Constanta, 2001; Popescu, I., Dumitras, C., Savu, T., Dumitrescu, A., Purcarea, M., Tonoiu, S. – Technology for processing parts from classical and composite materials (2 vol.), MATRIX ROM Publishing, Bucuresti, 2000].

The main materials used in the industry are metals. Of these, cast iron and steel account for about 90%, with the remaining 10% being non-ferrous metals and alloys. Cast iron is made in the furnace, and due to its high carbon content, it is hard and brittle and cannot be used in this state. Its mechanical properties can be improved by adding elements that transform the lamellar graphite into nodular graphite (Mg, Si, Ca, Ba), as well as by applying malleability annealing or by alloying it with various elements (Si, Mn, Cr, Ni, Mo, Al, Cu). Steel contains less carbon and has good mechanical properties. Increasing the carbon content leads to an increase in hardness and breaking strength but also to a decrease in ductility and toughness. By alloying it with 10% chromium, nickel and molybdenum, it becomes stainless [Dobrovici, D., Prisecaru, I., Banciu, M. – *Source metallurgy*, Technical Publishing, Bucuresti, 1966; Popescu, V.I., Chiriac, C. – High speed steels, AGIR Publishing, Bucuresti, 2002; Sha, W., Guo, Z. – *Maraging Steels: Modeling of Microstructure, Properties and Applications*, Woodhead Publishing Limited, 2009;

Suciu, V., Suciu, M.V. – Study of materials, FAIR PART-NERS Publishing, Bucuresti, 2008]

The non-ferrous metals and alloys are more expensive, rarer and are used in areas where special physical-mechanical or chemical properties are required. Some of them are very old and have been of great importance in the development of human society, such as the bronze that was discovered around 3500 BC in Mesopotamia and Sumer with such importance that the second millennium BC received the name the Bronze Age in history. Then, it came the aluminium, titanium, and magnesium alloys, which are prized for their low weight and high strength and are widely used in the aerospace construction and the automotive industry [Amza, Gh., Rîndasu, V.O., Dumitru, G.M., Amza, C.Gh. – *Treated by materials technology (second edition)*, Romanian Academy Publishing, Bucuresti, 2002; Brabie, V., Avram, N., Moldovan, P. – *Alloy making*, Didactic and Pedagogical Publishing, Bucuresti, 1978; Reed, C.R. – *The Superalloys: Fundamentals and Applications*, Cambridge University Press, 2006].

Plastics were discovered in the last century, and today, they have surpassed in volume the metal materials due to their beneficial properties: they are cheap and light, resistant to oxidation and corrosion and allow the properties to be modified by using additives. Some can be recycled by solubilization or melting, and their applications cover almost every area of human activity, from the common shopping bags and toys to the underground water and gas pipelines that are gradually replacing metal ones [Kulshreshtha, A.K., Vasile, C. – *Handbook of Polymer Blends and Composites* (vol.2), Rapra Technology Ltd., Shawbury, 2002; La Mantia, F. – *Handbook of Plastics Recycling*, Rapra Technology, Shrewsbury, UK, 2002]. Recycling plastics is very important given that over 90% of it comes from oil and natural gas – valuable and increasingly scarce raw materials. As a result, recycling aims not only at waste processing (mechanical recycling) but also at the use of advanced technologies based on depolymerization, which breaks down the hydrocarbon chains that make up plastics and synthetic rubber, obtaining monomers (chemical recycling) [Buschow, K.H.J. (editor) – *Concise Encyclopedia of Magnetic and Superconducting Materials* (second edition), PDF, Elsevier Science, 2006].

The replacement of conventional materials used so far in the construction industry has led to an increase in service life, an increase in thermal and noise insulation, the vibration absorption for external insulation, as well as a reduction in the actual construction time due to the advent of new assembly technologies based on the use of composite materials. Composite materials, especially polymer composites, can be used to make all kinds of elements that go into the structure of a construction. The development of this field is observed especially in the case of modular constructions [Higgins, R.A. – *Engineering Metallurgy*, ELBS, Kent, 1986; Lee, S. – *Dictionary of Composite Materials Technology*, CRC Press LLC, Palo Alto, California, 1995; Lupescu, M.B. – Reinforcing fibers for composite materials, Technical Publishing, Bucuresti, 2004].

# 2. MATERIALS AND THEIR IMPACT ON THE QUALITY OF LIFE

## *2.1. Classical / Traditional Materials (Metallic, Plastic and Ceramic)*

In modern technology, metallic materials (metals and alloys) are widely used to make parts and various products. Metals are chemical elements with characteristic lustre, good conductors of heat and electricity, malleable and ductile, but they are rarely used due to their unfavourable properties and high price. Alloys are metallic materials obtained by melting together two or more metals or metals and metalloids, having properties suitable for the desired fields of use and lower price.

By their nature, the metallic materials [Bolundut, I.L. – Metallic *materials*, AGIR Publishing, Bucuresti, 2004; Fleser, T. – Changing the condition of steels subjected to thermomechanical stresses, Polytechnic Publishing, Timisoara, 2002.

Gale, W.F., Totemeier, T.C. – *Smithells Metals Reference Book* (8 edition), ASM International, 2004] can be grouped into two categories:

a) **ferrous materials** (iron, cast iron and steel) which represent about 90% of the world's consumption of metallic materials.

Iron and carbon alloys called cast iron and steel are the best-known metallic materials used in the technological processes due to the wide spread in the earth's crust of the raw materials they come from, relatively simple metallurgy, good physical-mechanical properties and due to their capability of being modified to a large extent by alloying and heat treatments, their relatively low-cost price and processing possibilities through all existing technological processes and recycling by remelting.

Iron is a metal that is well processed by hot and cold plastic deformation, it welds, glues, and has a good cutting.

The main alloying element of iron is carbon, which, even in small quantities, changes its properties, the carbon content being, in fact, the main criterion for the classification of cast iron and steel. Also, iron can be alloyed with any amount of carbon.

b) **non-ferrous materials** (copper, aluminium, magnesium, zinc, lead, tin, nickel, tungsten, etc. and their alloys), representing the remaining 10% of the world consumption.

Non-ferrous metals and alloys are of great importance in technology due to their properties that are missing from cast irons and steels, such as low density (Al, Mg, Ti), high thermal conductivity, high electrical conductivity, malleability, ductility, high resistance to oxidation and corrosion, good anti friction qualities etc. They are used in the production of alloy steels (Cr, Ni, Mo, W, V, Co, etc.), in the construction of vehicles, ships, aircrafts and spacecrafts (Al, Mn, Ti, Zr, Mo, W), in nuclear technology (V, Th, Be), in medicine (Hg, Si, Pt, Ag, Au), in the chemical, food, printing and armament industries, etc., representing about 10% of the world metal consumption.

Their wider use Is limited by the fact that they are in short supply and generally have very high prices. For these reasons, it is necessary to use them as rationally as possible and to replace them, where possible, with ferrous alloys or plastics.

**Plastic materials** [Constantinescu R., Platon, M. – *Use of plastics in constructions*, Technical Publishing, Bucuresti, 1985; Fetecau, C., Oancea, N., Stan, F. – *Mechanical processing of plastics*, Documentary Infirmation Office for the Machine Building Industry, Bucuresti, 2000] are macro molecular synthetic products, used in industry due to their high plasticity and the favourable properties of the machined parts. Appeared during 1920-1950, today they exceed the consumption of metals due to the following advantages: they have low density, they are good electrical and thermal insulators, they are resistant to the action of chemical agents, they are easily processed by multiple technological processes, and they have a low price. At the same time, their use is limited by the following disadvantages: the mechanical properties are relatively low, they do not keep their properties at high temperatures, they have relatively high coefficients of expansion, and by burning, they release toxic waste.

Since the 1950s, we have witnessed a rapid development of petrochemicals as a result of the increasing demand for fuel in road transport. Petrochemistry ensures the emergence of new plastics due to the cracking of crude oil. About 10% of crude oil is used in refineries to obtain plastics.

Today, the world consumption of plastics has come to equal that of steel, in volume, and tends to exceed it. Given that over 90% of the plastics production comes from oil and natural gas, one of the most important issues is their recycling in order to limit the consumption of valuable and increasingly deficient raw materials. Recycling aims not only to process waste for reuse but also to transform it, through special processes, into petroleum products of origin. These technologies are based on depolymerization, eventually breaking the long hydrocarbon chains that make up plastics and industrial rubber and obtaining methane gas and crude oil (chemical recycling).

**Ceramic materials** [Krenkel, W.H. – *Ceramic matrix composites: fiber reinforced ceramics and their applications*, John Wiley, New York, 2008] are the third group of materials used in technology, after metal and plastic. They are inorganic materials with atomic and ionic bonds, whose complex crystalline structure is obtained by sintering. The word ceramic comes from the Greek language (keramicos = burnt clay), and the human activity related to pottery and the production of bricks has its origins in prehistory. Over time, there are three stages in the development of pottery:

– utilitarian pottery is related to pottery and appeared before the use of metals, pottery and bricks being the first products obtained by man by burning clay

– art ceramics derived from the previous one, moving away from the utilitarian function and focusing on the decorative and aesthetic value

– industrial ceramics developed after 1950 as a result of the emergence of the leading industries, which use materials based on oxides, carbides, nitrides, borons and various forms of carbon.

They are considered to be ceramic and glass materials, concrete, and graphite, as they use specific ceramic processes, as well as refractory materials that are obtained at high temperatures and are used in lining furnaces and metallurgical furnaces. Until the 1950s, ceramic materials were utilitarian and art ceramics, the main products being bricks, tiles, faience, porcelain, as well as cement, concrete, and glass. Starting with the 1950s, new ceramic materials have appeared, called industrial, with various applications in the new fields. Thus, in 1953, ferrite cores were used in the construction of computers, and since 1965, bioceramics have been used as bone implants. The silicon nitride ceramics were discovered in the 1980s, as well as those for the manufacture of semiconductors and superconductors, and in the late 1980s, composite ceramics.

### 2.2 Polymeric Materials

Polymeric materials appeared in the period 1920... 1940, knowing a significant development and being used today in all branches of activity, 75% of them being represented by acronitrile-butatidien-styrene (ABS), polyesters (PET), polycarbonates (PC) and polyamides (PA) [Lendlein, A. – Shape-Memory Polymers, Springer, 2010; Mitelea, I. – Materiales science (vol. II), Polytechnic Publishing, Timisoara, 2010; Popescu, V., Horovitz, O., Rusu, T – Polymeric materials and the environment, Mediamira Publishing, Cluj-Napoca, 2005].

The temperature of use of ordinary and technical plastics does not exceed 70... 120°C, this being their major disadvantage. In the second half of the last century, American aviation material laboratories received the task of making polymers with which to obtain light composite material with operating temperatures of up to 300°C, which would replace the heavy metal parts in aviation and aerospace construction. The French did the same thing for the manufacture of the Concorde plane, followed by the Japanese. Today, 60% of the high-temperature polymers are produced in the United States, 20% in France, 10% in Japan, and 10% in Russia and China. In terms of operating temperature, it even reached 400°C, for short periods of use.

Depending on the degree of spread and performance, the polymers can be classified as follows:

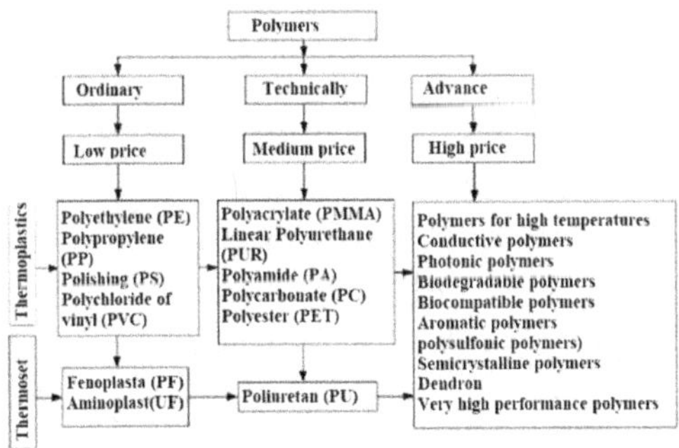


**Fig. 1** Classification of Polymers

Polymers are generally good electrical insulators, but there are also polymers that conduct electricity. Thus, the scientists Hideki Shirakawa, Alan G. MacDiarmid and

Alan J. Heeger were awarded the Nobel Prize in Chemistry in 2000 when they demonstrated that in order to conduct electricity, a polymer must have, alternatively, simple and double bonds between its carbon atoms. It must also be doped – its electrons taken away (by oxidation) or given to it (by reduction). The doping of the polymers leads to changes in their molecular structure, as well as the appearance of the electrical co-ductivity. Compared to metal conductors, conductive polymers are lighter, have a high corrosion resistance, are transparent and have a lower price. Therefore, conductive polymers combine oxidation and corrosion resistance, flexibility, elasticity, easy processing possibilities and low cost of plastics with the good electrical conductivity of metals. As a result, their fields of application are numerous: energy storage and conversion, extra-flat screens for TVs, solar panels, optical amplifiers, and display screens for mobile phones. In the future, transistors and other electronic components will be produced from a single conductive polymer molecule, which will lead to the miniaturization and the dramatic increase in computer speed. The main types of conductive polymers are polyacetylene, polypyrrole, polythiophene, polyaniline and paraffinylene polyvinyl [Simionescu, Gh. – Materials technology: plastics; protective coatings, Alma Mater Publishing, Bacau, 2001; Saban, R., Dumitrescu, C. – Treatise on the science and engineering of metallic materials. Metals. Alloy. Special materials. Composite materials (vol.3), AGIR Publishing, Bucuresti, 2009].

The photonic polymers, also called electroluminescent polymers (LEPs), were discovered in the 1960s but found their applicability only after 2000, along with the conductive polymers. The Organic Light-Emitting Diode (OLED) was patented and introduced in 1987 by Kodak. The first generations of light-emitting diodes (LEDs) had a crystalline structure and were not very cheap. Over time, the idea of using semiconductor polymers in their manufacture materialized. The diameter of such a diode shall not exceed 1 mm. each pixel (picture element) on an OLED screen consists of three adjacent diodes (one red, one green, and one blue).

The organic light-emitting diodes have low power consumption, very good colour rendering, very good contrast, more diffused light, a very short response time and a relatively simple manufacturing process. The disadvantages are the short operating time (14,000 hours for the blue ones), the sensitivity to moisture and the monopolization of the manufacturing right by the companies that patented it.

Areas of application include screens for mobile phones, digital cameras, large flat screens (home-cinema), head-up displays for controlling airplanes and cars, discreet ambient lighting, or various gadgets (clothes, ribbons, pens, or light key chains). As for their use for longer-lasting products (TV monitors and computers), this remains a problem for the future.

Another technology inspired by the science fiction literature is the technology of polymeric displays (LED – Light-Emitting Polymers) which replaced the liquid crystal monitors (LCD) – Liquid Crystal Display) [Collings, P.J. – Liquid Crystals (second edition), Princeton University Press, 2002;

Crisp, J., Elliott, B. – *Introduction to Fiber Optics* (third-edition), Newnes, Oxford, 2005; Radhakrishnan, V.M. – *Wel-ding Technology & Design*, New Age International Publishers, New Delhi, 2005].

Compared to LCD screens, LEP displays have the following advantages: the brightness is ten times higher than that of ordinary fluorescent lamps; very good contrast and a better definition of dark scenes; the image quality is exceptional; low weight; the possibility of obtaining extra-flat screens; low energy consumption.

Polymeric displays can be rigid or flexible, and the fields of application are very wide, from small devices (watches or mobile phones) to ordinary monitors and huge display panels. In many cases, they replace the on-board appliances of cars or airplanes, their installation being possible on any type of surface (monitors, house walls, tabletop). Electronic literature (e-ink) and electronic paper (e-paper) have already appeared in literature, imitating classic text and images, which can be stored at any time without additional processing and power consumption.

High-performance polymers can be processed by various technological processes (casting, extrusion, cutting) and are used in aeronautics, electronics, as well as in the manufacture of medical instruments combining exceptional wear resistance with robustness, thermal and dimensional stability, and resistance to chemical agents. These polymers are also used in the manufacture of semiconductors, housings, and sockets for checking printed circuits.

## *2.3 Composite Materials*

The composite material is a combination of two or more immiscible materials but with a high adhesion capacity and with superior properties than the materials from which it derives. Such material consists of a frame called a reinforcement which provides mechanical strength, and a connecting material called a matrix which ensures the cohesion of the structure and the transmission of the stresses to which the parts are subjected. They also contain fillers that significantly change the mechanical, electrical, and thermal properties, improve the surface appearance and reduce the cost price. The materials thus obtained are heterogeneous (have different properties at different points) and anisotropic (do not have the same properties in all directions) [Cobzaru, P. – *Composite Materials*, Didactic and Pedagogical Publishing, Bucuresti, 2004; Lozovan, M., Dobrea, V., Craus, M.C., Cornei, N. – Advanced materials, Alfa Publishing, Iasi, 2008; Nanu, A. – Unconventional Tehnology, Augusta Publishing, Timisoara, 2003].

The first composite material used by man was wood (natural composite), and later adobe, concrete, and reinforced concrete. In 1823, Charles Macintosh invented the raincoat by rubberizing a cotton fabric, and in 1892, Francois Hennebique made the reinforced concrete.

The composite materials have the following advantages: low weight, good tensile strength, low coefficient of expansion, high fatigue strength, high resilience, good vibration damping ability, resistance to moisture, heat, corrosion, and the action of chemicals (oils, solvents, oil), short manufacturing cycle and acceptable cost price, and high operational safety. At the same time, they cannot replace metallic or ceramic materials in areas that require specific physical-mechanical or chemical properties.

The first classification into three categories of the composite materials can be made starting from the type and method of combining the materials, and thus there can be obtained the fibrous composite material consisting of materials in the form of fibres introduced into a base material called matrix, the laminated composite materials formed from the superimposed layers of different materials and the special composite materials composed of particles introduced into the matrix.

Another classification into four groups of composite materials can be made starting from the manner in which the combinations of materials are made, being able to obtain fibre-reinforced composites, hybrid composites, layered composites, and particle-reinforced composites [Sha, W., Malinov, S. – *Titanium Alloys: Modeling of Microstructure, Properties and Applications*, Woodhead Publishing Limited, England, 2005; Surugiu, I. – Modern technologies. EDM processing, (vol. I), Electra Publishing, 2008].

A layered and fibre-reinforced composite material is obtained by gluing several sheets (layers) with different fibre orientations. If two or more successive laminae (sheets) have the same fibre orientation, they form a group of laminae. The placement of the fibres in sheets or groups of sheets is done depending on the mechanical performance required for the structure made of the respective material (rigidity, resistance to certain stresses, etc.). The laminate is characterised by the number of sheets that make it up, as well as by the angle, q, that indicates the orientation of the fibres in the sheet (laminae) [Cardwell, D.A., Ginley, D.S. (editors) – Handbook of Superconducting Materials (vol I) • *Superconductivity, Materials and Processes*, Institute of Physics Publishing, Bristol and Philadelphia, 2003; Jaoul, D.B. – *Etude de la plasticité et application aux métaux*, Presses de l'École des Mines de Paris, 2008].

## 3. SPECIFIC APPLICATIONS

The replacement of conventional materials used so far in the construction industry has led to an increase in the service life, improved thermal insulation and absorption of noise and vibration for exterior insulation, as well as a decrease in the actual construction time due to the advent of the new assembly technologies based on the use of the composite materials.

The composite materials and especially the polymer composites can be used to make all types of elements that are part of the structure of a construction. The development of this field is particularly noticeable in the case of modular constructions.

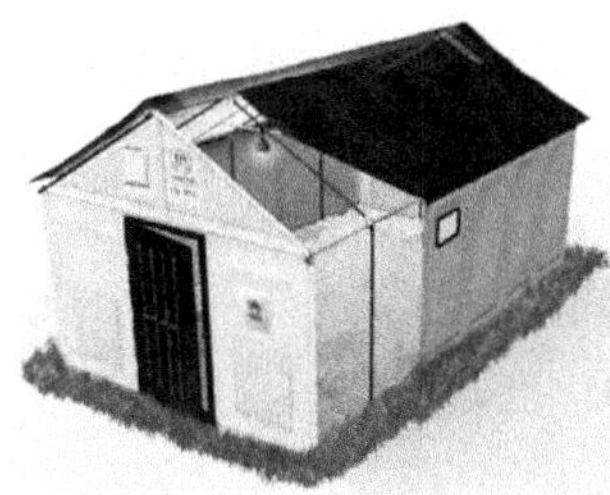

*Refugee shelter*

*Emergency shelter*

**Fig. 2** Shelters

The composite materials have been developed mainly for the aerospace field due to the need for lightweight but durable materials for various demands [Marinescu, N.I., Gavrilas, I., Visan, A., Marinescu, R.D. – Unconventional machining (vol. II), Technical Publishing, Bucuresti ; Morris, D.G., Naka, S., Caron, P. – *Intermetallics and Superalloys*, Willey – VCH Verlag GmbH, 2000]

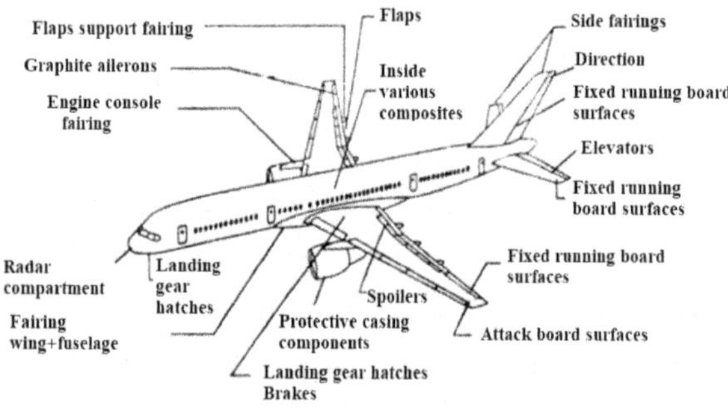


Fig. 3 The structure of the component parts of a Boeing 777

As composite materials develop, their properties make their applicability possible in the machine building industry as well. Thus, the Machine Design magazine published that, in 1995, the Ford Explorer and Ranger cars had a thermoplastic composite carburettor, produced at Cambridge Industries Madison Heights, Mich. The material is thermoplastic composite reinforced with 40% glass fibres. The weight of this product, as a whole, is reduced by 10%, it provides better heat exchange and saves fuel.

If an analysis is made of the lifespan of the new car models, it is observed that the time period until the appearance of a new model is getting shorter. If a few decades ago, the companies were releasing new car models with a frequency of 4-5 years, lately this period has decreased. Thus, almost all car companies launch an improved model on the market in a very short time. This shortening of the new models' life is due to the speed with which technology is advancing, the requirements of comfort and safety imposed and the competition in the car market. In addition to the improvements made, the new models need to be differentiated from the previous ones by means of both exterior and interior design. Thus, a large volume of raw materials and flexible manufacturing technologies is needed to ensure a large number of interior components, differing in shape and structure from one model to another [Anghel-Sprânceana, F., Anghel, D. – *Technological methods and procedures* (vol. II), Printech Publishing, Bucuresti, 2006; Bujoreanu, L.Gh. – *Intelligent materials*, Junimea Publishing, Iasi, 2002].

Against the background of the need for a sustainable resource of raw materials, as well as the environmental problems caused by plastics and metals, which are difficult to degrade, car manufacturers are always looking for new materials, especially composites, with low impact on the environment, provide the possibility to use the waste from other manufacturing processes and to be easily recyclable and biodegradable after the end of their life cycle, are able to ensure the same performance, but to be produced in the most environmentally friendly way possible. In the search of viable solutions to these problems, science and industry, in turn, have taken natural fibres into account. Lately, the reintroduction of ligocellulosic materials into the structure of automotive components has been pursued worldwide.

Electric and hybrid vehicles are seen as vehicles that have nothing to do with oil or emissions. These vehicles are also dependent on the use of composite materials, as the weight gain of the vehicle must be offset by the use of batteries.

Researchers at London Imperial College, including Volvo Corp., have developed a prototype of a carbon fibre electric vehicle, which stores electricity in the composite material from which the body is made. The latest nano-materials made from extremely thin and strong carbon fibres replace the car's steel body panels and can be used to make the roof, doors, hoods, and the floor. The patented composite, made of carbon fibre and polymer resin, could change the construction of hybrid electric vehicles. The material is designed to easily store and supply electricity, but it is strong enough to be used to make structural components or body panels. The car itself could become a battery. The material is able to store and supply large amounts of energy much faster than conventional batteries. The recharging process does not involve any of the chemical reactions that cause the batteries to degrade over time [Lagoudas, D.C. – *Shape Memory Alloys: Modeling and Engineering Applications*, Springer, 2008; Lozovan, M., Dobrea, V., Craus, M.C., Cornei, N. – Advanced materials, Alfa Publishing, Iasi, 2008; Mihaila, I – Unconventional Tehnology (second edition), Publishing University of Oradea, 2003].

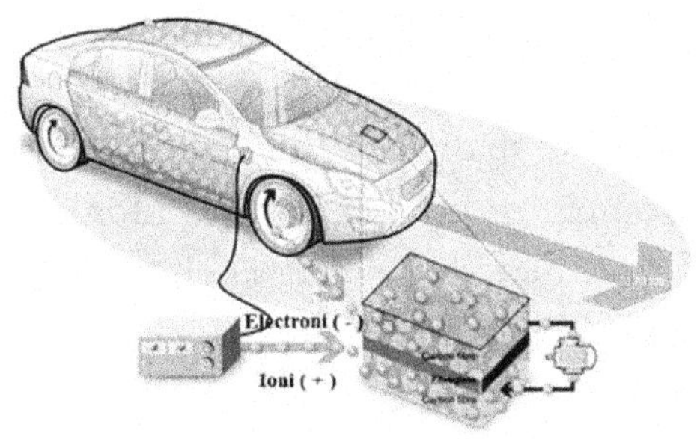


**Fig. 4** Energy-generating composite body elements

Well-known automotive companies such as Ford, Mercedes, Volkswagen, Audi Group, BMW and Opel are currently using new wood and plastic composite materials, or reinforced with various vegetable fibres, for various applications [Vlase, S. – Composite materials. Calculation methods, „Transilvania" University Publishing, Brasov, 2007].

In the field of shipping, polyester resins, reinforced with fibreglass, carbon fibre and aramid fibres, are mainly used as composite materials, especially for light boats, with low weights and high stiffnesses.

# 4. CONCLUSIONS

Composite materials are being used more and more and place themselves in the category of new materials especially designed to meet special requirements in terms of mechanical strength, rigidity, corrosion resistance, lightweight, fatigue strength, shock, wear, and dimensional stability [Amza, Gh., Rîndasu, V.O., Dumitru, G.M., Amza, C.Gh. – *Treated by materials technology (second edi-*

*tion)*, Romanian Academy Publishing, Bucuresti, 2002] thus, being used more frequently in the aeronautical industry, but also in many other fields (automotive industry, sports equipment or others). In the automotive industry, the use of these materials increases the strength while the weight of the vehicles decreases, which translates into reduced fuel consumption and increased performance.

According to an insurance company, 616 cities around the world are exposed to natural disasters such as floods, earthquakes, tsunamis or hurricanes, and due to the way they are assembled, composite houses can be a solution for people who face such problems, but also for people living in a poor environment, such as countries in Africa, Central America and Asia.

The polymer composite houses are proving to be a solution for the disasters that arise in people's daily lives, even for the countries that are protected from natural disasters, with a decent standard of living. The modular assemblies obtained have a low cost and a short assembly time, so they can also be used for emergencies.

## REFERENCES


Amza, Gh., Rîndasu, V.O., Dumitru, G.M., Amza, C.Gh. – *Treated by materials technology (second edition)*, Romanian Academy Publishing, Bucuresti, 2002.

Anghel-Sprânceana, F., Anghel, D. – *Technological methods and procedures* (vol. II), Printech Publishing, Bucuresti, 2006.

Ashby, F.M., Jones, R.H.D. – *Engineering Materials 1. An Introduction to Properties, Applications and Design* (fourth edition), Cambridge, 2009.

Bailley, D., Wright, E. – *Practical Fiber Optics*, Newnes, Oxford, 2003.

Bolundut, I.L. – *Plastics and composites technology*, Junimea Publishing, Iasi, 2010.

Bolundut, I.L. – Metallic *materials*, AGIR Publishing, Bucuresti, 2004.

Bolundut, I.L. – *Materials science and engineering*, Junimea Publishing, Iasi, 2010.

Brabie, V., Avram, N., Moldovan, P. – *Alloy making*, Didactic and Pedagogical Publishing, Bucuresti, 1978.

Bujoreanu, L.Gh. –I*ntelligent materials*, Junimea Publishing, Iasi, 2002.

Buschow, K.H.J. (editor) – *Concise Encyclopedia of Magnetic and Superconducting Materials* (second edition), PDF, Elsevier Science, 2006.

Callister, W.D.Jr. – *Materials Science and Engineering – An Introduction*, Ed. John Wiley & Sons (5 th edition), New York, 2000.

Cardwell, D.A., Ginley, D.S. (editors) – *Handbook of Superconducting Materials* (vol I) • *Superconductivity, Materials and Processes*, Institute of Physics Publishing, Bristol and Philadelphia, 2003.

Cobzaru, P. – *Composite Materials*, Didactic and Pedagogical Publishing, Bucuresti, 2004.

Cojocaru-Filipiuc, V. – *Irons. Obtaining*, Samia Publishing, Iasi, 2002.

Colan, H., Tudoran, P., Ailincai, Gh., Marcu, M., Drugescu, E. – *Study of metals*, Didactic and Pedagogical Publishing, Bucuresti, 1983.

Collings, P.J. – *Liquid Crystals* (second edition), Princeton University Press, 2002.

Constantinescu R., Platon, M. – *Use of plastics in constructions*, Technical Publishing, Bucuresti, 1985.

Crisp, J., Elliott, B. – *Introduction to Fiber Optics* (third edition), Newnes, Oxford, 2005.

Dimitriu, S., Gheorghe, C, Dimitriu, A., Butu, M. – *Heat treatment of welded joints*, BREN Publishing, Bucuresti, 2002.

Dobrovici, D., Prisecaru, I., Banciu, M. – *Source metallurgy*, Technical Publishing, Bucuresti, 1966.

Fetecau, C., Oancea, N., Stan, F. – Mechanical processing of plastics, Documentary Infirmation Office for the Machine Building Industry, Bucuresti, 2000.

Fleser, T. – Changing the condition of steels subjected to thermomechanical stresses, Polytechnic Publishing, Timisoara, 2002.

Gale, W.F., Totemeier, T.C. – *Smithells Metals Reference Book* (8 edition), ASM International, 2004.

Gambhir, M.I. – *Concrete technology* (third edition), Tata McGraw-Hill, New Delhi, 2004.

Gheorghe, C., Stefan, M. – Metal guide. Obtaining. Properties. Uses, Technical Publishing, Bucuresti, 1997.

Gladcov, P., Petrovici, A., Alexandrescu, V., Cosmulescu, D. – Materials technology (vol. I, II), PROINVENT Foundation of the "Politehnica" University of Bucharest, 1998.

Gutt, G., Palade, D.D., Gutt, S., Klein, F., Schmitt, K.T. – Testing and characterization of metallic materials, Technical Publishing, Bucuresti, 2002.

Higgins, R.A. – *Engineering Metallurgy*, ELBS, Kent, 1986.

Jaoul, D.B. – *Etude de la plasticité et application aux métaux*, Presses de l'École des Mines de Paris, 2008.

Krenkel, W.H. – *Ceramic matrix composites: fiber reinforced ceramics and their applications*, John Wiley, New York, 2008.

Kulshreshtha, A.K., Vasile, C. – *Handbook of Polymer Blends and Composites* (vol.2), Rapra Technology Ltd., Shawbury, 2002.

La Mantia, F. – *Handbook of Plastics Recycling*, Rapra Technology, Shrewsbury, UK, 2002.

Lagoudas, D.C. – *Shape Memory Alloys: Modeling and Engineering Applications*, Spriger, 2008.

Lee, S. – *Dictionary of Composite Materials Technology*, CRC Press LLC, Palo Alto, California, 1995.

Lendlein, A. – *Shape-Memory Polymers*, Springer, 2010.

Lozovan, M., Dobrea, V., Craus, M.C., Cornei, N. – Advanced materials, Alfa Publishing, Iasi, 2008.

Lupescu, M.B. – Reinforcing fibers for composite materials, Technical Publishing, Bucuresti, 2004.

Marinescu, N.I., Gavrilas, I., Visan, A., Marinescu, R.D. – Unconventional machining (vol. II), Technical Publishing, Bucuresti

Mihaila, I – Unconventional Tehnology (second edition), Publishing University of Oradea, 2003.

Miravete, A. – *Materiales Compuestos*, Editorial Reverté S.A., Barcelona, 2007.

Mitelea, I. – *Materiales science* (vol. II), Polytechnic Publishing, Timisoara, 2010.

Morris, D.G., Naka, S., Caron, P. – *Intermetallics and Superalloys*, Willey– VCH Verlag GmbH, 2000.

Motoasca, S.D. – Study of the magnetic characteristics of soft magnetic materials, PhD student thesis, „Transilvania" University of Brasov, 2010.

Murray, G.T. – *Introduction to Engineering Materials*, Library Publishing Company, New York, 1992.

Nagy, I.I. – Ultrasound and their use, Scientific and Encyclopedic Publishing, Bucuresti, 1982.

Nanu, A. – Unconventional Tehnology, Augusta Publishing, Timisoara, 2003.

Newmann, J., Choo, B.S. (editors) – *Advanced Concrete Technology*, Ensevier Butterworth-Heinemann, Oxford, 2003.

Nocivin, A. – Advanced materials: composite materials; metallic materials with special properties, „Ovidius" University Press, Constanta, 2001

Popescu, I., Dumitras, C., Savu, T., Dumitrescu, A., Purcarea, M., Tonoiu, S. – Technology for processing parts from classical and composite materials (2 vol.), MATRIX ROM Publishing, Bucuresti, 2000.

Popescu, V.I., Chiriac, C. – High speed steels, AGIR Publishing, Bucuresti, 2002.

Popescu, V., Horovitz, O., Rusu, T – Polymeric materials and the environment, Mediamira Publishing, Cluj-Napoca, 2005.

Popovici, E., Dvininov, E. – Advanced nanostructural materials. Present and future (vol. I), Demiurg Publishing, Iasi, 2007.

Radhakrishnan, V.M. – *Welding Technology & Design*, New Age International Publishers, New Delhi, 2005.

Rakhit, A.K. – *Heat Treatment of Gears – A Practical Guide for Engineers*, ASM International, 2000.

Reed, C.R. – *The Superalloys: Fundamentals and Applications*, Cambridge University Press, 2006.

Sha, W., Guo, Z. – *Maraging Steels: Modeling of Microstructure, Properties and Applications*, Woodhead Publishing Limited, 2009.

Sha, W., Malinov, S. – *Titanium Alloys: Modeling of Microstructure, Properties and Applications*, Woodhead Publishing Limited, England, 2005.

Simionescu, Gh. – Materials technology: plastics; protective coatings, Alma Mater Publishing, Bacau, 2001.

Singh, O., Bhavikatti, S.S. – *Introduction to Mechanical Engineering*, New Age International Publishers, New Delhi, 2006.

Suciu, V., Suciu, M.V. – Study of materials, FAIR PARTNERS Publishing, Bucuresti, 2008.

Surugiu, I. – Modern technologies. EDM processing, (vol. I), Electra Publishing, 2008.

Saban, R., Dumitrescu, C. – Treatise on the science and engineering of metallic materials. Metals. Alloy. Special materials. Composite materials (vol.3), AGIR Publishing, Bucuresti, 2009.

Serban, V.A., Raduta, A. – Materials science and engineering, Politehnica Publishing, Timisoara, 2010.

Toderas, M. – Material testing, Focus Publishing, Petrosani, 2008.

Totten, G.E. – *Steel Heat Treatment: Metallurgy and Technologies* (2 edition), CRC Press, New York, 2006.

Vlase, S. – Composite materials. Calculation methods, „Transilvania" University Publishing, Brasov, 2007.

# GDP and Inflation - Macroeconomic Indicators that may Reflect an Improved Economic Well-Being

**Ramona Mariana Călinică** Cross-Border Faculty, "Dunărea de Jos" University of Galati ramona.calinica@ugal.ro

## ABSTRACT

Within each national economy, a range of economic activities is carried out, resulting in a diverse range of goods and services, which can be assessed in physical or value terms using macroeconomic indicators. One of these is the gross domestic product, which is used to measure a nation's economic activity and is considered to be an index that can reflect the health of an economic system. When analysing the state of an economy, inflation is another important indicator. It has a significant impact on the evolution of the GDP and can have considerable damaging effects to the economic growth. The aim of this paper is to analyse the evolution of both GDP and inflation in the context of the economic and monetary integration of Eurozone countries.

**Keywords:** *gross domestic product, inflation, macroeconomic indicators, economic welfare.*

## 1. INTRODUCTION

It is known that the higher the GDP value, the better the economic situation in the country in question. In addition, since it is not possible to draw sufficient conclusions about the competitiveness of a country's economy from a single observation of GDP in order to understand the dynamics and prospects for its development, it is necessary to carry out an analysis aimed at comparing the country in question with other countries in terms of the current value vs. other values previously recorded. Since the GDP is calculated according to a clear methodology, it allows such comparisons between countries or regions and between different time periods.

In the technical literature, economic growth is defined as a global process that expresses the upward trend of the aggregate economic magnitudes over a time frame, at a national or international level, with favourable effects on economic and social life. In a narrower sense, economic growth expresses the real size of an aggregate economic indicator over a given period of time, such as the GDP, per total or per capita in a given economic area. In a broader sense, economic growth is the form in which all the quantitative, structural and qualitative transformations occurring in economic life over a long period of time are manifested, giving the aggregate indicators an upward trend [Popescu, C. (2001), Dictionarul de Economie, Editia a II-a, Editura Economica, p. 138-139].

inflation is considered to be one of the most powerful macroeconomic imbalances which, to varying degrees, affects all national economies. This process is characterised by the following trends: increases of the generalized price, decreases of the purchasing power of money and the depreciation of the national currency.

# 2. THE ANALYSIS OF THE EVOLUTION OF THE GROSS DOMESTIC PRODUCT IN THE EUROZONE COUNTRIES BETWEEN 2004 AND 2020

The GDP is the first analysed indicator, and this represents „the final result of production activity for resident productive units, for a certain period" [National Institute of Statistics, Products, Data, Gross Domestic Product, http://www.insse.ro/cms/en/content/gross-domestic-product].

Table 1 and table 2 show the GDP values/per capita recorded by the Eurozone Member States referred to the above-mentioned period. It is important to emphasise that the countries adopting the Eurozone in 2004 were also included: Slovenia (2007), Cyprus and Malta (2008), Slovakia (2009) Estonia (2011), Latvia (2015).

Also, for an in-depth GDP analysis, Table 3 shows the percentage of yearly changes in this macro-economic indicator, highlighting the years when both the economic growth and the recession were recorded.

**Table 1** GDP per capita in Eurozone countries between 2004-2015

| Year<br>Country | 2004 | 2007 | 2008 | 2009 | 2010 | 2012 | 2015 |
|---|---|---|---|---|---|---|---|
| Belgium | 28,700 | 32,500 | 33,100 | 32,300 | 33,500 | 35,100 | 36,500 |
| Germany | 27,900 | 31,000 | 31,700 | 30,600 | 32,100 | 34,300 | 37,100 |
| Estonia | 7,100 | 12,100 | 12,300 | 10,600 | 11,000 | 13,600 | 15,600 |
| Ireland | 38,400 | 44,800 | 41,700 | 37,300 | 36,400 | 38,100 | 46,200 |
| Greece | 17,700 | 21,100 | 21,800 | 21,400 | 20,300 | 17,300 | 16,200 |

| Spain | 20,100 | 23,900 | 24,300 | 23,300 | 23,200 | 22,300 | 23,300 |
| France | 27,300 | 30,400 | 31,000 | 30,000 | 30,800 | 31,800 | 32,800 |
| Italy | 25,000 | 27,400 | 27,600 | 26,400 | 26,800 | 26,700 | 26,900 |
| Cyprus | 19,000 | 22,800 | 23,900 | 22,900 | 23,000 | 22,500 | 20,600 |
| Latvia | 5,200 | 10,300 | 11,200 | 8,700 | 8,500 | 10,800 | 12,300 |
| Lithua-nia | 5,400 | 9,000 | 10,200 | 8,500 | 9,000 | 11,200 | 12,800 |
| Luxem-bourg | 60,300 | 76,500 | 77,000 | 72,800 | 77,900 | 82,000 | 91,600 |
| Malta | 12,100 | 14,200 | 15,000 | 14,900 | 15,900 | 17,200 | 20,400 |
| Austria | 29,600 | 34,000 | 35,100 | 34,300 | 35,200 | 37,600 | 39,100 |
| Nether-lands | 32,200 | 37,400 | 38,900 | 37,400 | 38,000 | 38,500 | 40,000 |
| Portugal | 14,500 | 16,600 | 16,900 | 16,600 | 17,000 | 16,000 | 17,300 |
| Slovenia | 13,900 | 17,400 | 18,800 | 17,700 | 17,700 | 17,500 | 18,700 |
| Slovakia | 6,400 | 10,400 | 12,200 | 11,800 | 12,400 | 13,400 | 14,400 |
| Finland | 30,300 | 35,300 | 36,500 | 33,900 | 34,900 | 36,900 | 37,800 |

Source: elaborated by the author based on the [EUROSTAT databases]

In 2007, in comparison to 2004, the GDP per capita was higher for all Eurozone countries. The increasing trend was registered in 2008, as well. However, for Ireland, a lower GDP value was recorded compared to 2007 and, also, to 2004. Therefore, regarding the GDP value per capita, Ireland, as the second country, registers an increasing trend in 2007 compared to 2004, from 38,400 euro/per capita to 44,800 euro/per capita; also, in **2012 compared to 2010, from 36,400 euro/per capita**

**to 38,100 euro/per capita reaching up to 48,200 euro/ per capita in 2015.** Nevertheless, during 2008-2010 a frequent contraction of the GDP indicator was registered caused by the financial economic crisis and its subsequent impact.

Throughout these years, Luxemburg has registered the highest GDP value per capita. Also, except for the year 2009, this indicator kept increasing continuously from 60,300 EUR/per capita in 2004, up to 91,600 EUR/per capita in 2015.

The following five countries which have recorded the highest GDP per capita value are Belgium, Austria, Finland, Germany, France, and Italy. These countries have had quite a similar development with an increasing trend (except for the year 2009) and a relatively high GDP indicator.

In contrast, a group of countries among which Latvia, Lithuania, Slovakia, and Estonia (non-EU countries at that time) has registered a relatively low GDP per capita which was lower than the one in 2004 and below the value of 10,000 euro/per capita. Despite this, and excepting the year 2009 from the trend, these countries have registered a GDP growth, exceeding the previously mentioned level.

Greece and Cyprus are the only two countries where a GDP decreasing tendency has been recorded within 2012 – 2015 compared to 2010. Thus, Cyprus had a GDP decrease from 23,000 EUR/ capita in 2010 up to 20,600 euro/ capita in 2015. Also, Greece, where the GDP grew from 17,700 EUR/ capita in 2004 to 21,400 EUR/ capita in 2009, recorded a compression of 16,200 EUR/ capita in 2015, a value below the one registered in 2004. Also, in 2015, all countries, except Greece, recorded higher values of GDP per capita, compared to 2012.

**Table 2** The GDP per capita in Eurozone countries between 2018-2020

| Year<br>Country | 2018 | 2019 | 2020 |
|---|---|---|---|
| Belgium | 40,260 | 41,620 | 39,580 |
| Germany | 40,620 | 41,800 | 40,490 |
| Estonia | 19,570 | 20,930 | 20,190 |
| Ireland | 67,080 | 72,360 | 74,870 |
| Greece | 16,730 | 17,090 | 15,420 |
| Spain | 25,750 | 26,420 | 23,690 |
| France | 35,070 | 36,050 | 33,960 |
| Italy | 29,580 | 30,050 | 27,820 |
| Cyprus | 24,840 | 26,090 | 24,160 |
| Latvia | 15,130 | 16,020 | 15,530 |
| Lithuania | 16,250 | 17,490 | 17,710 |
| Luxembourg | 99,150 | 100,890 | 101,760 |
| Malta | 26,730 | 27,850 | 25,360 |
| Austria | 44,920 | 46,880 | 42,540 |
| Netherlands | 43,610 | 44,780 | 45,870 |
| Portugal | 19,950 | 20,840 | 19,430 |
| Slovenia | 22,140 | 23,170 | 22,310 |
| Slovakia | 16,420 | 17,250 | 16,860 |
| Finland | 42,320 | 43,440 | 42,680 |

Source: elaborated by the author based on [EUROSTAT databases]

In 2020, Luxembourg remained the country with the highest GDP per capita in the Eurozone, namely 101,760 EUR /capita, followed by Ireland with 74,870 EUR /capita, the Netherlands with 45,870 EUR /capita, Finland with 42,680 EUR /capita, Austria with 42,540 EUR /capita, and Germany with 40,490 EUR /capita. At the other end of the scale, there are countries with a lower indicator, below 20,000 EUR per capita, namely Greece (15,420 EUR / capita), Latvia (15,530 EUR / capita), Slovakia (16,860 EUR /capita), Lithuania (17,710 EUR /capita) and Portugal (19,430 EUR /capita).

Table 3 clearly shows that the GDP decreased in all Eurozone countries in 2009 under the impact of the 2008 economic crisis. Even the highly developed states had trouble maintaining the indicator level at least at the level of the previous year.

The Baltic countries have registered the highest GDP reduction: Estonia (-14.7%), Lithuania (-14.8%) and Latvia (14.3%) (non-Eurozone countries at that time).

Some countries registered the impact a year earlier, in 2008. Thus, Estonia, Ireland, Greece, Italy, Latvia, and Luxembourg recorded decreases in the GDP values in 2008. In 2010, the GDP value increased due to the economic growth in more Eurozone countries. Except for Greece (-5.5%), where the recession continued its increment. Latvia also registered a GDP decrease (-3.8%), but, as mentioned above, Latvia was not a Eurozone country at that time.

As recession ended in 2010, the Eurozone countries had to cope with the same phenomenon in 2012. As a result, Spain (-2.6), Italy (-2.8), Cyprus (-2.4), Luxembourg (-0.8) Portugal (-4), Slovenia (-2.7) and Finland (-1.4) could not avoid entering recession. The same trend continued in Greece (-7.3), the recession process deepening. By contrast, Estonia had the highest economic growth (5.2%). In 2015, all Eurozone countries, except Greece, had economic growth. The highest GDP values were reported by Ireland (+ 7.8%), Malta (+ 6.3%) and Luxembourg (+ 4.8%).

The year 2020 was marked by the manifestation of the COVID-19 pandemic in Europe, with the economies of the countries being affected. Thus, as can be seen in Table 3, the Eurozone countries, with the exception of Ireland, recorded decreases in the GDP as compared to the previous period. The largest contraction was recorded in Spain (-10.8%), but other countries such as Italy (-8.9%), Portugal (-8.4%), Malta (-8.2%) and France (-7.9%) also recorded considerable decreases in GDP.

**Table 3** The annual GDP increase and decrease

| Country \ Year | 2004 | 2007 | 2008 | 2009 | 2010 | 2012 | 2015 | 2018 | 2019 | 2020 |
|---|---|---|---|---|---|---|---|---|---|---|
| Belgium | 3,6 | 3.4 | 0.7 | -2.3 | 2.7 | 0.2 | 1.4 | 1.8 | 2.1 | -5.7 |
| Germany | 1.2 | 3.3 | 1.1 | -5.6 | 4.1 | 0.4 | 1.7 | 1.1 | 1.1 | -4.6 |
| Estonia | 6.3 | 7.7 | -5.4 | -14.7 | 2.5 | 5.2 | 1.1 | 4.1 | 4.1 | -3.8 |
| Ireland | 4.4 | 5.5 | -2.2 | -5.6 | 0.4 | 0.2 | 7.8 | 9.0 | 4.9 | 5.9 |
| Greece | 5.1 | 3.3 | -0.3 | -4.3 | -5.5 | -7.3 | -0.2 | 1.7 | 1.8 | -9 |
| Spain | 3.2 | 3.8 | 1.1 | -3.6 | 0 | -2.6 | 3.2 | 2.3 | 2.1 | -10.8 |
| France | 2.8 | 2.4 | 0.2 | -2.9 | 2 | 0.2 | 1.2 | 1.9 | 1.8 | -7.9 |
| Italy | 1.6 | 1.5 | -1.1 | -5.5 | 1.7 | -2.8 | 0.8 | 0.9 | 0.4 | -8.9 |

| Cyprus | 4.6 | 4.9 | 3.7 | -2 | 1.4 | -2.4 | 1.6 | 5.7 | 5.3 | -5.2 |
| Latvia | 8.3 | 10 | -3.6 | -14.3 | -3.8 | 4 | 2.7 | 4.0 | 2.5 | -3.6 |
| Lithuania | 6.6 | 11.1 | 2.6 | -14.8 | 1.6 | 3.8 | 1.6 | 4.0 | 4.6 | -0.1 |
| Luxembourg | 4.4 | 8.4 | -0.8 | -5.4 | 5.7 | -0.8 | 4.8 | 2.0 | 3.3 | -1.8 |
| Malta | 0.4 | 4 | 3.3 | -2.5 | 3.5 | 2.8 | 6.3 | 6.1 | 5.9 | -8.2 |
| Austria | 2.7 | 3.6 | 1.5 | -3.8 | 1.9 | 0.8 | 0.9 | 2.4 | 2.0 | -6.7 |
| Netherlands | 5.1 | 7.2 | 3.9 | 2.6 | 3.7 | 1.6 | 3.6 | 2.5 | 1.5 | -3.8 |
| Portugal | 1.8 | 2.5 | 0.2 | -3 | 1.9 | -4 | 1.5 | 2.8 | 2.7 | -8.4 |
| Slovenia | 4.4 | 6.9 | 3.3 | -7.8 | 1.2 | -2.7 | 2.9 | 4.4 | 3.3 | -4.2 |
| Slovakia | 5.3 | 10.8 | 5.7 | -5.5 | 5.1 | 1.5 | 3.6 | 3.8 | 2.6 | -4.4 |
| Finland | 3.9 | 5.2 | 0.7 | -8.3 | 3 | -1.4 | 0.5 | 1.1 | 1.2 | -2.8 |

Source: elaborated by the author based on [EUROSTAT databases]

The GDP analysis reveals as a rough guide a picture of the Eurozone countries' economic development, their vulnerabilities to some negative global phenomena and even their „regeneration" capacity and tools to cope with severely difficult conditions.

It is worth noting that the GDP analysis is not sufficient to clearly understand all aspects of a country's development level, its real economic development or its living standard. To this end, further analysis of other macro-indicators such as the inflation rate is proven necessary.

## 3. THE ANALYSIS OF THE INFLATION RATE EVOLUTION IN THE EUROZONE COUNTRIES IN THE PERIOD 2004-2020

Inflation is a major imbalance caused by specific aspects of each country's economy. It represents an economic phenomenon not easily controllable, with a significant impact on the economy in general and, upon the economic agents and population, in particular.

Inflation is a dynamic phenomenon, a result of the increase in prices and is relevant for the so-called main price indicator. Deflation is opposed to inflation; the lack of these two processes signifies a price balance. Thus, as inflation consists of "a general increase in prices and fall in the purchasing value of money and services during a long period, causing a fall of the currency value and thus of the purchasing value, deflation is frequently noted as a general fall of prices during a long period. When inflation or deflation is absent, we can talk about prices stability, when, on average, prices neither increase nor decrease but are stable in time" [Gerdesmeier, D. (2009), *Stabiltatea preturilor: de ce este importanta?* Banca Centrala Europeana, 2009, p. 24].

One of the conditions mandatory to the Euro currency-adopting countries is to maintain the inflation rate to a level that does not exceed the 1.5% average level of the first three countries which report the lowest rate. The indicator of these Eurozone countries is shown in Table 4, based on EUROSTAT data; as well, the following chapters analyse the inflation rate for the years 2004, 2007, 2008, 2009, 2010, 2012, 2015, 2018, 2019 and 2020.

**Table 4** The Inflation rate in Eurozone countries

| Year \ Country | 2004 | 2007 | 2008 | 2009 | 2010 | 2012 | 2015 | 2018 | 2019 | 2020 |
|---|---|---|---|---|---|---|---|---|---|---|
| Belgium | 1.9 | 1.8 | 4.5 | 0.0 | 2.3 | 2.6 | 0.6 | 2.3 | 1.2 | 0.4 |
| Germany | 1.8 | 2.3 | 2.8 | 0.2 | 1.1 | 2.1 | 0.1 | 1.9 | 1.4 | 0.4 |
| Estonia | 3.0 | 6.7 | 10.6 | 0.2 | 2.7 | 4.2 | 0.1 | 3.4 | 2.3 | -0.6 |
| Ireland | 2.3 | 2.9 | 3.1 | -1.7 | 1.6 | 1.9 | 0.0 | 0.7 | 0.9 | -0.5 |

| Greece | 3.0 | 3.0 | 4.2 | 1.3 | 4.7 | 1.0 | -1.1 | 0.8 | 0.5 | -1.3 |
|---|---|---|---|---|---|---|---|---|---|---|
| Spain | 3.1 | 2.8 | 4.1 | -0.2 | 2 | 2.4 | -0.6 | 1.7 | 0.8 | -0.3 |
| France | 2.3 | 1.6 | 3.2 | 0.1 | 1.7 | 2.2 | 0.1 | 2.1 | 1.3 | 0.5 |
| Italy | 2.3 | 2.0 | 3.5 | 0.8 | 1.6 | 3.3 | 0.1 | 1.2 | 0.6 | -0.1 |
| Cyprus | 1.9 | 2.2 | 4.4 | 0.2 | 2.6 | 3.1 | -1.5 | 0.8 | 0.5 | -1.1 |
| Latvia | 6.2 | 10.1 | 15.3 | 3.3 | 1.2 | 2.3 | 0.2 | 2.6 | 2.7 | 0.1 |
| Lithuania | 1.2 | 5.8 | 11.1 | 4.2 | 1.2 | 3.2 | -0.7 | 2.5 | 2.2 | 1.1 |
| Luxembourg | 3.2 | 2.7 | 4.1 | 0.0 | 2.8 | 2.9 | 0.1 | 2.0 | 1.6 | 0.0 |
| Malta | 2.7 | 0.7 | 4.7 | 1.8 | 2 | 3.2 | 1.2 | 1.7 | 1.5 | 0.8 |
| Austria | 2.0 | 2.2 | 3.2 | 0.4 | 1.7 | 2.6 | 0.8 | 2.1 | 1.5 | 1.4 |
| Netherlands | 3.6 | 2.6 | 2.2 | 4.0 | 0.9 | 3.7 | -0.7 | 1.6 | 2.7 | 1.1 |
| Portugal | 2.5 | 2.4 | 2.7 | -0.9 | 1.4 | 2.8 | 0.5 | 1.2 | 0.3 | -0.1 |
| Slovenia | 3.7 | 3.8 | 5.5 | 0.9 | 2.1 | 2.8 | -0.8 | 1.9 | 1.7 | -0.3 |
| Slovakia | 7.5 | 1.9 | 3.9 | 0.9 | 0.7 | 3.7 | -0.3 | 2.5 | 2.8 | 2.0 |
| Finland | 0.1 | 1.6 | 3.9 | 1.6 | 1.7 | 3.2 | -0.2 | 1.2 | 1.1 | 0.4 |

Source: elaborated by the author based on [EUROSTAT databases]

In 2004, the three (3) countries with the lowest inflation rate were: Finland 0.1%, Lithuania 1.2%, and Germany 1,8%, the average being 1.033%. Taking into consideration one of the convergency criteria referring to the inflation rate in 2004, the countries interested in joining the Economic and Monetary Union had to achieve an inflation rate lower than 2.533% (1.5%+1.033%). Leaving aside the countries that joined the EU in 2004 and those that have joined later, we can assert that the indicator mentioned above was higher in several EU Member States: Greece 3%, Luxembourg 3.2%, Spain 3.1%, and The Netherlands 3.6%, all four countries being Eurozone Member States.

Latvia (6.2%) and Slovakia (7.5%), non-Eurozone countries at that time, but among the newest EU Member States, registered the highest inflation rate levels.

In 2007, things changed. The first two countries which had stable prices from the ones targeted by this research were France with 0.7% and Finland with 1.6%. Thus, the average was 1.3%, the level changing up to 2.8%. A significant increase of the inflation rate was noted in the Baltic countries: Estonia 6.7%, Latvia 10.1%, and Lithuania 1.2 to 5.8%. Other countries such as France, Italy, Malta, The Netherlands, and Slovakia managed to decrease this indicator.

In 2008, the inflation rate increased in all countries except The Netherlands. The average of the first three countries with the lowest inflation rate (The Netherlands 2.2%, Portugal 2.7%, and Germany 2.8%) reached 2.57%, under the condition to join the Monetary Union.

In 2009, as an impact of the economic crisis, a sudden fall in the inflation rate in all European countries was registered, even negative values in some countries, hence the deflation phenomenon. (Portugal -0.9%, Spain -0.2%, and -1.7% Ireland). Latvia, Lithuania, and The Netherlands had the highest rates, 3.3%, 4.2% and 4.0%, respectively; the first two were, later, in 2010, the only countries getting a reduction in the inflation rate in comparison with the others.

In 2012, the first three countries with the lowest rate were: Greece 1.0%, Ireland 1.9%, and Germany 2.1%, their average being 1.66%. Estonia was the country with the highest inflation rate increase (from 0.2% to 4.2%).

In 2015, the inflation rate significantly decreased all over the Eurozone, even reaching negative values, except for Malta which had a 1.2% rate (the highest of the countries mentioned). Although the deflation phenomenon means a decrease of the consumer prices, it can have negative effects on both the countries in question and the Eurozone in its entirety. Thus, „the term deflation refers to a broad-based and lasting decline in prices, with negative effects on economic growth. In the euro area context, deflation risks must be analysed for the euro area as a whole, taking into consideration that, within a monetary union, negative inflation in individual countries may reflect relative price changes in order to regain competitiveness" [European Central Bank (2014), Monthly Buletin, June 2014, p. 69, https://www.ecb.europa.eu/pub/pdf/other/mb201406_focus05.en.pdf].

In 2020, the inflation, in all Eurozone countries, did not exceed 2%, and some of them recorded negative values of this indicator, namely: Estonia (-0.6%), Ireland (-0.5%), Greece (-0.3%), Italy (-0.1%), Cyprus (-1.1), Portugal (-0.1%), and Slovenia (-0.3%). As can be seen, the highest inflation rate was recorded in Slovakia, reaching 2%, and the lowest was recorded in Greece at -1.3%.

It is worth mentioning that, based on the monetary policy enforced by the European Central Bank, which aims at maintaining the purchasing power of the euro currency and the stability of prices, it is generally considered that „maintaining the inflation rate at 2 % is low enough for the economy to make the best of the benefits of prices stability" [Comisia Europeană, (2013), *Uniunea economică și monetară (UEM) și moneda euro*, p. 5].

# 4. CONCLUSIONS

It is widely known that the phenomenon of economic growth in a country reflects the positive variation in the production of goods and services within its economy over a certain period of time. Thus, the indicator most often used to measure growth is the gross domestic product (GDP).

The GDP is often regarded as the most consistent and relevant macroeconomic indicator and, together with the monetary policy, plays a particularly important role in the long-term investment planning.

Economic growth is the increase in the quality of life reflected in the continuous upward trend of economic indicators, in the process of increasing the economic performance with favourable effects on the economic and social life, and it is influenced by a multitude of direct and indirect factors. As far as inflation is concerned, it is a complex process and can cause serious distortions in the functioning of the economic system in a country. The causes of this phenomenon are multiple being of economic, social, and political nature, and they must be analysed and prioritised by countries and groups of countries.

Preventing inflation is important, but it is complicated to put into practice. A country can avoid a too high inflation through a series of measures such as rigorous monetary policies, avoidance of currency surpluses, appropriate budgetary policies, combating budget deficits, and efficient resizing of public expenditure.

Although it has many negative effects, it is considered that there are situations where inflation could stimulate economic growth. If the inflation in a country is close to zero, a slight increase in the inflation rate is sometimes considered to have a positive impact on the economic growth in the medium term. Also, where there is moderate inflation, individuals and companies may tend to save or invest to forgo borrowing, and the economic growth may be felt over time.

Maintaining the economic balance in the Eurozone Member States was a difficult issue to achieve during the period under review, as they were not spared by global events, such as the economic and financial crisis in the US in 2007 and the subsequent effects of the COVID-19 pandemic. However, maintaining the balance of these countries is an important factor in determining the role of the Euro on the international money market. Under these circumstances, it is of major importance to implement a set of measures through various European policies, which will contribute to ensuring the economic growth of the region.

# REFERENCES

Comisia Europeană, (2013), *Uniunea economică și monetară (UEM) și moneda euro*, European Central Bank (2014), *Monthly Buletin*, June 2014, p. 69, https://www.ecb.europa.eu/pub/pdf/other/mb201406_focus05.en.pdf

Eurostat, Database, *http://ec.europa.eu/eurostat/data/database*

Gerdesmeier, D.(2009), *Stabiltatea preturilor: de ce este importanta?*, Banca Centrala Europeana, 2009, p. 24

National Institute of Statistics, Products, Data, *Gross Domestic Product*, http://www.insse.ro/cms/en/content/gross-domestic-product

Popescu, C., *Dictionarul de Economie, Editia* a II-a, Editura Economica, 2001, pg. 138-139http://europa.eu/pol/emu/flipbook/ro/files/na7012001roc_002.pdf

# International Legal Standards for the Protection of Government Officials During the Performance of Their Duties

**DRĂNICERU Mihai** Cross-Border Faculty,
"Dunărea de Jos" University of Galati, mihai.draniceru@ugal.ro

Annotation. The topicality of the research undertaken is due to the importance of the public service in carrying out the tasks and functions of the state, or the current state organisation is inextricably linked to the need to form a modern state apparatus, one whose activities should be based on effective international principles and practices.

The chapter presents a comparative analysis of the legal aspects regarding the rights and guarantees offered to government officials both by the legislation of international institutions and of some reference countries. Particular emphasis has been placed on the protection by legal-criminal instruments of civil servants against pressure from third parties, which, by most laws, are considered crimes. The paper focuses on the persons placed under the protection of the law, the main sanctions, and the circumstances of committing the offences.

The main conclusions of the research are related to the fact that the states of continental Europe are similar in terms of legal and criminal protection of civil servants, the differences being related to the sanctioning regime and the status of victims. Commonwealth member states also protect public representatives but under different laws.

Given its millennia-long evolution, public service has acquired some key features due to specific historical circumstances, society's level of economic development, geographical factors, national traditions, the population's cultural level of development and others. However, regardless of the above-mentioned conditions and the different perspectives on the concept of state and its role in society's dynamics, the tendency to define, develop, and consolidate the legal status of the state's civil servants remained unchanged. They act as direct representatives of the state's interests, as intermediaries between the civil society and the state, conveying the will of that state.

The optimal functioning of state institutions is only made possible by the high professionalism of civil servants, which have skills and moral qualities that enable them to thoroughly, scrupulously, and responsibly fulfil the duty of exercising public power functions. Meanwhile, the successful training of the state's staff is only possible based upon a consistent policy that combines material elements, social security, legal protection, stimulation of disinterested work for society's and the state's welfare, as well as a high degree of labour discipline. The social vector of state policy is stipulated in most state constitutions worldwide (Art.1 para.3 Constitution of Romania, Art.1 para.3 Constitution of the Republic of Moldova, Art.2 Constitution of the Russian Federation, and others), representing public interest, and civil servants themselves are subject to social relations and, as any other member of the society, in need of social security. By consolidating the legal status of government officials, including the proper level of judicial protection, the state solves an important problem, thus raising the confidence level of society's members in the state.

The organization of public services, as well as the activity and legal status of civil servants, is stipulated in the national law. However, there are some common trends that could be identified at an international level, especially in the European Union, to create a unique legal framework pertaining to civil servants' deontology (Recommendation No. R (2000)10 of the Committee of Ministers of the member states of the Council of Europe "On codes of conduct for civil servants" ) or to the measures to provide insurance and social protection for civil servants in the EU (Regulation No 1023/2013 of the European Parliament and of the Council of 22 October 2013 amending the Staff Regulations of Officials of the European Union and the Conditions of Employment of Other Servants of the European Union).

The above-mentioned issues require comparative theoretical research and analysis with regard to the legal protection of civil servants, in order to further improve the institution of public functions, in accordance with society's expectations and the complexity of the civil servant's missions. The comparative judicial analysis method allows highlighting the general, special, and unique character of normative regulations for the legal status of civil servants in various contemporary legal families and systems.

There are several international general provisions referring to the people's right to take part in the administration of public affairs. On these lines, article 21 of the Universal Declaration of Human Rights states: "Everyone has the right to take part in the government of his country, directly or through freely chosen representatives. Everyone has the right of equal access to public service in his country." (The Universal Declaration of Human Rights), while article 25 of the International Covenant for civil and political rights stipulates: "Every citizen shall have the right and the opportunity, without any of the distinctions mentioned in article 2 and without unreasonable restrictions:

(a) To take part in the conduct of public affairs, directly or through freely chosen representatives;

(b) To vote and to be elected at genuine periodic elections which shall be by universal and equal suffrage and shall be held by secret ballot, guaranteeing the free expression of the will of the electors;

(c) To have access, on general terms of equality, to public service in his country" (International Covenant on Civil and Political Rights, adopted on 16 December 1966).

Following the analysis of European practice, we identify the following categories of rights for civil servants:

1. The right to legal protection reflected both in guaranteeing stability in office and in the defence against assault or other forms of illicit physical or psychological violence;

2. The right to social security (salary, rest, social insurance, medical insurance);

3. The right to take part in the organisation of public service and the elaboration of statutory rules;
4. The right to benefit from continued professional training;
5. The right to a career (which implies the perennial character of holding public office, as well as promotion in rank and function);
6. The right to associate in trade unions (not for all categories of public servants);
7. The right to go on strike (in some states, there are limitations for certain categories of civil servants);
8. The right to an opinion (limited with regards to expressing opinion when exercising public office). (Vieriu , 2009, p.78-86)

European multilingualism determines that public service be named in different ways: in France, the words used are „fonction publique" (public function), in Great Britain – „civil service", in Germany – „öffentlicher Dienst" (public service). Although these terms are not perfect matches, they are used to define civil servants, becoming synonyms with administration in daily language. (Ziller, 1993, p.349)

The process of designing and formalising public policy at a worldwide level differs depending on the legal family the state belongs to. Consequently, in their first form, the civil servants' status in countries of the Anglo-Saxon legal family is defined through the fact that the norms of reference are not consolidated through a single legal document but included in a set of laws. As a case in point, in Great

Britain, the statutes regulate certain categories of relations related to exercising public functions, such as:

1. The use and storage of official state information (Official Secrets Act, 1989);
2. Functions of certain categories of civil servants (Minister of the Crowns Act, 1975 and Civil Service Management Functions, 1992);
3. General employment aspects (Employment Relations Act, 1999);
4. Employee's financing (Ministerial and Other Salaries Act, 1975).

In Canada, public service regulations started in 1918 through the Civil Service Act, modified in 1938 and 1961. In 1967, the law was replaced by the Public Service Employment Act and the Public Service Staff Relations Act. These documents were later modified through the Public Service Reform Act in 1992. The act on public service employment, issued in 1967, was replaced by the Public Service Employment Act in 2003.

Unlike other common-law states, the United States of America aimed to issue a unifying legal document regulating public service. As a result, many separate provisions related to public service have been unified in Title 5 of the United States Code.

Another approach, mainly used in states pertaining to the Roman-German law system, is creating a single comprehensive special law on public service. The regulations of public functions in such countries are based both on constitutional norms and on complex special laws (to exemplify, the French Law on the rights and duties of civil servants 13 July 1983, Italy's Framework Law on Public Employment from 29 March 1983, the German Framework Law regarding the standardisation of public service from 1 July 1957, modified on 27 February 1985, etc.). The advantage of this approach to regulating the civil servants' status consists in the law's structure, consistency, and transparency. However, this order determines a high degree of law inflexibility and a rather late response to a change in circumstances.

We shall continue by referring particularly to the comparison between penal law regulations on the protection of civil servants during the exercise of public duties.

One of the specific traits of American penal law consists of the fact that there is no unified penal law system. This is why USA's penal law refers to many sources and provisions, which include: 1) federal law – the USA's Code, the Penal Model Code from 1962, and a series of statutory laws, among which one of the most significant is the Organized Crime Control Act; 2) the legislation of the federation's subjects, mainly represented by the States' penal codes. (Spatari, Nedelcu, 2017, p.12-17)

American legal language defines the intentional acts resulting in putting another person in harmful or offensive contact by the terms of assault and/or battery. In order to exemplify, we shall analyse the content of section 22.01 of Title 5 of the Texas Penal code, according to which a person commits an assaultive offence if they intentionally, knowingly, or recklessly cause bodily injury to another person. A person can also be accused of offence if they intentionally or knowingly threaten others with imminent bodily injury, even if there is no actual physical contact. In most cases, such crimes are considered Class A offences and incur prison sentences of maximum one year and a fine of maximum 4.000 USD. ( https://statutes.capitol. texas.gov )

When such acts are committed against civil servants, they are to be deemed a level three crimes, which incur prison sentences of 2 to 10 years and fines amounting to maximum 10,000 dollars, as well as other long-time consequences. The law stipulates that such crimes are committed when there is an aggression against another person and the aggressor is aware that the victim is a public servant in the course of legally exercising an official duty or takes revenge on that civil servant or acts following the exercise of official power or the fulfilment of the official duty of a civil servant. Civil servants consist of police officers, judges, jurors, lawyers, arbiters, political candidates, elected officials and government employees. An important aspect is that a key component of the prosecution's case for assault on a civil servant involves providing that the subject had knowledge of the fact that the victim is a civil servant.

The most important penal law sources in Great Britain are statutes. This is due to the fact that all attempts to codify penal legislation have failed. The last attempt to elaborate a British Penal Code was made in 1989. A final version of this law project had been developed, consisting of two parts: *General Principles of Liability* and *Crimes*, but they are not in place so far. This is why in Great Britain, penal law liability for offences against authority is established through separate laws, some of them tracing back to the XIV[th] century. As a case in point, the Treason Act from 1351 introduced in Great Britain's criminal regulations the concepts of *high treason* and *petty treason*. High treason referred to crimes against the state: the intentional killing of the king, queen or heir, the rape of the king's wife, of his eldest unmarried daughter or of the wife of his eldest son or of his heir; waging war against the king in his own kingdom; supporting the king's enemies in his kingdom or granting support or assistance in the kingdom or elsewhere; killing the chancellor, the chief of the treasury or the royal judge while in the exercise of their function; forging fake royal seals; forging coin.

During the XV century, this list of crimes was completed by adding a new offence, called criminal conspiracy. Subsequently, Great Britain adopted several laws stipulating liability for crimes against the state: the Official Secrets Act 1911, 1920, 1939, 1989, the Forgery and Counterfeiting Act 1981 and others. (Borzencova, Komissarova, p.466)

In Great Britain, judicial precedents are also sources of law. Presently, the best-known such precedents are the Weekly Reports (All-England Court) and the Reports on penal appeals. In our opinion, regulating offences against civil servants through different laws and the lack of a unique penal law in the form of a penal code is an omission in Great Britain's penal law system. The lack of a unique penal law determines the impossibility to systematise the criminal component and also generates difficulties in understanding its essence.

Italy's penal code contains, in art. 276, stipulations regarded the attempted murder of the Republic's President. Consequently, any person endangering the life, security or personal freedom of the Republic's President is sentenced to life in prison. ( https://www.brocardi.it/codice-penale/ )

It is of importance that Part II of the Italian Penal Code, called "Special offences", starts with this article in particular. Further on, Article 277 sanctions the attempt on the Republic President's freedom, except for the cases provided in the previous article. Article 278 punishes offences to the honour and dignity of the Republic's President.

Part II, Title II, Chapter II of the Italian Penal code deals with crimes committed by private persons against public administration. Thus, art. 336 incriminates violence against or threats to a civil servant, with the intent to oblige such servant to act against his/her duties or to omit the fulfilment of an act resulting from his/her service duties. Art. 337 sets out the punishment for resisting a civil servant or a person responsible for a public service while exercising service duties. Art. 337 also incriminated the modification of transportation that could endanger the safety of policemen. Such a legal provision has not been identified in the penal regulations of other states, thus suggesting that the incrimination of such an act resulted from social realities, namely from the occurrence of such instances, which led to the necessity of penal incrimination.

Article 338 of the Italian Penal Code incriminates acts of violence or threats against a political, administrative or judiciary organ. Consequently, whoever uses violence or threatens political, administrative or judiciary officials, the members, or representatives of any public authority to determine it, fully or partially, even temporarily to suspend its activity is sentenced to prison from one to seven years. At art. 339, the Italian legislator stipulates the aggravating form of the three crimes presented above, referring to whether a weapon was used to commit the crimes, whether the crime was committed by several persons, whether dangerous sharp objects had been used or whether any form of intimidation occurred. We should note that the Italian legislator has not stipulated the occurrence of serious consequences as an aggravating circumstance.

Article 341 bis of the Italian Penal Code refers to the assault against civil servants. Whoever offends, in a public place or in a place opened to the public and in the presence of several persons, the honour or prestige of a public servant during the execution of an official act and because or throughout the exercise of his/her duties, can be sentenced to prison of up to three years. The subsequent articles 342 and 342 regulate the acts of outrage against a public, administrative or judiciary organ, respectively, against a magistrate during the hearings. The Italian Republic is one of the European states that still incriminates verbal assaults which harm the honour and prestige of a public servant during the exercise of an official act and because or throughout the execution of his/her duties. ( https://www.brocardi.it/codice-penale/ )

A thorough examination of the legal provisions of the Spanish Penal Code leads to the finding that an object of penal protection is life, freedom of the Crown (the King, the Queen, their Descendants), given that the government from Spain is a constitutional monarchy. Title XXI of the code called "Crimes against the Constitution", in chapter II, stipulates the crimes against the Crown. Hence, art. 485 sets for that anyone who murders the King or any of his ascendants or descendants, the Queen consort or the Queen's consort, the Regent or any other member of the Regency or the heir to the Crown shall receive a prison sentence from twenty to twenty-five years. The one-degree lower penalty shall be decided for the attempted murder of such a crime. Art. 487 stipulates that anyone depriving the King or any of his ascendants or descendants, the Queen consort or the Queen's consort, the Regent or any other member of the Regency or the Heir of the Crown from freedom shall receive a prison sentence from fifteen to twenty year, except when there are harsher sentences in other provisions of the code. The Spanish Penal Code incriminates, in art. 489, even the coercion through violence or serious intimidation of the above-mentioned persons to act against their will.

The honour and dignity of the King are also subject to penal protection according to the provision of the Spanish Penal Code, thus art. 490 incriminating the King's or the King's family slander or defamation during or because and with the occasion of the fulfilment of their service duties. Considering that the Kingdom of Spain is a monarchical government form, it is duly justified to provide the King's penal protection, and we note that the protection of the King's authority is so accentuated that the crimes committed against him are deemed crimes against constitutionality.

Further on, we shall tackle the penal protection of the public authority representatives. The Spanish penal code stipulates under art. 550, the assault, the threat or the active resistance against public authority, agents or servants or the use of force against such while they are fulfilling their duties or on the occasion of exercising their duties. Art. 551 sanctions the same act committed against the members of the cabinet, the governmental councils of the autonomous communities, the Congress of Deputies, the Senate or the Legislative Assemblies of the Autonomous Communities, the members of the General Council of the Judiciary or the Magistrate of the Constitutional Court. Art. 552 provides more serious sentences in case the act is committed by use of weapons or other dangerous means or if the offender takes advantage of his/her condition of public authority, agent, or servant. ( https://www.boe.es/buscar/act.php)

In order to complete our comparative analysis, we shall proceed with an analysis of the German Penal Code. In Section 90 of the code, defamation of the Federation's President is incriminated. Hence, any person insulting the President publicly, in a meeting or through the distribution of written material, faces a sentence from three months to five years in prison. (https://www.gesetze-im-internet.de)

Penal prosecution can start, in such cases, only following the authorisation of the Federation President. Chapter

VI, called Resistance against state authority, stipulates, under Section 113, Resistance to Enforcement Officers, that anyone who, by force or by threatening with force, opposes resistance or assaults a public official or a soldier of the armed forces entrusted with the fulfilment of the law, ordinances, court decisions of orders which act for the execution of official duties is facing a prison sentence of maximum two years or a fine. The article also sets forth the aggravating circumstances of the offence: the offender or an accomplice carry a weapon in order to use it while committing the offence or when the offender violently places the victim in danger of death or severe injury.

An innovative element of German regulations is that when the act (action) of the authority's representative is illegal or illicit, the offence committed against such representative shall not be qualified, according to this article. The same rule applies when the offender wrongly believes that the official's action is legal. German penal code incriminates, under section 114, opposing resistance to persons equal to enforcement officers invested with the attributions and duties of police officers that are not civil servants, such officials being deemed equivalent to civil servants. The sentence is applicable mutatis mutandis to persons called to assist in the execution of an official act.

As for French legislation, we mention that the French Penal Code of 1992, which replaced the 1810 one, has a very complex structure, consisting of a Legislative Part and a Regulatory Part. For this research, the provisions included in Book IV Felonies and misdemeanours against the nation, state and public peace, Title III Violations on the authority of the State are of particular interest, as Chapter II refers to offences against public administration committed by public servants and included in the category of abuses of authority directed against the administration, which consists of offences such as: discrimination, passive corruption, traffic of influence, misappropriating property, violating the confidentiality of correspondence or of the domicile, etc.

Chapter III, entitled Offences against the public administration committed by private persons, is split into 12 sections, out of which we shall put emphasis on sections 2 and 4. In Section 2 of the chapter, the focus is on threats and intimidation committed against persons holding public functions. Article 433-3 punishes with 3 years of imprisonment and a 45,000-euro fine the threat to commit a felony or a misdemeanour against persons or property made against a person holding elected public office, a magistrate, a juror, a lawyer, a public or ministry officer, a soldier of the national Gendarmerie, a member of the national police, customs, labour inspection, prison administration or any other person holding public authority, a professional or volunteer firemen, a building warder or an agent carrying out security and surveillance duties on behalf of a tenant, in the exercise or on account of his functions or mission, when the capacity of the victim is known or apparent to the perpetrator.

The threat to commit a felony or a misdemeanour against persons or goods is punished the same if it is committed against an agent of the public transport network operator, a teacher or any other member of the staff employed in education units or other, any other person entrusted with a public service mission, as well as a health care professional in the exercise of his function, when the capacity of the victim is known or apparent to the perpetrator. The same sanctions apply when the threat is made against the spouse, ascendants or direct descendants of the persons mentioned above or against any other person who usually resides in their house, because of the function carried out by these persons.

In case of a death threat against civil servants, the penalty increased to 5 years of imprisonment and a 75,000 euro fine, while the use of violence, threats or other intimidating acts are punishable by a 10 year prison sentence and a fine of 150,000 euro.

The French penal code also incriminates, under Section 4, contempt. Hence article 433-5 sets forth the punishment for words, gestures or threats, written documents, or images of any kind that are not made public or the sending of any objects addressed to a person executing a public service mission, acting in the exercise or on the occasion of such mission, liable to undermine the dignity or respect owed given the office he is invested with. Contempt is punishable when directed to a person holding public authority. Contempt is criminally sanctioned when addressed to a person who has been entrusted with a public service mission, and the act is committed inside or in the surroundings of a school or an education unit when pupils are arriving or leaving the premises.

Section 5 incriminates opposing resistance. Article 433-6 stipulates that obstruction constitutes a violent resistance to a person holding public authority or being entrusted with a public service mission who acts, while in the exercise of his functions, for the purpose of enforcing laws, public authority's orders, judicial decisions, or mandates. (https://www.legifrance.gouv.fr )

In France, offences against the representatives of the state are traditionally considered to be the worst type of crime in penal law. However, there is a deviation regarding this concept towards a better personality protection. A study on the sentences related to the persons holding public functions and their interpretation by the court reveals that punishment is excessive and that the law regulating them is precarious. ( https://www.lemonde.fr )

Conclusion. Following the comparative analysis presented in this research, we conclude the following:

1. In Romania, similarly to other states, protection of social relations related to state activities and the civil servants' personality is a priority. This attitude is a natural one, given that a prerequisite for any modern society is a state system, its subjects benefiting from increased protection, including by means of the criminal law.

2. The main role in the efficient execution of state functions lies with the public servants, who, through their judicial status, have rights and obligations whose fulfilment depends on being offered legal guarantees of their inviolability. Considering that the essence of state power requires the imposition of its will on the citizens, public servants, through their organisational and legal role, are inevitably faced with conflictual resistance from various individuals.

- Aggressive and intimidating behaviour against public servants during the execution of their duties is an affront both to state authority and to the public servant, resulting in the obstruction or the cessation of the performance of duties and in offences to the state authority.
- Most penal legislations worldwide have special chapters (parts, sections, paragraphs) regulating liability for offences against state authority. By comparing criminal provisions applicable in states of the Romanian-German legal families, there are similarities in terms of indictment, sentencing and defining the beneficiaries of special penal protection.
- The level of legal protection granted to public servants differs depending on the function and attributions. Consequently, public servants enforcing public order and justice (policemen, prosecutors, magistrates) benefit from a legal-penal protection with a sentencing regime more severe than persons committing illicit acts related to the fulfilment of service duties by other state representatives.

## REFERENCES

The Universal Declaration of Human Rights, adopted by the UN General Assembly. By Resolution 217 A (III) of 10.12.1948, in New York

Recommendation No. R (2000) 10 of the Committee of Ministers of the member states of the Council of Europe "On codes of conduct for civil servants", adopted at its 106th session on 11 May 2000 (https://wcd.coe.int/

ViewDoc.jsp?id=354025&Site=CM&BackColorInternet=C3C3C3&BackColorIntranet=EDB021&BackColorLogged=F5D383) accessed at 19.01.2022

Regulation No. Regulation (EC) No 1023/2013 of the European Parliament and of the Council of 22 October 2013 amending the Staff Regulations of Officials of the European Union and the Conditions of Employment of Other Servants of the European Union (https://eur-lex.europa.eu/legal-content/RO/TXT/?uri=CELEX%3A32013R1023) accessed at 27.01.2022

The International Covenant on Civil and Political Rights, adopted on December 16, 1966 in New York, ratified by the Republic of Moldova by Parliament Decision no. 217-XII of 28.07.1990 (in force since 26 April 1993).

Italian Criminal Code approved October 19, 1930, n. 1398, updated on November 27, 2019, available on the website https://www.brocardi.it/codice-penale/ accessed at 1.02.2022

Criminal Code of the French Republic of 22.07.1992 available on the site https://www.legifrance.gouv.fr/affchCode.do?cidTexte=LEGITEXT000006070719 accessed at 19.01.2022

German Criminal Code of 15 May 1871 (published in the Official Gazette no. I, p. 3322, MOIII-FNA450-2) subsequently amended by the Law of 02.08.2000 (published in OJ no. 1, p. 1253) – republishing Criminal Code of the German Reich of May 15, 1871 (published in the Official Gazette of the Reich p. 127). See website https://www.gesetze-im-internet.de/englisch_stgb/englisch_stgb.html accessed at 18.02.2022

Spanish Criminal Code – Law no. 10/23.11.1995, updated on 30.03.2015, published in the Spanish Official Gazette no. 281/24.11.1995. available on the site https://www.boe.es/buscar/act.php?id=BOE-A-1995-25444 accessed at 18.02.2022

Texas Penal Code approved in 1856 revised in 1973 https://
statutes.capitol.texas.gov/Docs/PE/htm/PE.22.
htm#22.01 accessed at 18.02.2022 https://web.archive.org/
web/20070703131234/http://www.psc-cfp.gc.ca/research/
timeline/psc_timeline_e.htm accessed at 7.02.2022

Public Service Employment Act of Canada: https://laws-lois.
justice.gc.ca/eng/acts/p-33.01/ accessed at 13.12.2021

United States Code, Title 5 : https://www.govinfo.gov/content/
pkg/USCODE-2009-title5/html/USCODE-2009-title5-
partI.htm accessed at 9.02.2022

Law No. 83-634 of July 13, 1983 on the rights and obligations
of civil servants. Law known as Le Pors law: https://www.
legifrance.gouv.fr/loda/id/JORFTEXT000000504704/
accessed at 18.01.2022

Framework law on the civil service of 29.03.1983: https://www.
cliclavoro.gov.it/Normative/Legge_29_marzo_1983_n.93.
pdf accessed at 20.01.2022

Framework law for the standardization of civil service law:
https://www.bgbl.de/xaver/bgbl/start.xav?start=
%2F%2F*%5B%40attr_id%3D%27bgbl157s0667.
pdf%27%5D#__bgbl__%2F%2F*%5B%40attr_
id%3D%27bgbl157s0667.pdf%27%5D__1642515746317
accessed at 20.01.2022

Official Secrets Act 1989 https://www.legislation.gov.uk/uk-
pga/1989/6/contents accessed at 5.01.2022

Ministers of the Crown Act 1975 https://www.legislation.gov.
uk/ukpga/1975/26/contents accessed at 5.01.2022

Civil Service (Management Functions) Act 1992 https://www.
legislation.gov.uk/ukpga/1992/61 accessed at 5.01.2022

Employment Relations Act 1999 https://www.legislation.gov.
uk/ukpga/1999/26/contents accessed at 10.01.2022

Ministerial and other Salaries Act 1975 https://www.legisla-
tion.gov.uk/ukpga/1975/27 accessed at 10.01.2022

Spatari M., Nedelcu V., Some peculiarities of coercive measures, regulated by the criminal law of the United States of America and Great Britain in Law and Life Number 3 (303), 2017, pp 12-17

Vieriu E. The rights of civil servants in the Public Administration Magazine № 2/2009 pp. 78-86.

Ziller, J., Comparative Administrations. The politico-administrative systems of the Europe of the Twelve, Paris: Editions Montchtrestien, 1993.. p.349

Borzenkov G.I., Komissarov V.S., Handbook of Criminal Law, Moscow, 2002, 512 p.

# Progress and Suitability of Life Quality Indicators in Imagistic Analysis

**Alina-Mihaela CEOROMILA,** Cross-Border Faculty,
"Dunărea de Jos" University of Galati alina.cantaragiu@ugal.ro

Generally, an indicator is defined as a perfectible multi-dimensional concept (a mathematical model) applied to a theory. The life quality indicators represent noticeable variables which indicate unnoticeable variables, describing the health and well-being degrees of worldwide citizens. Life quality is often defined by means of some confusing descriptors, known as umbrella-terms, in order to express a wide-ranging human life aspects (Buligescu & Țoc, 2021).

Worldwide, there are many concerns regarding the research of life quality by means of public politics, namely improvement of living and working conditions, which implies the increase of life quality and society quality, respectively. At a European level, these data are collected and statistically analysed by means of the European Union Agency (ec.europa.eu, 2021), and in Romania, they were reported by Precupețu (Precupețu et al., 2018).

According to the Organisation for Economic Co-operation and Development (OECD), on the one hand, a set of social indicators was developed, but on the other hand, many life indicators were made out (Buligescu & Țoc, 2021) (Figure 1). The OECD Better Life Index compares the current well-being across countries based on 11 topics (Figure 2) and grouped in two fundamental areas, such as material living conditions and quality of life, respectively (ince.ro, 2019). As a suggestion, four new topics have been proposed for future well-being resources, as we can see in Figure 2. Also, according to the Eurostat database (ec.europa.eu, 2022), the specialists have proposed the measurement of life quality indicators by nine dimensions (Table 1).

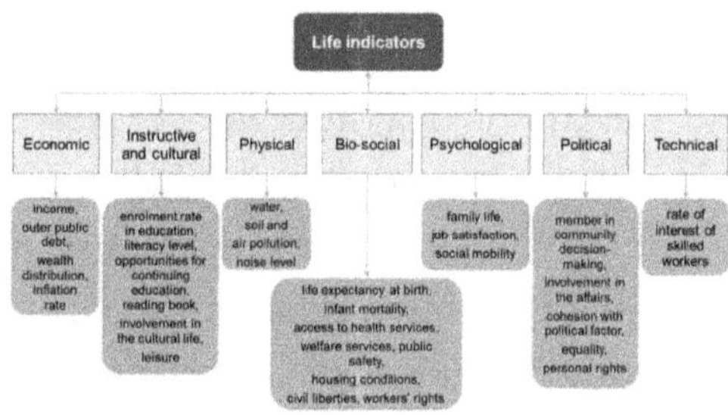

**Fig. 1** Classification of multi-dimensional indicators for
life quality measurement

To report the social progress, in addition to the economical indexes (objective indicators), the experts took

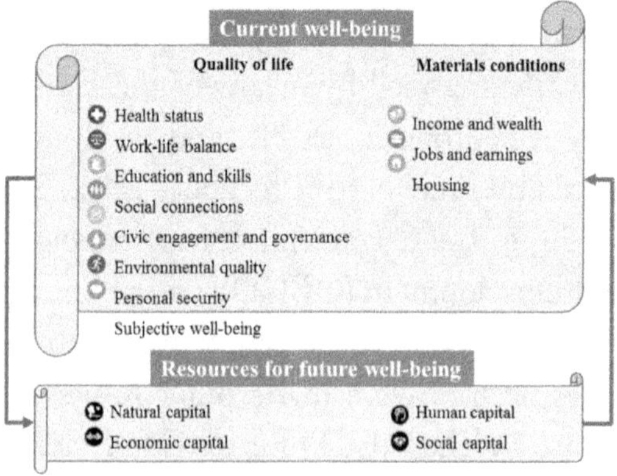

**Fig. 2** OECD Better Life Index

into consideration the social parameters developed in th period 1960-1970 (Buligescu & Țoc, 2021). In other words, both economic growth and social costs contribute to social progress (Land et al., 2012).

Bache pointed out the idea that for a better society, people are more careful to set quality goals than to use a larger amount of goods. It has led to the development of new public policies regarding the subjective indicators (increased satisfaction with life, happiness, health, financial resources, job, and welfare) (Bache, 2013). Between 1990 and 2016, the field of life quality research expanded, obtaining scientific results and laying the foundations of various European decision-making forums with statistical programs (e.g., European Community Household Panel, European Union Study on Income and Living Conditions, European Foundation for the Improvement of Housing and Working Conditions – Eurofound). These researches have studied some aspects related to the environment and social development at European and national levels.

Nationally, Chiriac et al. analysed the data obtained from the Diagnosis of life quality between 1990 and 1993 (Chiriac et al., 1994). One of the conclusions is related to the „good" perception of the population regarding the quality of the environment, in the context of increasing pollution and environmental degradation (Toc, 2021). Quality of human life depends on the life conditions made by each citizen. The people's perception, thinking, getting and effects of their actions have a major impact on the living conditions.

**Table 1** Measurement of life quality indicators by 9-dimensions according to Eurostat

| Dimension | The standard of living | Efficient (main) activities | Health | Education, Leisure time and social interactions | Economic and physical security, Fundamental rights | The natural and living environment |
|---|---|---|---|---|---|---|
| Sub-Dimension | Incomes, Intake, Material conditions | Number of jobs, Quality of jobs | Results, Healthcare services | Competences and skills, Lifelong learning, Leisure time, Social interactions | Economic and physical security, Institutions and public services, Participatory citizenship | Physical and chemical pollution, Recreation spaces |
| Indicators | Incomes, Constrained low consumption, Non-market consumption, Materials deprivation, Housing conditions | Employment and unemployment rate, Low employment rate (quantitative), Low unemployment rate (qualitative), Income and benefits from employment, Work/ life balance, Health and safety at work | Life expectancy, Morbidity versus health status, Factors: Healthy and less healthy behaviours, Healthcare services | Level of education, Self-reported skills, Assessed skills, Lifelong learning, Quantity and quality of leisure time, Access to leisure time, Social cohesion, Supporting relationships | Wealth, Debt, Job insecurity, Misdemeanour, Urban security, Perception of physical security, Reposal in institutions/ public services, Quality of public services, Quality of society, Participatory citizenship, Equal chances | Physical and chemical pollution, Recreation spaces, Green space systems, The ratio between built space and green space |

Over the last years, in the life sciences, namely agricultural, food, microbiology, water, soil, air, medical, and healthcare, the imaging techniques represent valuable methods which allow obtaining a large amount of information about specific properties and quality criteria, generally. Among the imagistic methods, it can be mentioned the optical microscopy, scanning electron microscopy, transmission electron microscopy, scanning tunnel microscopy, fluorescence microscopy, confocal microscopy, and atomic force microscopy.

In order to improve the resolution of images, find out the advanced functional materials for new applications, and store and process the large amount of data from the microscopic images, it is suggested to combine the conventional imaging methods with the integrating advanced technologies (Abdullah et al., 2004. Therefore, modern digital microscopy requires algorithms for the automatic analysis of information for different purposes (Chen et al., 2011; Dubey & Jalal, 2015). The dedicated imaging system integrates the classical optical microscope, data acquisition software, digital images and digital videos processing software, analysis systems, monitor, camera, and colour scanners.

Thus, the new imaging systems will allow increasing the spatial (3D) resolution and the depth of field. For example, researchers from the biomedical area are now capable to develop tests *in vivo* conditions and in dynamic and non-invasive regimes (Chen et al. 2011). Also, the micro-computed tomography represents an advanced imaging technique which, by means of specialized algorithms, is able to characterise the 3D-microstructure of materials in engineering (Sharma et al., 2018) and histology fields (Armi & Fekri-Ershad, 2019)through the identification of chemical elements or cells and textures in accordance with the reference values. In practical terms, ImageJ software in different versions is an example of the image processing algorithms in order to analyse the microstructures (Rasband).

Air pollution is one of the physical indicators for life quality measurement. Ambient air pollution represents a concern due to global industrial activities and is one of the environmental risk factors for health, causing people death (World Health Organization (WHO), 2021). Therefore, it is essential to control and improve the air quality through accurate microscopy techniques. The particulate matter (PM) can be quantified by some algorithms used in microscopy analysis. PM represents a composition of solids and liquids particles suspended in the air, being an important indicator of air pollution. From the chemical point of view, the major elements of PM are carbon, oxygen, hydrogen, sulphur, nitrogen, sodium, chlorine, and mineral dust. Two types of PM are known: PM with a diameter $\leq$ 10 $\mu$m (PM10), which can affect the lungs and the vascular system, and PM whose diameter is $\leq$ 2.5 $\mu$m (PM2.5) are more health-unsafe particles, causing even cancer even at very low concentrations (Loomis et al., 2013). PM derived from different types of sources, such as smokestacks, industrial areas, automobiles, constructions, house heating can reduce atmospheric visibility. Another method to monitor the outdoor air pollution degree is atmospheric modelling, further contributing to the development of warning guidelines for people and industrial areas.

Wu *et al.* have analysed the PM morphology using a conventional microscope (Wu et al., 2017).

The advantages of this imagistic technique are the accuracy (93%) of the particle counting and sizing, the rapid recognition of particle shape, and the elemental identification (the type of aerosols). However, the lens-based microscopy techniques in the field present some limitations, such as the higher costs of the air-quality monitoring system, heavy-handed design, not portable system and an expert to prepare the sample and operate the equipment. Therefore, this group of authors has proposed a new method to analyse the aerosol samples: a portable lens-free based microscopy (Greenbaum et al. 2012), using an image sensor chip below the sample and a mobile application interface. The chip lens-free based microscope works on the basis of specific machine learning algorithm for remote data processing and to analyse the particles.

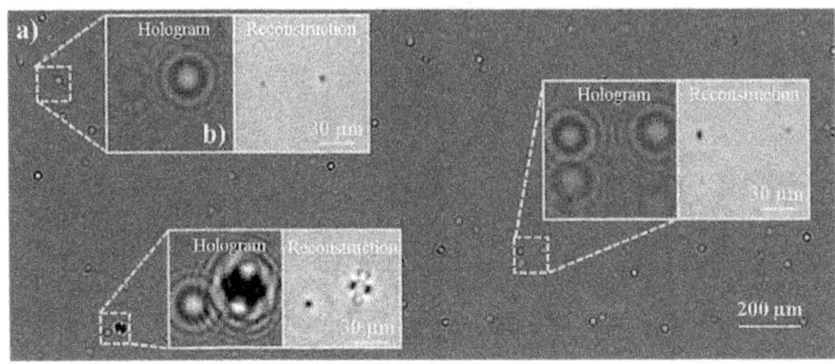


**Fig. 3** Microscopic analysis of an aerosol sample: (a) overall view during the sampling (200 µm); (b) detailed from different regions as a hologram and its reconstruction (30 µm) (Wu et al., 2017)

Figure 3 shows the holographic microscope images and their reconstructions for aerosol particle statistical measurements. These results regarding the air quality were validated with those obtained by means of an Environmental Protection Agency (EPA) device, and a good agreement was noted.

Food quality is defined by the synthesis method and the physico-chemical characteristics of products, the quality control parameters, and the human subjective perspective (the sensory evaluation) (Figure 4) (Mihafu et al., 2020).

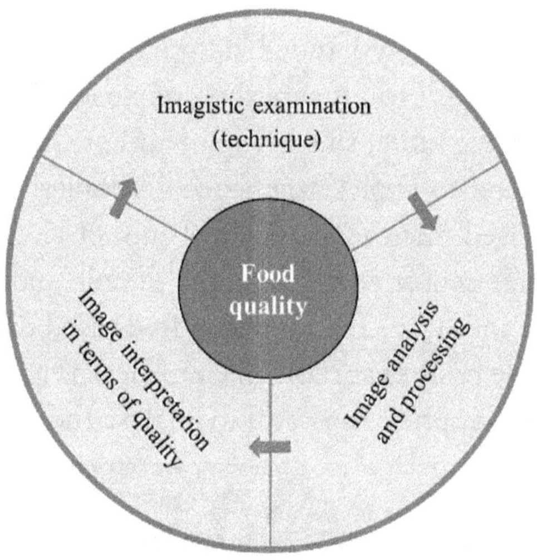


**Fig. 4** Food quality prediction stages by means of imaging methods

The quality in food industry is highly developed due to the diversity, adaptability, and performance of newly synthesized products as a function of consumer requirements. For instance, Petrescu et al. showed the results of some case studies applied to consumers from two different European regions (Petrescu et al., 2022). They studied the impact of different food quality indicators on the socio-environmental, health, choice, origin, and trustworthiness factors. Therefore, the answer of participants would predict the consumers' behaviour related to environmental sustainability.

Some researchers noted that the choice of the proper technology and working parameters could generate an innovative product, that must be rigorous and precisely measured, accomplishing the quality criteria (Møller, 2012). The stabilisation of milk chocolate (fat dispersion) was obtained by adding proper emulsifiers such as carrageenan and guar gum (Danisco, 2011). In the case of yoghurt, its quality is defined by the texture, viscosity, whey separation, and the probiotic effect is due to the lactose fermentation. Figure 5 shows the casein microstructure modification and the electron micrographs of casein aggregated during fermentation.

Another criterion for food quality is represented by the fruits and vegetable classification using automatic detection systems. Their level of recognition is directly reflected in the final price through the bars code; thus it can automatically sort and differentiate a variety of unpacked fruits and vegetables from the distribution centre. The fruits and vegetables' quality and quantity evaluation can be measured through the intelligent systems of some image indicators based on size, texture, colour, appearance cues, firmness, histograms, and defects.

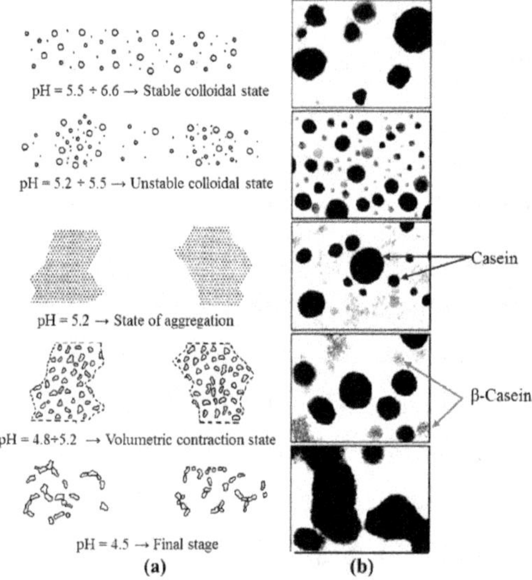


Fig. 5 Model of: (a) the microstructure of acid milk gels, modified during the lactose fermentation; (b) transmission electron micrographs – the aggregation of casein (McMahon, 2009)

For example, Bolle *et al.* developed the Veggie Vision recognition system with 95% accuracy, which analyse the colour, texture, and density of foods (Bolle et al., 1996). Another method with a higher level of precision (99%) has used a set of binary grading algorithms (K-Means clustering method) (Figure 7) for determining the species and variety of products (Dubey & Jalal, 2015).

The algorithms for image processing represent a key element for the agricultural industry due to the difficult processing of the captured images of foods (variant colours, non-ideal shapes, size, and texture). Wan Nurazwin Syazwani et al. have studied a novel approach for fruits image processing when applying a machine learning method (namely, Artificial Neural Networks (ANN) optimised with variance analysis tool (ANOVA)) in order to increase the detection efficiency of pineapple crown (Wan et al., 2022). The most common fruit grading is represented by morphological characteristics such as size and shape. Therefore, Mustafa and co-authors have proposed an automatic method for sorting and classification of 5 types of fruits based on their morphology and colour (Mustafa et al., 2011). They have applied the Digital Image Processing and ANN techniques and controlled by MATLAB/SIMULINK programs obtaining an efficiency ranging from 79 to 90%.

Another classification criterion of food quality can be considered the antioxidant activity using template validation tools. Plants contain many antioxidant components such as ascorbic acid, alpha-tocopherol, lycopene, or anthocyanins. The obtained results by the group of Patrasa allowed identifying different species of fruits and vegetables through the correlation of all parameters (i.e., total phenols, anthocyanin content, ascorbic acid, total carotenoids) (Patrasa et al., 2011).

Other researchers have found that the physiological ability to grow maize is to use the Seed Analysis System as a tool for image analysis and for controlling the seeds and seedlings quality (Mariucci et al., 2018). Pinto et al. have adapted their proper methodology in order to obtain a higher efficiency in the developing process of maize seeds. They have studied the growth of maize from seeding on a white paper towel at 25°C for a period of three days, using SAS instrument (Pinto et al., 2015).

On the one hand, the preliminary method allows monitoring the health or stress conditions of fruits and vegetables, and on the other, it is an uneconomical method and a long-time process. As an alternative, the experts have proposed a biomolecular method, namely the polymerase chain reaction, as a new solution for early detection, identification and controlling the degradation state and the availability of foodstuffs (Bonilauri et al., 2016).

A new opportunity that opens up the quantification of properties of single cell (even a microbial cell) and the communities functions was studied by Jeckel and Drescher (Jeckel & Drescher, 2021). They have presented some semantic and instance segmentation methods based on fluorescence microscopy and convolutional neuronal network (Figure 7). Also, the results of Christiansen et al. showed a possible association between the fluorescence microscopy and neuronal network to anticipate some quantitative parameters, having minimum phototoxicity reaction of cells.

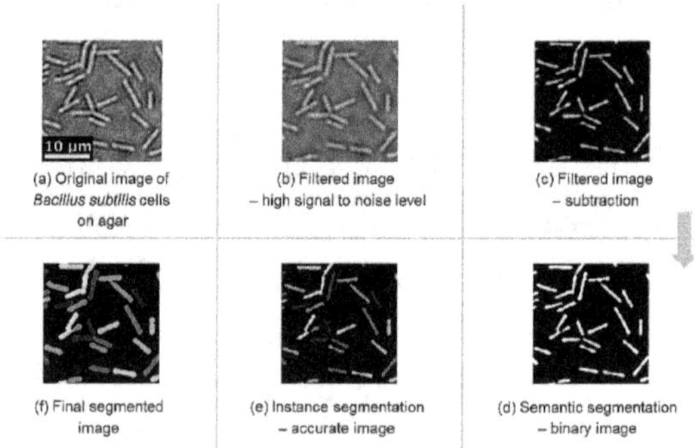


Fig. 7 Segmentation and filters applied in traditional image to improve the process efficiency (O'Neil et al., 2016)

In conclusion, the research shows that both optical and electronic microscopy combined with intelligent image processing techniques have an important role in the clinical imaging evaluation of cells, molecules, and genes (Rasband). Indeed, future perspectives may investigate how image processing methods allow predicting the human perception. In recent years, the scientific papers have indicated the progress of the imagistic technologies and modelling algorithms as non-invasive, rapid, high resolution and low-cost approaches for food quality evaluation. Therefore, the new proposed strategies have allowed measuring the morphological, microbiological, chemical, defects, ripeness, and contamination characteristics. The development of new adaptative microscope imaging techniques combined with artificial intelligence machines will contribute to real time measurements both at the laboratory and industrial scale.

# REFERENCES


B. Buligescu, S. Țoc, Abordări conceptuale și metodologii de măsurare a calității vieții. O analiză descriptivă. *Calitatea vieții*, 32(3), 1-19, 2021. https://doi.org/10.46841/RCV.2021.03.03

https://ec.europa.eu/info/strategy/priorities-2019-2024/economy-works-people/jobs-growth-and-investment/european-pillar-social-rights/european-pillar-social-rights-20-principles_en (Accessed on 13.02.2022)

I. Precupețu, F. Mihalache, C. Petrescu, C.E. Pop, L. Tufă, M. Vasile, Calitatea vieții în România în context european. Institutul de Cercetare a Calității Vieții, București, 2018.

http://www.ince.ro/Evenimente/8_aprilie_2019_I_Preucupetu_ICCV_Indicatori_si_indici_ai_calitatii_vietii.pdf (Accessed on 12.02.2022)

https://ec.europa.eu/eurostat/web/quality-of-life/data (Accessed on 20.02.2022)

K. Land, A. Michalos, J. Sirgy (eds.), Handbook of social indicators and quality of life research. Dordrecht Heidelberg, London-New York, Springer Science & Business Media B.V., ISBN 978-94-007-2420-4, p. 593, 2012. DOI:10.1007/978-94-007-2421-1

I. Bache, Measuring quality of life for public policy: an idea whose time has come? Agenda-setting dynamics in the European Union. *Journal of European Public Policy*, 20(1), 21-38, 2013. https://doi.org/10.1080/13501763.2012.699658

D. Chiriac, L.L. Pascal, M. Tatu. Calitatea mediului înconjurător în România și percepția populației, *Calitatea vieții*, 5(3-4), 257-264, 1994.

S. Toc, Cercetarea calității vieții în România. O analiză a studiilor publicate în Revista „Calitatea Vieții" în intervalul 1990-2020, *Calitatea Vieții*, 32(3), 1-25, 2021. doi:10.46841/RCV.2021.03.05

M.Z. Abdullah, L.C. Guan, K.C. Lim, A.A. Karim, The applications of computer vision system and tomographic radar imaging for assessing physical properties of food. *Journal of Food Engineering*, 61(1), 125-135, 2004. https://doi.org/10.1016/S0260-8774(03)00194-8

X. Chen, B. Zheng, H. Liu, Optical and digital microscopic imaging techniques and applications in pathology. *Analytical Cellular Pathology (Amsterdam)*, 34(1-2), 5-18, 2011. doi: 10.3233/ACP-2011-0006

S.R. Dubey, A.S. Jalal, Application of Image Processing in Fruit and Vegetable Analysis: A Review. *Journal of Intelligent Systems*, 24(4), 405-424, 2015. https://doi.org/10.1515/jisys-2014-0079

B.N. Sharma, D. Naragani, B.N. Nguyen, C.L. Tucker, M.D. Sangid, Uncertainty quantification of fiber orientation distribution measurements for long-fiber-reinforced thermoplastic composites. *Journal of Composite Materials*, 52(13), 2018. https://doi.org/10.1177/0021998317733533

L. Armi, S. Fekri-Ershad, Texture Image Analysis and Texture Classification Methods – A Review. International Online *Journal of Image Processing and Pattern Recognition*, 2(1), 1-29, 2019. https://doi.org/10.48550/arXiv.1904.06554

W.S. Rasband, *ImageJ*. National Institutes of Health, Bethesda, Maryland, USA, 1997-2015. http://imagej.nih.gov/ij

World Health Organization (WHO), Ambient (outdoor) air pollution, 2021, https://www.who.int/en/news-room/fact-sheets/detail/ambient-(outdoor)-air-quality-and-health (Accessed on 17.02.2022).

D. Loomis, Y. Grosse, B. Lauby-Secretan, F. El Ghissassi, V. Bouvard, L. Benbrahim-Tallaa, N. Guha, R. Baan, H. Mattock, K. Straif, The carcinogenicity of outdoor air pollution. *Lancet Oncology*, 14(13), 1262-1263, 2013. doi:10.1016/s1470-2045(13)70487-x

Y.-C. Wu, A. Shiledar, Y.-C. Li, J. Wong, S. Feng, X. Chen, C. Chen, K. Jin, S. Janamian, Z. Yang, Z.S. Ballard, Z. Göröcs, A. Feizi, A. Ozcan, Air quality monitoring using mobile microscopy and machine learning. *Light: Science & Applications*, 6, e17046, 2017. doi:10.1038/lsa.2017.46

A. Greenbaum, W. Luo, T.W. Su, Z. Göröcs, L. Xue, S.O. Isikman, A.F. Coskun, O. Mudanyali, A. Ozcan, Imaging without lenses: achievements and remaining challenges of wide-field on-chip microscopy. *Nature Methods*, 9, 889-895, 2012. https://doi.org/10.1038/nmeth.2114

F.D. Mihafu, J.Y. Issa, M.W. Kamiyango, Implication of Sensory Evaluation and Quality Assessment in Food Product Development: A Review. *Current Research in Nutri-*

*tion and Food Science*, 8(3), 690–702, 2020. http://dx.doi.org/10.12944/CRNFSJ.8.3.03

D.C. Petrescu, I. Vermeir, P. Burny, R.M. Petrescu-Mag, Consumer evaluation of food quality and the role of environmental cues. A comprehensive cross-country study. *European Research on Management and Business Economics*, 28(2), 100178, 2022. https://doi.org/10.1016/j.iedeen.2021.100178

F. Møller, *Imaging Food Quality*. PhD Thesis, Technical University of Denmark, Kongens Lyngby, Denmark, IMM-PHD-2012-288, p. 137, 2012.

A.S. Danisco, *Chocolate milk*. In Technical Memorandum. A.S. Danisco, 2011.

D.J. McMahon, H. Du, W.R. McManus, K.M. Larsen, Microstructural changes in casein supramolecules during acidification of skim milk. *Journal of Fairy Science*, 92(12), 5854-5867, 2009. https://doi.org/10.3168/jds.2009-2324

R.M. Bolle, J.H. Connell, N. Haas, R. Mohan, G. Taubin, VeggieVision: a produce recognition system. In *Proceedings of the 3rd IEEE Workshop on Applications of Computer Vision*, WACV'96, 244-251, Sarasota, USA, 1996. doi: 10.1109/ACV.1996.572062

R. Wan Nurazwin Syazwani, H. Muhammad Asraf, M.A. Megat Syahirul Amin, K.A. Nur Dalila, Automated image identification, detection and fruit counting of top-view pineapple crown using machine learning. *Alexandria Engineering Journal*, 61(2), 1265-1276, 2022. https://doi.org/10.1016/j.aej.2021.06.053

N.B.A. Mustafa, K. Arumugam, S.K. Ahmed, Z.A.M. Sharrif, Classification of fruits using Probabilistic Neural Networks – Improvement using color features. In *TENCON 2011-2011 IEEE Region 10 Conference*, 264-269, 2011. doi: 10.1109/TENCON.2011.6129105

A. Patrasa, N.P. Bruntona, G. Downeya, A. Rawsona, K. Warrinerb, C. Gernigonc, Application of principal component and hierarchical cluster analysis to classify fruits and vegetables commonly consumed in Ireland based on in vitro antioxidant activity. *Journal of Food Composition and Analysis*, 24(2), 250–256, 2011.

G.E.G. Mariucci, A.K. Suzukawa, A.L. Braccini, C.A. Scapim, L.H. da Silva Lima, P. Angelotti, R.M. Ponce, D.C.V. Marteli, Physiological potential of maize seeds submitted to different treatments and storage periods. *Journal of Seed Science*, 40(1), 60-66, 2018. https://doi.org/10.1590/2317-1545v40n1184456

C.A.G. Pinto, M.L.M de Carvalho, D.B. de Andrade, E.R. Leite, I. Chalfoun, Image analysis in the evaluation of the physiological potential of maize seeds. *Revista Ciência Agronômica*, 46(2), 319-328, 2015. doi: 10.5935/1806-6690.20150011

P. Bonilauri, L. Bardasi, R. Leonelli, M. Ramini, A. Luppi, F. Giacometti, G. Merialdi, Detection of Food Hazards in Foods: Comparison of Real Time Polymerase Chain Reaction and Cultural Methods. *Italian Journal of Food Safety*, 5(1), 5641-5645, 2016. https://doi.org/10.4081/ijfs.2016.5641

H. Jeckel, K. Drescher, Advances and opportunities in image analysis of bacterial cells and communities. FEMS Microbiology Reviews, 45(4), 1-14, 2021. http://orcid.org/0000-0002-7340-2444

E.M. Christiansen, S.J. Yang, D.M. Ando, A. Javaherian, G. Skibinski, S. Lipnick, E. Mount, A. O'Neil, K. Shah, A.K. Lee, P. Goyal, W. Fedus, R. Poplin, A. Esteva, M. Berndl, L.L. Rubin, P. Nelson, S. Finkbeiner, In Silico Labeling: Predicting Fluorescent Labels in Unlabeled Images. *Cell*, 173(3), 792-803.e19, 2018. doi: 10.1016/j.cell.2018.03.040

# The Criminal Policy in The Republic Of Moldova in the Attempt to Increase The Quality of Life

**Andrei NASTAS** Faculty Cross-border, "Dunărea de Jos" University of Galați andrei.nastas@ugal.ro

## SUMMARY

The population's quality of life is an indicator that reflects the changes and social processes that take place, and, at the same time, it reflects the degree of development.

From its independence to the present day, the Republic of Moldova has faced various economic and social problems (political instability, income gap, government instability, etc.), which have directly influenced the quality of life of Moldovan citizens (Musin & Sura, 2020: 131-133) and have also increased the number of crimes against life and health.

Concerns about the protection of a person's life date back to antiquity, when it was protected by various means, including moral and religious norms.

At the current stage of societal development, the right to life, as the supreme social value, is protected by the rules of law, among which there is the most effective mechanism – that provided by criminal law.

**Keywords:** *Quality of life, right to life, victim, crime,violence*

Quality of life is a socio-economic concept through which the living conditions, the standard of living, standard and lifestyle of the population of the Republic of Moldova can be assessed in all its complexity. In this sense, quality of life integrates the characteristics of needs, possibilities, living conditions, way of life, lifestyle, and value orientations. These, in turn, represent an important element of the whole of the daily standard of a person (Danii, 2004).

According to the results of the 2021 Social Progress Index on Quality of Life and Social Welfare, conducted by the non-profit organisation Social Progress Imperative, with the support of Deloitte, Moldova climbed eight positions and ranked 60th out of 168 countries in the world ranking on quality of life and social welfare with 73.67 points out of 100, a slightly higher score than in 2020 (72.58 points).

Undoubtedly, a person's life is the most precious social value, the protection of which, through the criminal policy of the Republic of Moldova, has always been one of the most pressing problems of the Republic of Moldova society.

Concerns about the protection of a person's life date back to antiquity, when it was protected by various means, including moral and religious norms.

Each social group has been concerned with ensuring, by all means, the protection of the lives of individuals, whether it resorted to traditional (customary) rules, religious rules, moral rules, or legal ones. Among the legal means of defence, the criminal law has had an increasingly important role, the criminal law being the most effective form of protection of social relations and protection of the fundamental values of society. In all the laws, starting with the Hammurabi Code (18th century BC), the Chinese codes (13th century), the Egyptian sacred books, the laws of Manu (11th century), the laws of Lycurgus, Solon, Dracon (7th century) -IX), the Roman laws, the laws of the Germanic peoples, and even the laws of the modern age, the care for the protection of human life is at the centre of the legislator's attention (Dumneanu, 2009: 82-83).

At the current stage of development of society, the right to life, as the supreme social value, is protected by the rules of law, among which there is the most effective mechanism – that provided by criminal law.

The protection of the individual, and especially of life, is a constant concern common to all legal systems. Life as a social value designates the main attribute of the person. The life of the person represents his social existence, that is, the realisation of the possibility to participate in social relations, exercise his rights and interests and execute his obligations (2009: 82-83).

The European Court of Human Rights considers the right to life to be an indispensable right of the human being, one of the fundamental values of our society, thus conferring protection in the field of human rights at the international level. The Universal Declaration of Human Rights establishes in art. 3 the right of every person to life and inviolability. Article 2 of the European Convention provides that the right to life is protected by law, and the International Covenant on Civil and Political Rights states that the right to life is inherent for every human being (Tratate internaționale, 1998, *Declarația Universală a Drepturilor Omului*).

Criminal regulations of all times and in all social orders have recognised the particularly high degree of social danger posed by crimes against the life and health of the person, the killing of a person being one of the most serious acts. The violation of the right to live creates a state of social insecurity, a dangerous imbalance for the very existence of society.

At present, in the Republic of Moldova, as evidenced by official statistics, out of the total number of criminal cases examined by the courts, a constant share has crimes against the life and health of the person.

Thus, in the Republic of Moldova, the number of cases of crimes against the life and health of the person registered in recent years is: 1,615 – in 2009; 1,806 – in 2010; 1,707 – in 2011; 1,647 – in 2012; 1,519 – in 2013 (Brânză, 2015: 146); 1,389 – in 2015; 1,505 – in 2016; 1,250 – in 2017; 1,218 – in 2018; 1,127 – in 2019 (Statistica Moldovei, *Nivelul infracționalității în Republica Moldova în anul* 2019); 908 – in the year 2020 (Statistica Moldovei, *Nivelul infracționalității în Republica Moldova în anul* 2017); 639 – in the first 9 months of 2021 (Poliția.md, Raport privind activitatea Poliției. 9 luni anul 2021).

The most representative crime in the series of crimes against the life and health of the person is that of intentional murder, with the legislative headquarters within art.145 of the Criminal Code of the Republic of Moldova.

In the Republic of Moldova, the number of intentional homicides recorded in recent years are: 243 – in 2006; 209 – in 2007; 223 – in 2008; 234 – in 2009; 249 – in 2010; 204 – in 2011; 212 – in 2012; 200 – in 2013; 172 – in

2014; 177 – in 2015; 189 – in 2016 (Statistica Moldovei, Justiție) ; 154 – in 2017; 170 – in 2018; 175 – in 2019; 169 – in the year 2020 (Statistica Moldovei, *Nivelul infracționalității în Republica Moldova în anul* 2017, 2018, 2019).

In 2018, the number of people who died according to the registered crimes was 608. Thus, almost every third person died according to road accidents (37.0%), followed by death due to homicide (23.5%) (Statistica Moldovei, *Nivelul infracționalității în Republica Moldova în anul* 2018).

According to the operative information of the Ministry of Internal Affairs regarding the state of crime (except for the classified criminal cases) on the territory of the Republic of Moldova, for 11 months of 2019, 19 murders were registered (Politia.md, *Raport privind activitatea Poliției. Anul* 2019).

In 2019, the number of people who died, according to the registered crimes, was 620. Thus, almost every third person died in a car accident (35.3%), followed by death due to homicide (20.6%) (Statistica Moldovei, *Nivelul infracționalității în Republica Moldova în anul* 2019).

Thus, during 2019, Police registered 416 moderate intentional injuries and 195 serious intentional injuries to bodily integrity, as a result of which 54 people died (Politia.md, *Raport privind activitatea Poliției. Anul* 2019).

For the first three months of 2020, the territorial subdivisions of the General Inspectorate of Police registered 6,185 crimes, including 267 crimes related to the category of those that threaten the life and health of the person. Out of the total number of murders (148), in which 39 people died, 14 crimes were committed in public places, 4 murders were committed with the use of a firearm, 1 crime was committed by people with a criminal record, 1 committed by minors, and 3 murders were committed by people fit for work, but not employed. At the same time, the Police registered 87 moderate intentional injuries and 45 serious intentional injuries of bodily integrity, as a result of which 15 people died (Statistica Moldovei, *Nivelul infracționalității în Republica Moldova în anul* 2020).

In terms of the day they have been committed, it can be noticed that crimes against life and health predominate on Sundays, Saturdays and Tuesdays, ranging between 34 and 47 crimes. For a period of 6 months in 2020, the Police subdivisions registered 11,130 crimes, of which 29% belonged to the municipality of Chisinau. Of the total number of offences, 4% are for crimes against life and health (418). Within the activities of criminal investigation and investigation of crimes, the Police established that 76.32% of the criminal cases have been against the life and health of persons.

The act of intentional murder is defined in art.145 of the Criminal Code of the Republic of Moldova in a standard version and an aggravated version. Intentional homicide, in the standard variant (simple homicide), is incriminated in paragraph 1 art. 145 of the Criminal Code of the Republic of Moldova. Most legislators define murder as the illegal deprivation of another person's life (see Dobrinescu, 1987, Bulai, 1975, Stoica, 1976, Nistoreanu & Boroi, 2002, Macari, 2003). Intentional murder, or simply murder, is the unlawful and intentional deprivation of another person's life. This definition of the notion of murder is applicable to all crimes committed through murder, provided in art.145-148 of the Criminal Code of the Republic of Moldova.

Literally, the expression "intentional murder", used in the name of art. 145 of the Criminal Code of the Republic of Moldova, is a pleonastic one. Par excellence, the act of murder can only be committed with intent. In accordance with the criminal law in force, the use of the phrase "reckless murder" is inadmissible. This phrase was appropriate in the context of the previous criminal law when art. 93 of the 1961 Criminal Code of the Republic of Moldova was called "reckless homicide". In the criminal law currently in force, the correspondent of this article is art. 149 of the Criminal Code of the Republic of Moldova, literally entitled "Reckless deprivation of life" (the equivalent of manslaughter). Any murder represents the loss of life, but not every loss of life is murder. In connection with this, it should be mentioned that as far art.145 of the Criminal Code of the Republic of Moldova is concerned, the legislator uses the term murder without the unnecessary circumstance of guilt manifested by the perpetrator (Brânză et. al., 2005).

By contrast, art.148 of the Criminal Code of the Republic of Moldova establishes the criminal liability for the crime of deprivation of life at the will of the person (euthanasia), i.e., for the deprivation of life of the person in connection with an incurable disease or the unbearable nature of physical suffering, at the request of the victim or, in the case of minors, their relatives.

In terms of law, euthanasia or mercy killing is defined as "the act or practice of painlessly putting to death persons suffering from painful and incurable disease or incapacitating physical disorder or allowing them to die withholding treatment or withdrawing artificial life-support measures" (www.britannica.com).

Today, euthanasia is understood as the so-called murder of compassion, that is, to submit one's desire to die so as to end the suffering. Euthanasia is always a form of homicide because it assumes that one person kills another, either by a positive act or by omitting attention and care. Regardless of society's attitude towards this subject, this is a crime.

The delimitation of the intentional homicide by euthanasia is based on the subjective side of the crime.

The signs that circumscribe the subjective side of the crime are as follows: guilt, reason, and purpose. The relevance of these signs is not a similar one, although all these, as a whole, characterise the internal psychic process of the criminal act (Botnaru *et. al*, 2005: 199).

In addition to these obligatory signs of the subjective side of the crime, the psychic attitude of the perpetrator is influenced by the emotional and affective components. The nature of the emotions allows perceiving more deeply the motives of the crime and the real intention of the person who commits the criminal act (Назаренко, 2002: 166). In some cases, the emotional component of the deed is taken into account by the legislator as mitigating circumstances; it is the case of the crimes mentioned by art. 146, 148, and 149 of the Criminal Code of the Republic of Moldova.

It is necessary to mention, from the beginning, that both the theory and the judicial practice of the Republic of Moldova state that intentional murder (or simply murder) is the illegal and intentional deprivation of another person's life. This definition of the notion of murder is applicable to all crimes committed through murder, provided in art.145-148 Criminal Code of the Republic of Moldova (Macari, 1999). It follows that euthanasia (the crime incriminated in art. 148 CP RM) is part of the category of murder committed in the presence of mitigating circumstances, although the form of guilt with which it is committed is undoubtedly the intention.

Paradoxically, however, the same Decision of the Plenum of the Supreme Court of Justice of the Republic of Moldova regarding the judicial practice in criminal cases regarding crimes committed by murder (art.145-148 Criminal Code of the Republic of Moldova) no. 11 of 24.12.2012, (Buletinul Curții Supreme, 2013) under point 9 offers the following explanations – in order to distinguish intentional murder from recklessness (art.149 Criminal Code of the Republic of Moldova), attention should be drawn to the fact that murder represents a form of manifestation of the perpetrator who has decided to suppress the life of a person and uses the means to achieve this goal, while in the case of recklessness we do not have an act of violence, but misconduct of the perpetrator in a dangerous situation, likely to produce, in certain circumstances, consequences in the form of brain death of the victim. Namely, these explanations are the basis for the delimitation of the title of the crimes in art. 145 Criminal code of the Republic of Moldova (intentional murder), on the one hand, and 149 CP RM (reckless life), on the other hand.

Regarding the classification of the crimes in terms of the day when they were committed, with reference to 2019, we can mention that the crimes against life and health predominate on Sundays and Saturdays (207 and 179 crimes) Thursday and Monday (136 and 137 crimes), the time of the crime: 18.00–24.00 and 12.00–18.00 (388 and 318 offences) (Politia.md, *Notă informativă privind activitatea în domeniul prevenirii criminalității și evoluția fenomenului pe parcursul a XII ale anului* 2019).

The population's quality of life is an indicator that reflects the changes and social processes that take place and, at the same time, reflects the degree of development of the country, from a political, economic, cultural, and social point of view.

From its independence and to this day, the Republic of Moldova has faced various economic and social problems (political instability, income inequality, government instability etc.), which have influenced the citizens' quality of life and have also increased the number of crimes against life and health (Musin & Sura, 2020: 131-133).

Among the cases that influence the quality of life of the Moldovan citizens and the crimes against the life and health of the person, without claiming to be an exhaustive list, there are included:

- *the precarious material and financial condition of the population*, induced by the economic crisis, which causes scandals and violent actions in families and people, in general. Its influence is exerted not only by the sudden and excessive decline of living standards but also by the emotional instability it causes.

Thus, the National Bureau of Statistics informs that the average consumer prices, in September 2021 compared to September 2020, increased by 6.68%, including food, by 8.31%, non-food goods by 8.62%, and services provided to the population by 1.52% (Statistica Moldovei, *Evoluția prețurilor de consum în luna septembrie* 2021).

The National Bureau of Statistics informs that the average consumer prices in November 2021 compared to November 2020 increased by 12.44%, including food products, by 15.49%, non-food goods, by 11.28% and services provided to the population, by 9.65%. The average consumer prices in November 2021 compared to October 2021 increased by 3.50% (worth mentioning is that in November 2020 compared to October 2020, they increased by 0.16%). The increase in average consumer prices was determined by the increase in food prices by 3.17%, non-food goods by 1.38% and services provided to the population by 7.07% (Statistica Moldovei, *Evoluția prețurilor de consum în Republica Moldova în luna noiembrie* 2021).

The average monthly consumption expenditures of the population, in 2020, amounted to an average of 2,791.2 lei per person. In real terms (with the adjustment to the consumer price index) the population spent on average 3.5% less compared to 2019.

Most of the expenditure is for food consumption – 43.5%. For housing and communal services, an average person allocated 16.1% of the total consumption expenditures, and for clothing and footwear - 8.8%. The other expenses were directed for housing (5.6%), transport services (5.5%), health (4.7%), telecommunications (4.7%) (Statistica Moldovei, *Veniturile și cheltuielile populației în 2020*).

• the <u>*drug/alcohol*</u> use. Thus, people in a state of intoxication commit 63% of intentional homicides and 65% of serious bodily injuries. An eloquent example in this respect is the following case: X has been found guilty of committing the crime provided by art. 145 para. 2 lit. e1) of the Criminal Code of the Republic of Moldova. In fact, X being in a cohabitation relationship for about seven years with VL and living together in their home, on 04.10.2017, at approximately 17:50, intentionally, understanding the prejudicial nature of his actions and being in a state of intoxication, as a result of a conflict, he stabbed VL twice with a kitchen knife, after which VL died on the spot (Judecătoria Bălți, Dosar nr. 1/2-250/17).

Thus, the data show that in 2016, every second case of an intentional murder (83 out 189) and every third case of bodily injury (80 out 250) were committed because of alcohol intoxication (Independent.md, *Numărul infracțiunilor comise în Moldova în creștere. Fiecare al doilea omor și violență în familie comise în stare de ebrietate*).

In an effort to reduce the crimes related to the use of alcohol and drugs, as well as the HIV risk associated with it, the police state that 3,607 activities have been carried out to this end. 35,289 citizens have been the beneficiaries, and 16,074 flyers with useful information and recommendations have been handed out during the activities. The mass media has been involved with a number of 181 materials (newspapers, TV, radio, web networks) (Politia. md, *Notă informative privind activitatea în domeniul prevenirii criminalității și evoluția fenomenului pe parcursul a XII luni ale anului* 2019).

- *conflict situations*. In some cases, they appear suddenly, and in others, they are the result of the development of long hostile relations. An important role here is played by the victim's behaviour, which serves as a victimogenic factor. The analysis of the data on the personality of the victims shows that in 65% of the murder cases, they were intoxicated, and in 39% of the cases, they were drinking alcohol together with the criminals, 4.5% of the victims were the initiators of beatings. In most cases, the offences are not premeditated. Usually, the intention to commit serious crimes against human life and health appears in the process of a situation with developing conflict.

- *deficiencies in the field of detecting crimes against the life and health of the person*: victims who are among the wanted or lost without a trace are not detected in a timely manner; in the criminal investigation process, up to the moment of the crime, the victim's behaviour is superficially studied; in the event of a serious bodily injury, the location of the incident is often not examined; also, there are organised faulty searches for the criminals according to their physical description. As a confirmation of the above-mentioned deficiencies, the statistical data of the internal affairs bodies of the Republic of Moldova state that on 01.07.2020, 21 corpses were declared unidentified (Politia.md, *Rapoarte și evaluări*).

- *the criminalisation process* which can be identified: in a percentage of people who are unemployed or are out-of-school minors; in people who come from bad neighbourhoods; in the increasing number of offenders with conviction with a conditional suspension of execution of punishment and offenders released on parole; and in the increasing number of people declared in a state of irresponsibility when committing social-dangerous actions against the life and health of persons. Thus, on 01.01.2020, 6,101 criminals were still classified as "in search for" of them, 159 criminals being wanted for crimes against the life and health of the person - and 141 for serious intentional damage to bodily integrity (Politia.md, *Raport privind activitatea Poliției. Anul 2019*).

- *the insufficient control over convicts in places of detention*. In terms of crimes committed in the penitentiary, the attacks on the life and health of persons constitute the majority. Most of them are committed because of hostile relations, mutual offences, and quarrels between groups of convicts formed as a result of the shared place of residence.

- *gaps in the prophylaxis of crimes* against life and health: There is a lack of proper control over the purchase, storage, and use of firearms and their removal from persons who systematically commit violations of the law. The high level of spread of the traffic of arms and the direct endowment of citizens; the installation, by separatist structures, in some enterprises of a special or adapted equipment for the manufacture of weapons and ammunition that are later sold on the "black market".

* *the negative influence of the media*, shows, movies, and books that propagate violence, hatred, and revenge as socially pleasing values
* *the low level of education* of some members of the society, who tend to solve all problems by using force, violence, or commit provocative actions
* *unemployment* seriously attacks the inner balance of the individual, making it impossible for him to achieve his aspirations by legal means. The "father authority" is profoundly diminished, his role as a supporter of the family being altered. Disruption of family roles can lead to confusion, inner imbalance, anxiety, alcoholism, and a desire for revenge against society (Nistoreanu, 1994).

The number of unemployed people estimated according to the definition of the International Labor Office in the first quarter of 2021 was 35,800, slightly higher than the first quarter of 2020 (34,200). Unemployment affected in a greater proportion the men, as they represent 66.1% of the total unemployed people, and the people in rural areas – 57.4% (Statistica Moldovei, *Forța de muncă în Republica Moldova: ocuparea și șomajul în trimestrul I 2021*)

* *the presence of the Covid-19 Pandemic*

The COVID-19 pandemic has created a number of impediments to day-to-day activities that have impacted the mood of the population.

The effects of the Covid-19 pandemic on the labour market have appeared at the end of the first quarter of 2020, with the establishment of a state of emergency in the Republic of Moldova (starting on March 17, 2020). The Covid-19 pandemic has continued to affect the labour market in the following quarters. The biggest effects were recorded in the second quarter of 2020 when every fourth person employed stated that the pandemic had affected their relationship with the labour market.

In 2020, the number of the employed population decreased by 4.4% compared to 2019. Decreases in employment took place in all quarters of 2020 compared to 2019. At the same time, the most significant decreases were recorded in the quarters in which the effects of the pandemics were most felt on the labour market, respectively, in the second quarter (-8.8% or 80,000 people less) and in the third quarter (-5.1% or 46,000 less). In the first and the fourth quarters, the reduction in the number of people employed was relatively smaller - by 2.7% in the first quarter and, respectively, by 0.5% in the fourth quarter compared to the respective period of 2019 (Statistica Moldovei, *Impactul Covid-19 asupra indicatorilor forței de muncă în anul 2020*)

The Covid-19 pandemic has significantly affected the quality of life of the citizens of the Republic of Moldova.

At the same time, the pandemic, by its magnitude, influenced the plans and intentions of the households.

Thus, about 9.8% of the households with members abroad mentioned that at least one of their members returned home because they lost their job. Another 13.3% of the households with members abroad stated that their members had difficulty returning to the country. Also, 61.0% of the households whose members planned trips abroad mentioned that they had to postpone them.

It can be observed that the respondents of the households that have lost their jobs in the country have 39.3% lower incomes compared to the members of the households that continue to work. The households with at least one member experiencing depression have also had about 11.0% lower incomes compared to those who did not report depression.

At the same time, there are some differences between the consumption expenditures of the households whose members faced difficulties during the pandemic. The households with at least one member returning from abroad due to loss of job have spent about 17.0% less on a person than the households whose members have continued to work abroad. The expenses of the households whose members faced depression, stress and anxiety are lower by 6.6% compared to those who did not face these problems.

The households that have reported difficulties as a result of the COVID-19 pandemic in terms of reduced or lost income have a 17.7% lower income per person and a 3.1% lower consumer spending compared to those who did not mention this. The households that have reported a reduction or loss of the remittances received from abroad have also had a 7.8% lower income per capita and a 16.4% lower consumption expenditure compared to those that did not record these reductions/losses (Statistica Moldovei, *Principalele rezultate ale cercetării „Influența pandemiei Covid-19 asupra gospodăriei" în trimestrul III 2020*).

The average life expectancy in the Republic of Moldova in 2020 was 69.8 years, decreasing by 1.1 years compared to 2019 (after a continuous growth from 2014 onwards) and 10.4 years less than the average level of life expectancy at birth in the 27 EU countries in 2019 (81.3 years). The life expectancy at birth in 2020, according to gender, was 65.9 years for men and 73.9 years for women.

In 2020, the average life expectancy for men decreased by 0.9 years compared to the previous year and for women by 1.2 years.

Over the last year, the decline in the indicator is largely due to the significant increase in the overall mortality rate for both men and women, as well as the infant mortality rate.

Thus, in 2020 compared to 2019, there was a significant increase in the number of deaths – 4,245 more cases (or 11.7%). One of the reasons for the increase in mortality was the Covid-19 pandemic. According to information provided by the Ministry of Health, Labour, and Social Protection, 2,853 people died in 2020 for this reason, of which 1,490 were men and 1,363 women.

The mortality rate in 2020 was 15.4 deaths per 1,000 inhabitants, men – 17.1%, women – 14.0%. The infant mortality rate increased to 8.7 deaths before reaching the age of one-year old per 1,000 live births compared to 8.4

deaths per 1,000 live births in 2019. The growth of the infantile mortality rate was up to 9.0% (from 8.5% in 2019) in boys and in girls up to 8.4% (from 8.2% in 2019) (Statistica Moldovei, *Durata medie a vieții în anul 2020*).

As it can be seen, the causes of the crimes against the life and health of the person have a certain specificity, as they do not act independently, but in the context of socio-economic, political, culturological and other factors.

The crimes against the life and health of the person, depending on the level of social danger and the seriousness of the consequences caused, go beyond many other criminal phenomena. They cause considerable damage to society. Thus, in 2017, according to the registered crimes, the number of people who died was 585. Thus, 19.5% of the people died because of homicides and 9.7% of intentional injuries. *For example, X. was found guilty of committing the crime provided by art. 151 para. 4 CP to RM. In fact, X., on 01.07.2017, at approximately 19.00–20.00, being in a state of alcohol intoxication and at his home in the village XX, pursuing the purpose of serious injury to bodily integrity and health, which is life-threatening, during a conflict with cet. S. I., applied multiple punches and kicks to the latter in different regions of the body, which led to the victim dying on the spot. According to the forensic report no. 133D of July 7, 2017, the cause of death of cet. S. I. is a reflective cardiac arrest due to neck trauma. The corpse cet. S.I. had: haemorrhages in the bilateral soft tissues of the neck, haemorrhages in the soft tissues of the hyoid bone, of the thyroid cartilage, in the wall and in the adjacent carotid tissues on the right of the third cervical vertebra, in the soft tissues of the occipital region, a nasal bone frac-*

*ture, contusion wounds, bruises, excoriations on the face, neck, chest and on the left and right arm, which as a whole qualify as serious, dangerous and life-threatening bodily injuries. The cause of death is directly related to the mild neck trauma* (Judecătoria Bălți, Dosar nr. 1-2/2018).

In a study conducted by the author Oxana Rotari, two main types of victims have been underlined, following the intentional murder, committed without aggravating circumstances, which it belongs to:

• Type 1 – men aged 19-29 or 30-39 years, rarely 40-49 years, with general or incomplete secondary education. Most of them do not work, and those who do work are employed in unskilled or medium-skilled physical work. Most are friends, close acquaintances, or casual acquaintances of the victim.

• Type 2 – women aged 30-39 or 40-49 years with incomplete secondary education or general education. Most of them do not work or are employed in unskilled physical work, less often with intellectual work that does not require special secondary and higher education (singing, controller, etc.) (Rotari, 2011: 426-428).

In a criminological study regarding manslaughter, conducted by Gheorghe Gladchi, a typology of victims has been developed based on the characteristics of the injured, the possible causes of the crime and other important circumstances of these type of cases. Thus, seven types of victims have been identified:

1) People whose victimisation is determined by their important role in the current business. They hold senior positions in strong private structures and have higher

education and rich work experience, including leadership in state structures. The probable causes of the threat to their lives could be as follows: the fierce competition between commercial structures and the division of spheres of influence, the non-compliance with agreements and contractual obligations issued by trade groups, the concealment of income by partners, etc.

2) People with a criminal record, including criminal authorities included in the business, as well as people who have not been convicted but have business connections with the underworld. These respective individuals have an inferior social status, secondary or incomplete secondary education, practice a non-prospective business, and own large sums of money. Their victimisation is generated by the fight for influence in the criminal environment, for the right to control the treasury, their tendency to submit to a control of the activity of the entrepreneurs, to carry out different types of deceptions, and others.

3) People engaged in small and medium business, who have private companies or are employed in private structures, usually with higher education. Their victimisation is caused by conflicts related to the inability of making payments on time. The victims, as a rule, have been in the role of creditors.

4) The persons whose victimisation is determined by their profession, the execution of certain services and public functions.

5) People whose victimhood is caused by long-standing hostile relationships in the family sphere.

6) People with increased victimisation, immoral behaviour, and chaotic intimate relationships.
7) Citizens whose victimisation is determined by external circumstances and not by certain personality qualities. These are the people who have been killed by mistake, being confused with those who really were the target (Gladchi, 2001: 129).

In 2017, the murder cases led to imprisonment for 1442 people, followed by those who committed serious intentional injury – 589 people.

In 2018, the number of people who died, according to the registered crimes, was 608. Thus, 23.5% of people died due to homicides and 8.6% due to intentional injuries (Statistica Moldovei, *Nivelul infracționalității în Republica Moldona în anul 2018*).

According to the MIA statistics, during the ninth month of 2019, 21,304 crimes were committed, of which: Intentional and Medium Injuries – 595, and Murders – 127 (Poliția.md, *Notă informativă privind activitatea în domeniul prevenirii criminalității și evoluția fenomenului pe parcursul a IX luni ale anului 2019*).

A pressing problem in the studied field is the increase in the number of crimes against human life and health among young people. When we talk about young people, we are talking about people between the ages of 16 and 35. They often commit murder, cause serious bodily harm, etc. Thus, in 2017, 11 minors were convicted of murder (Statistica Moldovei, *Nivelul infracționalității în Republica Moldona în anul 2017*).

Crimes against a person's life and health are increasingly embodying a female face. Relatively, but permanently, the number of crimes against the life and health of the person committed by women is increasing. For example, *T. N. was found guilty of committing the crime provided by art. 151 para. (1) Criminal Code in the RM. In fact, on November 28, 2017, around 20:00, T. N. was at the domicile of citizen C. L., located in the village. C., Fălești district, and following a conflict that arose spontaneously with R. Iu., injured him: closed thoraco-abdominal trauma with spleen injury with the development of hemoperitoneum, multiple bilateral rib fractures, closed craniocerebral trauma with concussion, contusion wound and bruising, which according to the forensic report no. 212D of 06.12.2017 qualifies as serious and life-threatening bodily injuries* (Judecătoria Bălți, Dosar nr. 1-2/2018).

It is worth considering that crimes against the life and health of a person of particular cruelty and committed by women are no longer a rare phenomenon in the Republic of Moldova. For example, *on December 11, 2020, a 40-year-old woman from Comrat was killed cold-bloodedly by his own daughter. The 21-year-old cut her mother open and took out her heart.*

*The horrific murder took place in an apartment. The woman was working in Germany for many years to support her child. According to the local press, the two quarrelled because the young woman was a drug user, and the woman wanted to cure her of this vice (*ȘtiriMD, *Fata care și-a ucis mama filmată cum râde pe banca acuzaților)*

The prevention of crimes against human life and health is characterised by the following features: it has a continuous character; it has a permanent character; targets both potential perpetrators and potential victims; acts on exogenous factors that influence the commission of a crime; promotes respect for the criminal law, the rights and freedom of citizens (Paraschiv *et. al.*, 2014: 104-105).

In some countries, the law states the compulsory participation of victims in the trial, taking into account their opinion during the case investigation, the examination of issues concerning the early release of convicts, the release on bail (during criminal proceedings), or the suspension of the case. Therefore, we support the opinion of some authors (Bîrgău, 2010: 175-177) that it would be welcome to establish the mandatory elaboration of the protocol regarding the announcement of the victim about the cessation of the case or the refusal to initiate it.

At this stage, even the most vulnerable layers of the population that have become victims are imperative. The prosecuting officers continue to follow the old procedure, announcing the victim's place of residence to the accused or their relatives and proposing them to get along with each other. In such situations, it cannot even be a question of defending the victims of crimes against the life and health of the person.

Of particular importance, it is the restitution of material and non-pecuniary damage as a result of the offence.

In judicial practice, there are still no limits to the recovery of non-pecuniary damage from criminal offences. The courts make different decisions in the case of almost identical circumstances of the crime. There are cases of moral damages for bodily injuries of greater proportions than in the case of death. Therefore, there is a need to develop clear criteria for determining the extent of non-pecuniary damage for various types of offences.

It requires further improvement and other legal rules regarding the restitution of moral and material damages to victims.

As specified in §12 of the UN Declaration, in cases where the full compensation cannot be received from the offender or other sources, the state must pay compensation to victims who have suffered serious harm as a result of crime or whose condition has physically or mentally worsened; families, especially people whose guardians have died or lost their ability to work as a result of the crime.

Based on the experience of other countries, in order to optimise the implementation of the decisions regarding the compensation of the victims, they should be given priority over other offenders' proceeds.

In the Republic of Moldova, there is currently no single obvious victimology statistic. Law enforcement bodies focus only on some victimological aspects, which does not allow them to determine the state of affairs in this field objectively. The MIA's statistical report on victims and their damages is imperfect, as it does not reflect specific data on the number of applicants or inform the relevant authorities on the commission of the crime, the number of victims, the types and extent of damages caused and recovered.

Finally, it must be mentioned that both the criminal legal framework and the system for preventing crimes against life and health are not without shortcomings, which involves studying them and organising the work of law enforcement agencies to ensure the high quality of life of Moldovan citizens.

## REFERENCES


Antoniu G. și alții. (1976) Dicționar juridic penal. București

Bîrgău M., (2010) Criminologie (Curs universitar). Ed. a 2-a rev. și compl. Chișinău

Botnaru S. și alții (2005) Drept penal, partea generală, V.II, Chișinău, Ed. Cartier Juridic

Brînza S, Stati V. (2015) Tratat de drept penal. Partea specială. Chișinău, Vol. I

Brânză, S. et. al. (2005) Drept Penal. Partea special, Volumul II, Ediția a II-a, Chișinău: Editura Cartier http://drept.usm.md/public/files/Dreptpenalspecialf2f52.pdf

Bujor V. (2003) Infracțiuni contra vieții și sănătății persoanei. Chișinău

Bulai C. (1975) Curs de drept penal. Partea specială București: Universitatea din București, p. 84

Convenția Europeană pentru Apărarea Drepturilor Omului și a Libertăților Fundamentale, adoptată la Roma la 4 noiembrie 1950 (ratificată prin Hotărârea Parlamentului RM nr.1298-XIII din 24.07.1997). În: Tratate internaționale (ediția oficială), (1998) Vol.1. Chișinău

Declarația Universală a Drepturilor Omului, adoptată la New York la 10 decembrie 1948 (ratificată prin Hotărârea Parlamentului RM nr.217-XII din 28.07.1990). În: Tratate internaționale (ediția oficială), (1998) Vol. I. Chișinău

Danii, Tudor, 2004, Calitatea vietii populatiei Republicii Moldova   http://www.cnaa.md/files/theses/2004/2786/tudor_danii_abstract.pdf

Dobrinescu I. (1987) Infracțiuni contra vieții persoanei București: Ed. Academiei RSR, p. 12

Dumneanu L. (2009) Infracțiunile contra vieții și sănătății persoanei în viziunea dreptului comparat. În: Revista Națională de Drept, nr.10-12, https://ibn.idsi.md/sites/default/files/imag_file/Infractiunile%20contra%20vietii%20si%20sanatatii%20persoanei%20in%20viziunea%20dreptului%20comparat.pdf

Gladchi Gh. (2001) Criminologie generală. Chișinău,

Buletinul Curții Supreme de Justiție a Republicii Moldova (2013) Hotărîre a Plenului Curții Supreme de Justiție a Republicii Moldova, cu privire la practica judiciară în cauzele penale referitoare la infracțiunile săvârșite prin omor (art.145-148 CP al RM) nr. 11 din 24.12.2012, nr.6, pag.4

http://independent.md/doc-numarul-infractiunilor-comise-moldova-crestere-fiecare-al-doilea-omor-si-violenta-familie-comise-stare-de-ebrietate/#.WqgePWrFLIU

http://politia.md/sites/default/files/nota_prevenire_ix_luni_2019_pentru_presa.pdf

http://www.statistica.md/newsview.php?l=ro&idc=168&id=5926&parent=0

http://www.statistica.md/newsview.php?l=ro&idc=168&id=6268

http://www.statistica.md/public/files/publicatii_electronice/Anuar_Statistic/2017/12_AS.pdf

https://politia.md/ro/advanced-page-type/rapoarte-si-evaluari?page=1

https://politia.md/sites/default/files/ni_violenta_in_familie_12_luni_2019_pagina_web_a_igp.pdf

https://statistica.gov.md/newsview.php?l=ro&idc=168&id=6929

https://politia.md/sites/default/files/nota_prevenire_12_luni_presa.pdf

https://politia.md/sites/default/files/nota_prevenire_3_luni_2020.pdf

https://politia.md/sites/default/files/raport_activitatea_politiei_12_luni_2019_.pdf

https://statistica.gov.md/newsview.php?l=ro&idc=168&id=6268

https://statistica.gov.md/newsview.php?l=ro&idc=168&id=6595

Macari I., (1999) Dreptul penal al RM, partea generală, Chişinău

Macari I. (2003) Drept penal al Republicii Moldova. Partea specială. Chişinău: USM, p. 68

Musin Roman, Sura Ana-Maria, (2020), Calitatea Vietii in Republica Moldova, Sesiunea nationala de comunicari stiintifice studentesti, Vol. I, p. 131-133 https://ibn.idsi.md/vizualizare_articol/102993

Nistoreanu Gh., Boroi A. (2002) Drept penal român. Partea specială. Bucureşti, p. 92

Nistoreanu Gh., Păun C., (1994) Criminologie, Bucureşti

Pactul Internaţional privind drepturile civile şi politice, nr. 1966 din16.12.1966. (1998) În: Tratate Internationale nr.1, din 30.12

Paraschiv G., Paraschiv D.-Şt., Paraschiv E. (2014) Criminologie: evoluţia cercetărilor privind cauzalitatea şi prevenirea infracţiunilor. Bucureşti

Rotari O. (2011) Criminologie. Chişinău

Sentinţa Judecătoriei Bălţi, sediul Făleşti din 01.03.2018. Dosar nr. 1-2/2018. În: jbl.instante.justice.md/apps/pdf_generator/base64/create_pdf.php

Sentința Judecătoriei Bălți, sediul Sângerei din 06.12.2017. Dosar nr. 1/2-229/2017. În: https://jbl.instante.justice.md/apps/pdf_generator/base64/create_pdf.php

Sentința Judecătoriei Bălți, sediul Sângerei din 15.12.2017. Dosar nr. 1/2-250/17. În: https://jbl.instante.justice.md/apps/pdf_generator/base64/create_pdf.php

Stoica O. A. (1976) Drept penal. Partea specială. Bucureşti, p. 75

Назаренко Г. В., (2002), Невменяемость, Санкт-Петербург, Юридический Центр Пресс,

https://statistica.gov.md/newsview.php?l=ro&idc=168&id=7141&parent=0

https://statistica.gov.md/newsview.php?l=ro&idc=168&id=7204

https://statistica.gov.md/newsview.php?l=ro&idc=168&id=6948

https://statistica.gov.md/newsview.php?l=ro&idc=168&id=7007

https://statistica.gov.md/newsview.php?l=ro&idc=168&id=7006

https://statistica.gov.md/newsview.php?l=ro&idc=168&id=6859

https://statistica.gov.md/newsview.php?l=ro&idc=168&id=7063

https://stiri.md/article/social/topul-calitatii-vietii-locul-ocupat-de-moldova-in-clasamentul-mondial

https://stiri.md/article/incidente/fata-care-si-a-ucis-mama-filmata-cum-rade-in-hohote-pe-banca-acuzatilor

https://www.politia.md/sites/default/files/raport_cu_privire_la_activitatea_politiei_9_luni_2021.pdf

# Learning Foreign Languages as a Social Practice

**LUPAȘCU Daniela Eugenia,** Cross-Border Faculty, "Dunărea de Jos" University of Galati *daniela.lupascu@ugal.ro*

## ABSTRACT

People develop social practices as a way to relate to one another and our environment. Besides cultural social practices such as traditions or religion, one of the characteristics that most distinguishes us as a society among other peoples is our spoken language. Linguistic social practices are an essential component of any society, country, or group of people. In this study, we aim to review the broad concept of SLA and its main theories in general and to focus on second language learning as a social practice in particular.

## 1. SLA THEORIES

There are several theories that attempt to explain second language acquisition. However, experts have not reached a common ground. It is complex for scientists and experts to explain second language learning since it's a process that cannot be observed directly.

Between the 1940s and 1970s, mimicry and memorization through audiolingual materials were the most common activities used in second language acquisition. This was also the basis for the Behaviourism perspective, an approach firstly developed on animal testing. The Audiolingual Method in second language acquisition involved teaching activities like repetition, inflection, replacement, and expansion. This method was validated by psychologists and linguists such as Skinner, Watson, Lado, and Bloomfield. Their hypothesis was that the learning process can become a habit. (Ellis, 1997).

On the contrary, Noam Chomsky's theory counterattacks the Behaviourism principle according to which language can be learned by developing a habit. According to his theory, children's brain is equipped with a basic set of language skills that allows them to acquire the language of their environment. This capacity is also referred to as the innate knowledge or the Language Acquisition Device (LAD), which is one of the principles of Universal Grammar (UG). Researchers and neurologists have looked into the relationship between language and the brain. For a long time, it was assumed that language processes were located in the brain's left hemisphere. Recent brain studies, on the other hand, demonstrate that, during the processing of first and second languages, different locations in both hemispheres of the brain are activated. These brain activation zones differ based on the learner's skill level and age.

The theory of first language acquisition meets the second language acquisition practices in the theory of Stephen Krashen, who considered that the innate capacity "continue to operate during SLL, and make key aspects of SLL possible, in the same way they make first-language learning possible." (Mitchell & Myles, 2004)

Krashen's theories are divided into five hypotheses that create a framework for teaching a second language: the Acquisition-Learning hypothesis, the Monitor hypothesis, the Natural Order hypothesis, the Input hypothesis, and the Affective Filter hypothesis. For Krashen, the difference between acquisition and learning is that the first one is seen as an unconscious learning process, while the latter is considered a conscious learning process. The monitor hypothesis points out the difference between the acquired system responsible for producing a spontaneous speech and the learned system that is compared to a monitor and is responsible for checking on what is being spoken. *The acquired system* refers to the acquisition process that is compared to the process that children experience when they acquire their first language. It is well known that the first language is acquired by children primarily through the relationship with their environment (Bates & MacWhinney, 1987). Moreover, from the perspective of conversation analysis (CA), language learning and language use are two elements that are interwired. According to Krashen's third theory, structures are acquired in a specific order, called *natural order*. The natural order applies both to first language acquisition and second language acquisition, but there may be differences between them. In what concerns the affective filter in learning a language, this refers to external and non-linguistic factors that may influence the acquisition process, such as motivation and self-confidence. According to this hypothesis, negative attitudes towards the language learning process will make the acquisition process harder. The input hypothesis points out the relevance of the exposure to a comprehensible input from the environment in language acquisition and it is also related to the innate capacity of learners in language acquisition.

In what concerns the cognitive perspective, the capacity of the mind, respectively the language acquisition process is compared to the storage, integration, and retrieval capacities of a computer. The information-processing paradigm, for example, is based on the assumption that second-language acquisition occurs through the accumulation of knowledge that could become automatic when speaking and understanding the second language. Firstly, learners should pay attention to a specific component of the language, such as pronunciation or grammatical form. Then, by practising these elements, learners should be able to process them effortless so as to use them automatically, thus becoming fluent. Used-based learning is another theory from the cognitive perspective. According to Nick Ellis (2006), this theory emphasizes the bond between linguistic elements and the context in which they appear and the frequency of their use by the learners. The competition model, a theory influenced by the cognitive perspective, emphasizes the importance of observing the similarity between two or more languages. In second learning acquisition, learners should observe many cues appropriate to the target language (MacWhinney, 1997). For example, word order varies in many languages. Romanian has a flexible word order, a sentence may start with an object, while English has a very strong word order, following the pattern *Subject, Verb, Object.*

According to the sociocultural perspective, when learners speak and write in the second language, they internalize what they say to others. The internalizing process occurs when the learner interacts with an interlocutor within his or her zone of proximal development. The sociocultural perspective has been applied in the second language learning, based on the idea that learners must pay attention to the language features they will use in order to get the message across successfully, whether it is written or oral language.

## 2. L2 LEARNING AS A SOCIAL PRACTICE

Language is seen as a social practice from the sociocultural perspective point of view. A social practice viewpoint implies treating bilingualism or multilingualism in terms of repertoires of linguistic or communicative resources rather than focusing on language as an entity, a system of arbitrary symbols (Hatch, 1992). There has been a shift in language studies from a modernist and positivist perspective to a critical and poststructuralist one. In the study of Gabriele Pallotti and Johannes Wagner (2011), learning a foreign language in a new country is compared to learning to drive on the left side while you know how to drive only on the right side. The biggest challenge is that, in both cases, there is a change of behaviour that needs to be taken into account in the learning process. There is and always has been an important bond between language and interaction, more specifically between language learning and conversational interaction, as Hatch (1992) pointed out since second language acquisition (SLA) just emerged as a research object. Several research studies on SLA in general and the importance of language learning and language use in SLA have appeared since then.

The concept of language as a social practice encompasses the spoken and the written language and also the indirect language, the gestures, the voice inflections, and the body language that people use in order to support the message that is transmitted. Rising intonation, for example, is used by language learners to be guided by native speakers (Ibidem). The idea of shifting away from a conception of *language as a discrete object* towards *language use as something fluid, complex, and dynamic* is more essential than the choice of which term to use (Zavala, 2018).

The interactionist theory focuses on language as a social practice and as a result of the sociocultural context in which it is used. The interactionist school of thought is associated with linguists and researchers such as Halliday, Bruner, Vygotsky and Gee. According to Halliday's theory, language develops from the learner's interactions with other people. He identified eight functions of language use as follows: the instrumental use – to communicate needs, the regulatory use – to communicate directions, the interactional use – to build relationships, the personal use – to express personal information, the heuristic use – to seek information, the imaginative use – to express creativity, the informative use – to provide information and the divertive use – to express jokes (Freeman, 1994). In what concerns Bruner's theory, he identified three learning modes that also apply to language acquisition – enactive, iconic, and symbolic. The enactive mode refers to learning through action, while in the iconic mode, the learner is using images and icons to acquire knowledge. The symbolic mode of learning refers to learning through abstract symbols. He also enriches the LAD using perspective with LASS – Language Acquisition Support System – which implies a familiar environment and a social routine during the language learning process. In addition to this idea, according to Vygotsky's theory, language and thought are very related, cognitive development being enriched through exchanges with more knowledgeable members of the social group. Thus, relationships may foster learning. The concept of Zone of Proximal Development distinguishes between what learners can acquire with guidance and what they can acquire unguided. It also points out the importance of the assistance of more knowledgeable people accompanying the learner in the process of learning (Walker, 2019). In addition to these theories comes James Paul Gee, who emphasizes the idea that all learning is language learning (Gee, 2003).

## 3. CASE STUDY

**Example of exercise – learning language through every day or occasional activities**

We propose a second language learning activity in which learners are supposed to construct linguistic knowledge while engaging in the production of collaborative dialogues.

This exercise was applied to a group of 10 foreign students learning Romanian in Preparatory Year with an A2 level in Romanian language, according to the Threshold level in Romanian. They are able to furnish simple information about themselves and their family or friends, and they have developed the ability to read and understand the message of a simple written text. Their language background is different as they come from different countries such as Iran, Egypt, Syria and Turkey. While applying this exercise, we have taken into consideration its utility and its social benefits for language learning. So, we have identified six everyday situations or social situations in which students might find themselves at some point during their stay in Romania.

| | Imagining and setting the communication situation | Implementation of the communication situation | Identifying language elements that need to be improved |
|---|---|---|---|
| At the supermarket / stores / market | – imagining the interaction/ dialogue between interlocutors of each communication situation<br><br>– writing the dialogue (expressing a request, a greeting, an apology) | – apply the dialogue in each communication situation<br><br>– take into account the unpredictability of the dialogue given the fact that the interlocutor is unknown | – based on the experience of the practised dialogue and the teacher's remarks, the student becomes aware of his own language learning needs, and he can identify the elements that need improvement in terms of vocabulary, grammar, written and oral expression |
| At the bank | | | |
| At the hospital | | | |
| In a bus station | | | |
| At a coffee shop | | | |
| At the faculty secretariat | | | |

# 4. CONCLUSIONS

This exercise proved to be an effective self-directed exercise of practising Romanian language in different communication situations. One of the objectives of the exercise was to develop students' interactional competence. We also envisaged observing the students' responses in repeated sequences. Students were able to express their needs depending on the situation encountered. Even if the exercise was prepared in advance, the students also faced the unpredictability of the dialogue with the interlocutor in question. When they did not find the words to answer the interlocutor's questions, they expressed themselves through mimicry. In these situations, the acquired vocabulary proved to be in the first place among the needs of the students. As the exercise was repeated for two weeks, the ease of expression and enrichment of the students' speech were noticeable. This is just an example of language learning and vocabulary enrichment in social contexts through the direct use of language in different and common contexts. The general and predictable conclusion is that learning a foreign language is directly proportional to improving the quality of life, especially when the learner moves to another country, in an environment where the learned language is spoken and used, as it is in the case of the students participating in the exercise. This study aims to be continued and extended to other target audiences, also considering the learning of other foreign languages.

# REFERENCES


Bates, E., & MacWhinney, B. (1987). Competition, variation, and language learning. In B. MacWhinney (Ed.), Mechanisms of language aquisition (pp. 157-193). Lawrence Erlbaum Associates, Inc.

Hatch, E. (1992). *Discourse and Language Education*. Cambridge University Press

Ellis, R. (2010). *Second language acquisition, teacher education and language pedagogy. Language Teaching*, 43(2). URL: doi:10.1017/S0261444809990139

Freyberg, Marie Louis. (2006). *Second Language Learning Theories–The Behaviouristic Approach as the Initial Theory towards Modern Researches*. GRIN Verlag

Freeman, D., Freeman, Y. (1994). *Between worlds: Access to second language acquisition*. Portsmouth, NH: Heinemann

Gee, J.P. (2003) *What Video Games have to Teach Us about Learning and Literacy*. New York: Palgrave/Macmillan.

Joan, K., Lauer, N. (2003) *LA 3.1 Language as a Social Practice*. PASTEP: Papua New Guinea-Australia Development Cooperation Program

Mitchell, R., Myles, F., & Marsden, E. (2019). *Second Language Learning Theories: Fourth Edition* (4th ed.). Routledge. https://doi.org/10.4324/9781315617046

Norbahira Mohamad Nor, Radzuwan Ab Rashid. (2018). *A review of theoretical perspectives on language learning and acquisition*. Kasetsart Journal of Social Sciences, Volume 39, Issue1

Nick, C. Ellis. (2006). *Cognitive Perspectives on SLA*. Themes in SLA Research edited by Kathleen Bardovi-Harlig, Zoltán Dörnyei, pp. 100-121

Pallotti, Gabriele, and Johannes Wagner. (2011) *L2 learning as social practice: Conversation-analytic perspectives*. Natl Foreign Lg Resource Ctr

Walker, R.A. (2010). *Sociocultural Issues in Motivation*, Editor(s): Penelope Peterson, Eva Baker, Barry McGaw, International Encyclopedia of Education (Third Edition), Elsevier
URL: https://doi.org/10.1016/B978-0-08-044894-7.00629-1.
Zavala, V. (2018) *Language as social practice: deconstructing boundaries in intercultural bilingual education.* Trabalhos em Linguística Aplicada n(57.3): 1313-1338
URL: https://doi.org/10.1590/010318138653255423542

# Comparative Analysis and the Evolution of Communication Services

**ENACHE Ciprian-Mugurel,** Cross-Border Faculty,
"Dunărea de Jos" University of Galati, mugurel.enache@ugal.ro

Emerging in the 1970s as a communication alternative for far too slow conventional mail, Internet services were limited to sending messages to a small community and usually concentrated on different university campuses. The speed with which the messages were sent from one side to the other created a mirage compared to the waiting days of a physically sent letter. However, the disadvantages of the new mode of communication were obvious, the costs of both equipment and communications through "switched" telephone lines being quite high. In fact, the computer systems were not available to everyone, because the technology used then and the first microprocessors (from the Z80 family) had prohibitive costs. Looking back at the performance of the technology of that time compared to that of the technology of today, we can see the huge technological leap that mankind has taken in the last 50 years.

At the same time, with the development of technology, the need for communication has also grown exponentially, for many of us it is inconceivable that today we should not start the day by reading our e-mails, scrolling news from online newspapers or viewing various videos posted on social networks. And yet, let's do a little recapitulation of the main landmarks in the history of communications and, in particular, that of the Internet, at the international level:

– In 1958, the American company Bell developed the first modem capable of transferring digital information via a telephone line using FSK (Frequency Shift Keying) and AFSK (Audio Frequency Shif Keying) modulations; a FSK modulation but which uses frequencies from the audio spectrum, which falls within the range of frequencies transmitted via normal telephone lines (350Hz-3.5kHz) and, later, PSK (Phase Shift Keying), modulations that were resistant to external disturbances.

– In 1962, the foundations of the theoretical concepts about the interconnection of some computing systems are laid through ARPA (Advanced Research Projects Agency - an institution subsidiary to the United States Department of Defense)

– After several computer connection tests at four US colleges, the first network (ARPANET) appeared in 1971, with 23 computers, and allowed Ray Tomlinson to test the world's first e-mail. At that time, the famous "@" symbol separated the user's name from the name of the computer system from which the e-mail was accessed. Later, it separates the user's name from the domain name to which the e-mail server belongs.

– A year later, in 1972, the first organization to manage this type of network, which had already been called "internet", appeared. This organization was called the InterNetworking Working Group, and the beneficiaries were 37 nodes.

– Over the ocean, in 1973, England and Norway joined
  this network with a computer.
– In 1979, they appeared as facilities of this network
  NewsGroups, the predecessor of today's forums, being an application dedicated to students on American
  campuses.
– In 1982, the word "internet" is associated for the first
  time with the ARPANET network of interconnected
  computer systems, and the first standardisation of the
  communication protocols used, through TCP / IP, appears.
– In 1983, name aliases were created for existing servers,
  making it easier to remember their addresses.
-As a numerical evolution, we can note that in 1984 there
  were 1,000 interconnected computer systems, in 1987
  – 10,000, in 1989 – 100,000 and in 1992 – 1,000,000.
– The disappearance of ARPANET in 1990 and the official launch of the "www" (World Wide Web) in 1991
  as well as the appearance of specialized browsers and
  the widespread use of operating systems with graph-
  ical interfaces from Microsoft (Windows) made the
  number of computer systems with internet access to
  be 10,000,000 in 1996 and over 500,000,000 in 2001.
  Nowadays, it's an estimated number of tens of billions
  for devices that can access the internet.

At the same time, the quality of communications between computing systems, a quality expressed here by
parameters such as ease of access, stability over time, mobility and data transfer speed, has increased significantly

with the development and improvement of new technologies such as radio modems, fibre optics for fixed internet and new protocols, expanding coverage and services for mobile technologies.

In fact, the development of technologies and the reduction of their size have allowed the emergence of mobility in the use of the Internet and smart phone devices, today called, generically, "smartphones". They appeared on the market in the late 1990s as a combination of PDA (Personal Digital Assistant) telephone equipment, and the first equipment in this regard is considered to be the one produced by IBM Simon and presented at the COMDEX International Fair in Las Vegas. in 1992. This equipment had a touch screen and was able to send and receive faxes and e-mails.

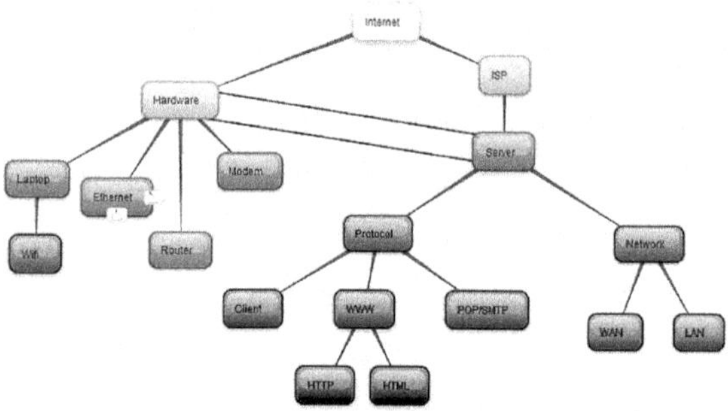


Fig. 1 The concept of the internet and the range of offered services
Source: https://sites.google.com/site/mobilecspdzenanm/reflections/internet-concept-map

Later, Nokia's Communicator series, as well as Black-Berry products, whetted the appetite of business people and the general public for mobile smart products. Nowadays, in the countries of our region (Ro-Md-Ua) there it's a large range of smartphones from over 65 manufacturers.

In parallel with the development of end-user technology, telephone companies around the world have invested in the assimilation of the latest communication protocols, which ensure faster and faster speeds. Thus, we can make a comparison between the GPRS protocol (General Packet Radio Services), from the mid-90s, which ensures a speed (average, approximate) of 20kb/s, where the BTS (Base Transceiver Station) – "antennas" of operators also allowed switching to packet data and today's 5G protocol that allows, in optimal conditions, the establishment of transfer speeds of over 600-700Mb/s and with a fairly high coverage. Depending on the type of coverage used, the data transfer speed via the 5G protocol can reach speeds of the order of Gb/s.

But, perhaps one of the most important facilities offered by modern communication technologies, particularly mobile ones, is the opening to IoT (Internet of Things). These equipments have an increasing involvement in our lives by increasing their quality, by taking on tasks from users and automating the various activities in the home or office. These IoT devices are derived from computing systems by reducing and dedicating some functionalities which lead to their miniaturization. Many of these require secure and permanent communication with the user or dedicated servers to operate at full capacity. These include, but are not limited to, smart solar panel or hot water heating systems, smart air conditioners, alarm systems, smart lighting systems, cleaning systems, and many other devices and modern appliances with these features. Also, many of these devices can be found in tourism or transport and most often, their presence is associated with the existence of a wide range of sensors.

Fig. 2 Example of using the IoT: A smart device that ultrasound monitors the amount of waste in a dumpster and warns via the internet when it needs to be emptied. My own project.

Information for users, one of the main purposes for which the Internet has emerged and developed, favouring websites for the speed with which information can reach users and offering the possibility to interact with them and many media outlets are abandoning traditional media for their information (especially print newspapers) in favour of websites for these thinks.

It has been found that many internet users prefer to follow sites and news with the possibility of posting their comments to the detriment of those who do not have this feature. In addition, thanks to the speed and mobility of the Internet, the multimedia area was able to bring live video and audio broadcasts from the venue in real-time. In fact, most radio and television stations in the world have live broadcasts and multimedia archives of their news on their websites as well as on social platforms, which allows them to follow the audience much easier than by conventional methods.

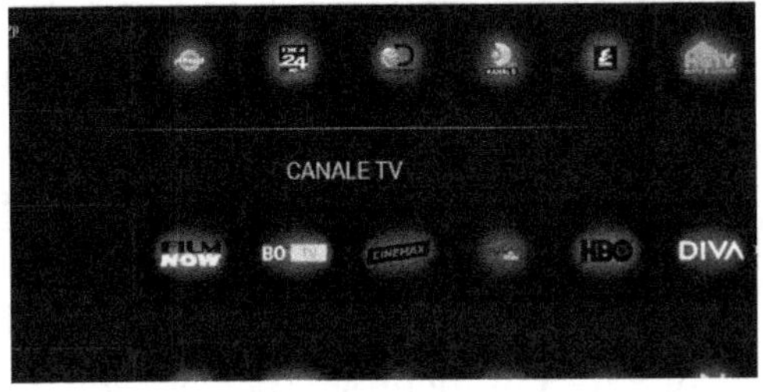


Fig. 3 Example of a dedicated platform for live TV viewing.
Screenshot from http://www.digionline.ro

Another important feature of the internet, highly appreciated by users, is entertainment. The very good transfer speeds it has gained, thanks to technology, the internet nowadays offers a diverse range of entertainment. Starting with the video streaming platforms that successfully replaced cinemas during the pandemic, there are many online gaming platforms, both in solidarity and for team games. Because current technology allows you to watch movies in UHD (4K or even 8K) technology, the internet bandwidth must ensure an optimal average transfer speed of 10Mb/s for full HD video resolutions (1920x1440pixels) and over 25Mb/s for UHD movies (for example, 4K has a frame size of 3840x2160 pixels for television).

When it comes to online gaming, the delay in sending packets of information between client and server is a very important factor, as is the loss of packets along the way. Delays are caused both by the time of processing and conversion of information into equipment but also by the "congestion" of the information transmission media at certain times. These delays in sending and receiving packets of data cause delays in the execution of actions in games (generically called "lag" by players), and ISPs that cannot provide such speed and security of packet transmission are avoided by them. Usually, these delays and packet loss occur in rural Internet providers and those that use a two-wire technology, such as DSL or ADSL, where the probability of external signal disturbances is very high.

In terms of entertainment, an increasing percentage is occupied, lately, by social networks. They have developed rapidly in the last 15-17 years and have become a way of life for most teenagers and beyond. If, in the early 2000s, the only popular social network was Hi5, nowadays, the battle is between Facebook, Twitter, Instagram and Tik-Tok. Of these, two belong to the same concern, Meta: Facebook and Instagram. Through these networks, users can communicate different information, both scriptural and multimedia, they can form different information or thematic groups. Also, knowing the magnitude of this phenomenon, many government organizations came to meet the users of social networks by bringing some of the official communications there and even started to take the opinions, criticisms, or suggestions of users there, in parallel with the official websites.

Many commercial companies have also used social media accounts to promote and sell various products, which is compounded by the isolation and lack of opportunities to visit physical stores during the pandemic. In fact, Facebook also has a sales area – Marketplace, which is very well targeted and promoted directly to the target audience. In fact, the pandemic and the closure of physical stores have made the use of online stores a daily occurrence for most of us. On the other hand, for retailers, the quality of life has increased with the reduction of operating costs, with an online store having much lower operating costs compared to physical stores.

Another extremely used feature of social networks is the messaging part, a part that ensures a much faster speed of messages to the target audience, given that it is statistically proven that accessing messages through this method is much easier and the inclusion of multimedia elements is also a favourable element. As for the speed of information transmission, for example, the Telegram application transmits seismic warnings, knowing that the speed of propagation of S waves in the event of an earthquake is much slower than the transmission through communications networks of a message, which has an advantage in warning the inhabitants of a city further away from the epicentre of an earthquake.

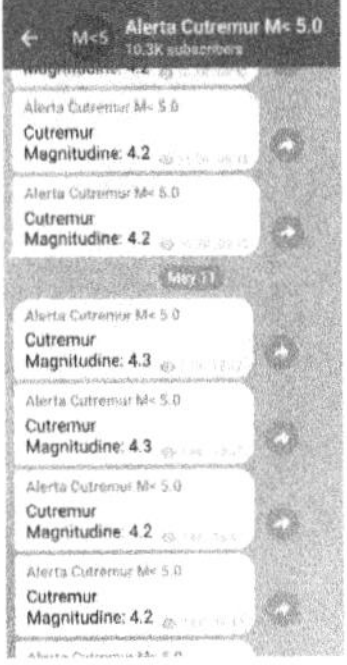

**Fig. 4** Use of messaging applications (Telegram) for transmitting seismic alarms.

Many of these applications are well known to users: Telegram, WhatsApp, Messenger by Facebook, Viber, etc. The miniaturization of telecommunications equipment (mobile terminals) and their endowment with quality multimedia elements (video cameras, displays) resulted in video calls between users gradually replacing conventional telephony and increased popularity of video calls, especially in situations where family members are at a distance. It played an important role here, in addition to the superior quality of calls and their lower and lower costs compared to traditional methods of communication.

## PARTICULAR CASE: RO-MD DURING THE LAST 15 YEARS.

Even though they are located in the same vicinity, in the same area of Europe, with a common border of over 680 km, the two countries have known different values for the development of communication networks and, implicitly, of the quality of life determined by their use.

## ROMANIA

In the middle of the first decade of the 2000s in Romania, the spread of the Internet was on the rise. The use of switched telephone lines (either voice or data) was declining due to very high costs but also due to the low access speeds that a conventional modem could offer, up to 90kb/s in terms of a very good line quality telephone. In addition, finding a free line at peak hours was also unknown. For example, the internet provider X-Net (part of

Connex, at that time) provided 100 lines in the "hunting" system for "dial-up" in the city of Galați, and the costs were shared both with the operator of Connex (as part of the subscription, and it was about 5USD) and with the operator who provided the telephone line, Romtelecom, which charged a local call fee, which, due to the low transfer speeds was in the order of hours, most of the time.

Many of the administrative institutions were in the process of migrating from the leased lines, which provided, with adequate modems, speeds of up to 256-384kb/s to fibre optics that could provide much higher speeds (of the order of tens of Mb/s) and whose price was about 0.33 USD/m and the related communication equipment (bi-directional fibre optic-UTP converters), about 250 USD.

An alternative to fibre optics had also become transmission via cable television networks, via cable modems with DocSys technology, modems that could provide a permanent connection, with decent speeds of over 128kb/s but still at prohibitive prices for people physical. Therefore, the so-called "neighbourhood networks" were very successful, in which an "entrepreneur" contracted a subscription with a higher speed and shared the costs with 20 ... 50 other users in the area (sometimes even larger, by bringing together several smaller networks), to which he had previously built a network in which, for entertainment, they could play interactively or even share files with each other. In fact, we cannot fail to mention here the scale of peer-to-peer applications or other file-sharing methods. Over time, this type of internet provision has disappeared, being either embedded in the networks of large internet providers or simply abolished as the prices of a direct subscription with a large provider had become accessible to many people. In the years 2008-09, an internet subscription with a maximum speed of 100Mb/s was approximately 15Euro. In fact, at a national level, the fixed communications market crystallized among the major operators, which were UPC, RCS-RDS, Romtelecom, and SNR.

The development of technology has led to cheaper services while increasing their quality and transfer speed. For example, nowadays, a fixed internet subscription, fibre optic connection, with a transfer speed of max. 1Gb/s is about 7-8 Euro, which places Romania in the top of countries with a very good access speed and quite low prices. The market for fixed internet operators remained the same during this period, although even larger groups were formed through acquisition or rebranding: RCS-RDS, Vodafone, Orange, Telekom, and SNR.

With regard to mobile communications, major changes have taken place during this period in terms of service quality. If, at the beginning of the reference period, the data coverage was quite low (almost non-existent outside the localities), the access speeds were up to 50kb/s (the technology used was GPRS), the prices were prohibitive for individuals. The market was divided at that time between Orange, Connex, Cosmorom and Zapp. Neither the communication equipment - the terminals, were not very efficient on the multimedia side and were used more as modems to ensure communication, and that's it.

The advent of smartphones and the reduction in their price have contributed to their widespread use and increased popularity among users. This has forced the data coverage of telephone operators to increase in quantity and quality. 3G, 4G and 5G technologies have been implemented one by one, which have allowed increasing access speeds to the Internet while reducing the price/quality ratio.

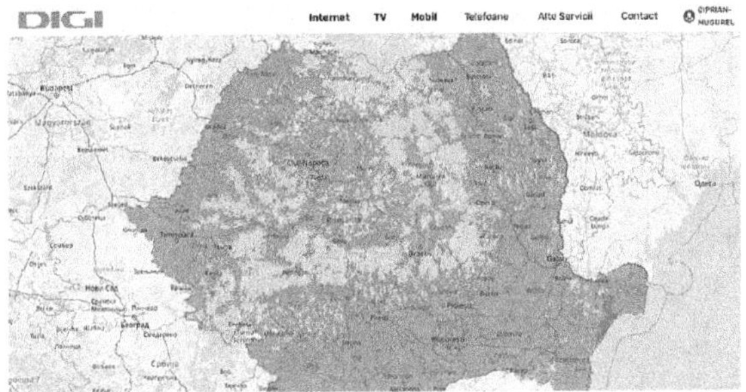

**Fig. 5** Example of mobile data coverage in 4G technology for the DigiMobil operator in 2022. Screenshot from https://www.digi.ro/asistenta/acoperire-servicii-portabilitate/acoperire-servicii

The emergence of another operator in the area of mobile communications (Digi Mobil, belonging to RCS-RDS) based on the fixed infrastructure of the main shareholder has made things accelerate on the coverage side since 2015. This has been fully contributed and the new legislative regulations pursued and applied by the National Authority in Communications – ANCOM, which verifies the assurance, from a technical point of view, of the quality of the services offered. In fact, all mobile telecommunications operators state that they have a population coverage of data (criterion imposed by ANCOM) of over 98%. The verification of the coverage at a national level for each operator can be done even on the portal provided by ANCOM, www.aisemnal.ro.

Therefore, the existence of data mobility in optimal quality parameters has contributed a lot in terms of increasing the quality of life, along with what the fixed internet offers. In 2022, according to the website www.worldpopulationreview.com, Romania is on the 4th place in the world, with an average download speed, for the fixed internet (232.17Mb / s) after Monaco, Singapore, and Hong Kong, and on the 46th place in the world ranking of download speeds for mobile telephony, with only 57Mb/s.

## MOLDAVIA

Although due to the existing legislative limitations, the development of the Internet in the Republic of Moldova has had a more difficult start, the efforts of the competent authorities and companies have made the country in a leading position in terms of high-speed internet coverage but also cheap in price.

1991, the year in which the Republic of Moldova gained its independence, was also the year in which it requested the country suffix ".su" for the specific domains of Internet pages. Three years later, in 1994, he applied for registration of the ".md" domain. The first officially recognized internet provider in the country was Relsoft, from 1992 and later; also three years later, others appeared (CRI, Relsoft Communications), able to provide dial-up internet. Prices were prohibitive for individuals at the time.

Since 1996, through the Soros Foundation and the aid received from Romania, the universities of the Republic of Moldova are connected to satellite Internet services, and the first direct connection to Bucharest through fibre optics is established. Two years later, the network is improved, and the distribution of fixed internet communications to schools and high schools begins through GlobNet, part of the DNT association. At the same time, Moldtelecom is starting to provide internet services, and Arax is also appearing on the market. In Transnistria, in 2000, Interdnestrcom appeared as a service provider, a company that remains in a dominant position even today.

The first internet services through ADSL technology were provided by Globnet in 2002 and in 2004 by Moldtelecom. The internet user market had already reached 100,000 users. At the same time, the provision of cable TV via SunCommunication, under the name SunInternet, is being inaugurated. StarNet also appeared on the market in 2003, and by 2005 the Internet user market had already reached 500,000 users. StarNet is also the one that initiated the development of its fibre optic networks, thus paving the way for high-speed internet.

The years 2007-2008 are the period when the main fixed internet providers in the Republic of Moldova started to offer fibre optic services to the users while in Transnistria, Interdnestrcom started to offer ADSL services.

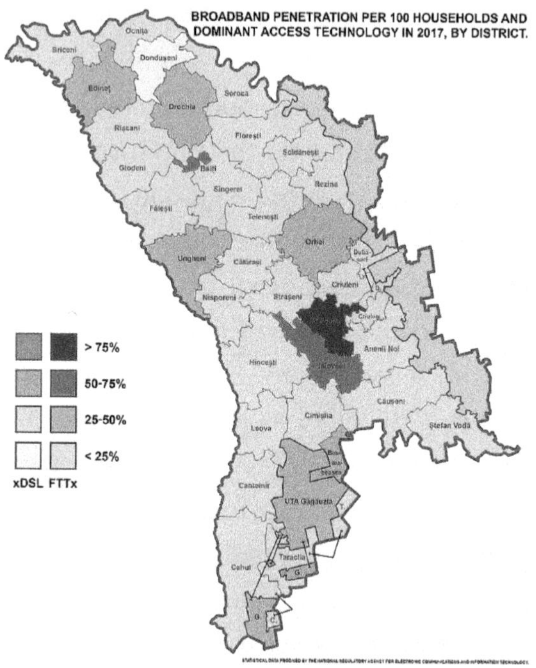



Fig. 6 District coverage of high-speed internet in 2017 for
the Republic of Moldova.
Source: https://en.wikipedia.org/wiki/File:Broadband_Penetration_by_
District_Moldova.jpg

In 2010, after the market of internet users in the Republic of Moldova had exceeded one million users, the first offers appeared (initially, from StarNet, then NordLinks, Arax and MoldTelecom) with unlimited traffic and download/upload speeds of 100/100Mb/s. Shyly, the high-speed internet has paved the way; the first to overcome the 100Mb/s barriers was Moldtelecom in 2012, and then Moldtelecom was the first to offer 1Gb/s speeds in 2014.

In 2016, SunCommunication was bought entirely by Orange Moldova. Prices also dropped significantly in 2022, the monthly price of a high-speed internet subscription (1Gb/s) being about 250-270 Moldovan lei, the equivalent of 11-12 Euros.

Regarding the Internet through mobile communications, the main players on the Moldovan market, Moldcell and Orange, launched the first 3G internet subscriptions for the public in 2008. Two years later, the Internet subscriptions provided by the 4G technology were also available. The network related to Moldtelecom, Unite, also launched its own 3G network. The last launch of LTE technology was in 2015.

Apart from these types of communications, the Wi-Fi spots provided by Orange and StarNet to its subscribers are very popular in the Republic of Moldova. In fact, most Moldovan public institutions, as well as many private companies, provide their users with free Wi-Fi internet hotspots, including in many places or restaurants, which in Romania is on the verge of extinction or is encrypted. Even in many public parks, the authorities provide free Wi-Fi internet access. Their users are happy, even if the transfer speeds available through these networks are lower than the rest of the internet.

In 2022, according to www.worldpopulationreview. com, Moldova ranks 29th in the world in average download speed for fixed internet (154.56Mb/s) and 59th in the world ranking of download speeds for mobile telephony, with only 42.99Mb/s.

Given the relatively small population and small size compared to other countries, Moldova boasts a third place in the world in terms of population coverage (90%) with high-speed internet services, 1Gb/s and low subscription costs, which gives a dominant position in the possibility of internet access and, implicitly, a high quality of life, starting from the facilities offered by the internet.

# REFERENCES


https://www.bbc.com/news/business-15856116

https://web.archive.org/web/20190329134941/https://www.sri.com/newsroom/press-releases/computer-history-museum-sri-international-and-bbn-celebrate-40th-anniversary

https://web.archive.org/web/20170926042220/http://elk.informatik.hs-augsburg.de/tmp/cdrom-oss/CerfHowInternetCame2B.html

https://books.google.ro/books?id=cNFOD_g7xXIC&pg=PA55 Schneidawind, J: „Big Blue unveiling" (23 noiembrie 1992). USA Today, pag. 2B

https://prezi.com/7v2bseijxzqv/the-history-of-the-smartphone/

https://worldpopulationreview.com/country-rankings/internet-speeds-by-country

http://gigabitmonitor.com/-/tPopulation

https://en.wikipedia.org/wiki/History_of_the_Internet

https://ro.wikipedia.org/wiki/Istoria_Internetului

https://www.bbc.com/news/business-15856116

https://ro.wikipedia.org/wiki/Orange_Rom%C3%A2nia

https://ro.wikipedia.org/wiki/Orange_Moldova

https://wikicro.icu/wiki/internet_in_moldova

https://en.wikipedia.org/wiki/Internet_in_Moldova

https://www.ancom.ro
https://www.vodafone.ro
https://www.orange.ro
https://www.digi.ro
https://www.digionline.ro
https://www.telekom.ro
https://www.moldtelecom.md
https://www.orange.md

# Well-Being For Migrants: Linguistic and Cultural Aspects to Improve Emotional Intelligence

**Alina Ionela Preda,** Cross-Border Faculty, "Dunărea de Jos" University of Galati, alina.preda@ugal.ro

## ABSTRACT

Migration is a universal phenomenon, which existed with the subsistence of the human beings on earth. People migrate from one place to another for several reasons, but the goal or main reason behind changing residence would be to improve their living conditions or escape from debts and poverty. Hence, migration has a great impact on any geographical area, and it is known as one of the three basic components of population growth in any particular region. Migration involves certain phases to go through; hence, it is a process. Moreover, subsequently it has a negative impact on the mental well-being of such population. Due to globalisation, modernisation, improved technologies and developments in all sectors, migration and its impact on human well-being is a contemporary issue; hence, here is an attempt to understand migration and its impact on the mental health of migrants based on the studies conducted around.

**Keywords:** *language, migrants, social, integration, culture, emotional intelligence*

# IF SOMEONE ASKED, "WHAT IS WELL-BEING?" WHAT WOULD THE ANSWER BE?

Obviously, the answer varies from person to person, or better said, there will be quite a few answers that will be the same but that, in most cases, will have a different value and meaning; but all the answers will refer to what is good for a human being. The experience of health, happiness, and prosperity is referred to as well-being. It entails good mental health, a high level of life satisfaction, a sense of meaning or purpose, and the ability to cope with stress.

Because it involves so many positive aspects, such as feeling happy, healthy, socially connected, and purposeful, well-being is something that almost everyone aims for.

## WHY IS WELL-BEING BENEFICIAL TO MIGRANTS?

Well-being combines mental health and physical health, leading in more comprehensive illness prevention and health promotion techniques.

According to the conclusions of experimental studies, well-being is related to self-perceived health, longevity, healthy habits that should be practiced, illness, both mental and physical, connectivity with others, productivity and environmental factors, both physical and social. Well-being is linked to many health, career, familial, and economic advantages. Higher levels of happiness, for example, are linked to a lower risk of sickness, illness, and injury, as well as improved immune function, faster recovery, and longer life. Individuals who are happy are more productive at work and more willing to give back to their communities.

As for the situation of migrants, it has become increasingly recognized that development cannot be assessed strictly in terms of economic indicators such as economic growth. Concepts and measures of migrant well-being and happiness can provide useful markers of human development. Because migrants frequently leave their countries in quest of a better life, subjective well-being indicators can help determine if they achieve their goals.

A happiness study has attempted a research on a variety of topics, including the relationship between money and happiness. According to the findings, while people with more earnings are usually happier, once a certain threshold is crossed, it appears to make little difference in terms of continued happiness gains. According to another study, people who live in high-income countries are happier than those who live in low-income countries. This suggests that a certain amount of economic growth is important and can affect a population's happiness and well-being. Other factors, including robust health, thriving social networks, religious belief, and advanced age, have been proven to have a favourable impact on happiness levels. In lower-income countries, particularly in relation to immigration, happiness research has been negligible. According to available evidence, migrants are often less satisfied than comparable people in their destination country and happier than similar groups who did not migrate. Although it could be assumed that as migrants become more integrated into their host community, happiness levels rise over time, multiple studies in Europe have indicated that migrants are less happy than native populations even after years of migration. The circumstances and drivers of migration have a significant impact on the mental well-being of some particular groups of migrants. Those who migrate in extreme situations, such as refugees and stranded migrants fleeing conflict and humanitarian crises, or those caught up in human trafficking and smuggling networks, may experience a great deal of suffering and trauma along the way, which can reverberate throughout their lives once they arrive in their destination country.

Therefore, the well-being of migrants is a subject that must be treated seriously and meticulously, depending on many internal and external factors.

The global immigration pattern of the 21st century was born in both rural and urban areas. Countries inexperienced with immigration became destinations for immigrants. The world economy is certain to continue to ensure the arrival of those looking for economic and cultural opportunities in new locations. At the beginning of the 20th century, Parks pointed out that migration is more than just a 'mere movement'. He wasn't optimistic about the status of immigrants, he believed he lived in two worlds, but he didn't belong in either. Immigrants are new associations and a new Venture. An important aspect of the Commission's immigration policy is economic opportunities, requiring 20 million migrant workers between 2010 and 2030 to support the ageing of the population (Europe). Such a change is slower than it looks, but mobility is expected to continue to improve. It is important that the host country is ready to do business with the bank. The lack of plans following the recent expansion of Europe in 2004 and 2007 suggests an underestimation of the resources needed to meet the social needs of migrants. Host societies usually play a role by providing bilingual access to public services in non-governmental languages. However, the national language is important to the coordination process as it provides a means of bridging links with new communities. Receiving societies can contribute to this process by providing language learning and training in the language of the state. Indeed, language learning is seen as an important mechanism for ensuring positive integration between immigrants and host societies. Such a language barrier is permeable and, at the same time, facilitates belonging to ethnic minorities and mainstreams. Low proficiency levels in the state language disable migrants' access to social services in the new country. Even with the political will to recognize "linguistic rights," many new destinations may not have the institutional infrastructure and skills to meet the new demand for language education and services. From this perspective, different forms of language integration are possible, and there are many possibilities for adapting individual language repertoires to new language environments. They reflect the different goals and needs of migrants (or other groups). Affected people have to decide for themselves whether the adjustment is satisfactory.

You can distinguish between:

- Low-level integration into the language repertoire: The majority of language resources are inadequate to effectively address communication situations without much effort, so no language resources are available in individual repertoires. The involvement of a third party is essential to this type of communication, and its success depends heavily on the linguistic goodwill of other speakers. Immigrants do not participate in certain activities or even avoid them because they are linguistically too demanding. They can consider their repertoire ineffective, and it may cause frustration. This may be the reason for their exclusion by the native speakers of the language.

Integration of languages into the repertoire: Immigrants actively reorganize their repertoire and integrate the languages of the majority. This is done with the language you are already speaking. It's no longer hard to rely on, as speakers can now switch languages and use them naturally, depending on the social situation. In this case, the native language, which may have been the only identity language, can retain a common identity status with the majority language. In this sense, the fact that there are multiple identity languages in the repertoire is similar to dual citizenship. The language of origin of immigrants can gain the value they want to convey to it. But from an identity perspective, what is important now is the reorganized repertoire.

These forms of integrating a language into an immigrant repertoire are abstract but probably depend on whether the language in the repertoire has a high or low rating before arriving at the host society (e.g., low integration, functionality, actual integration): These forms of language integration and their variants represent the options available to adult immigrants.

- The decision not to change the repertoire, that is, to systematically learn the main languages of the host society. Immigrants bear the functional pressure of not being able to use them, especially if they spend most of their time in an environment where their native language is dominant.
- Wanting to change their repertoire but not being able to change it due to lack of time or self-confidence, which leads to psychological and social problems.
- As part of a single identity language strategy, that is, the origin of immigrants, the aim is to reorganize the language repertoire to achieve "language naturalization". This involves a gradual abandonment of the native language and its permanent disappearance so that it is not passed on from generation to generation according to the language of the host society.
- Aimed to relocate the functional repertoire but uses two common identity languages.

A project that is helping migrants integrate easier is the ALL IN project, an innovative Erasmus+ project focused on the effective linguistic and cultural integration of European refugees and migrants. Currently, there is still a considerable gap between the demands of political experts and the reality of integration. ALL IN aims to build a bridge to fill this gap by providing innovative solutions in key areas. At the heart of the ALL IN project is the commitment of both members of the host society and the efforts of migrants and refugees to bring long-term results and benefits to all, for a successful social inclusion. Therefore, it makes it possible to build strong relationships in a multicultural society where the second language and cultural education are central to the mission of the ALL IN project.

## THE LINGUISTIC ASPECT OF IMPROVING A MIGRANT'S EMOTIONAL AND PHYSICAL STATUS

Language is the best tool in communication, and it gives the individual a series of privileges to adapt to a new society. Not only is it considered a valued aptitude, but a crucial one as well. Language proficiency establishes the actual key drive of immigrant integration, giving him this sort of "guarantee" of acceptance and support. However, from the perspective of the receiving society, there may exist the instability that most migrants are unable to use the foreign language, and this matter can compromise their job choices and consanguinity with the community. Anyway, travellers are similarly as ready to impart as others, maybe in various dialects. Numerous travellers can utilize more than one language since they come from multilingual nations (like African, Asian, or Balkan nations) or because in their interaction of relocation they had contact with different dialects. Also, due to their encounters with multilingualism, a significant number of them are substantially more mindful of etymological issues, similarities or contrasts among dialects, and the unique existing correspondence settings.

On the other hand, their adaptation competence and their large amount of culture and intelligence cannot always assure their status in a new territory, where the understanding might be a little different and difficult. There are multiple scenarios and stories. So, for instance, in some (uncommon) situations where bilingual transients have been important for minorities, they need to abandon a specific language after leaving their nation of origin since it is associated with viciousness and mistreatments of abusing power. By and large, anyway, transients consider their first dialects to be a fundamental component of their character, a fundamental connection to their very own, strict and social beginning, to their folks and their relatives and as the main link to a fundamental piece of their lives they needed to abandon. Their dialects may address the main figure of stability in their otherwise unreliable lives. This problem might cause different reactions, which is why the authorities of the receiving country might want to understand in a better way, a lot more empathetically, the fact that for most people, the first language belongs to the kernel of their identity - this being the language in which they started to understand the world and to hear their thoughts as a person, and it is what made them part of a group, a family, an entire community, also giving them a social identity, and in which they started developing important values for their lives, namely their cultural, religious identity. The more individuals need to abandon, the more significant their first language is. It is generally expected to be the main stable component in their lives. This is one of the reasons why the right to use one's mother tongue is one of the fundamental human rights.

So, there is no need to bring up the migrants who do not know any other foreign language. That is why the frequently asked question "If they want to live here, why don't they learn English faster?" Well, for you, an English native speaker, it is hard to understand that it is not easy to just switch your mind like that.

Language learning is not at all a straightforward undertaking, and many people promptly fail to remember that it requires around twelve years to gain proficiency with your first language. The initial five or six years from birth are committed to getting oral familiarity; and afterwards, an additional six years or so are expected to figure out how to peruse and compose, to gain the scholarly and printed aspects of a language, and to broaden linguistic designs, extend jargon and refine resembling patterns.
• So, what is the solution, then?

Language programs designed to inspire grownup migrants' second language acquisition must therefore meet the language needs of migrants and take into account their mental and psycho-social situations. Studying a second language in a migration context differs considerably from any type of standard foreign language learning. Three points are highlighted right here to show what this means for educating and the designation of levels:

– Firstly, language acquisition for migrants takes place now not solely with the aid of teaching but also simultaneously outside the classroom, to an exceptional extent, according to family, milieu, and job situation. This is one motive why the language gaining knowledge of the needs of migrants fluctuates considerably among individuals. Depending on unique language contacts and requirements beyond the classroom some need to exercise speaking or listening, and some need to practice reading. Here the issue of dialects also has to be discussed – the linguistic contacts of many migrants are not with people who use the popular variation of a language but rather with dialect speakers. And it may be necessary for surviving, social contacts, and expert success that one is able at least to recognize the dialect(s) spoken beyond the classroom.

– Secondly, getting to know the language takes place under significantly more (social, economic, legal) pressure than in regular classrooms. Migrants are normally properly aware that they need to master the language of the receiving states to survive, stay, and be successful there. Therefore, they often have very concrete linguistic needs: if a member of a family is in the hospital or someone gets a job there, a unique communicative situation exists in contrast to cases included in the training of children, issues regarding the form of dwelling, etc. are important.

The factors listed above – age, prior education, socio-economic status, gender, race, religion, luck – are by and large outside the control of the individual. What second language learning research shows above all is that learning another language is not an easy feat. It requires a considerable investment of resources, and it makes a huge difference whether you are learning in a supportive community or one that rejects you. The outcome of second language learning efforts is not purely an act of willpower or the result of the learner's personal choices.

## THE PROCESS OF ADAPTING

Migration is the phenomenon by which an individual leaves his or her place of birth to remain, permanently or temporarily, in a new location. This phenomenon offers the possibility for individuals to evolve from a personal, environmental, and educational point of view, but it is not without obstacles. Cultural barriers are caused by the contrast that is created between different mentalities, given the social, economic, political, and religious differences between countries. These bottlenecks must be identified, realised, and removed to ensure an improvement in the condition of migrants in the host country.

The process of adapting migrants is difficult because there are blockages from both the host country and those leaving their homeland for a good education or a more favourable life, but the reasons for these obstacles are often similar.

In order to remove the barriers that prevent adaptation and harmonious coexistence, it is important to understand the reasons behind them, and for the explanation, we will use the SCARF model, which proposes the theory that 5 universal buttons press, voluntarily or involuntarily, influence people's behaviour and attitudes. These "buttons" are certainty, familiarity, autonomy, status, and fairness.

I illustrate, with a fictitious model, the following situation: Aman is a 20-year-old boy from Saudi Arabia who came to Romania to study general medicine. In the host country, Aman observes cultural differences that materialize through the customs, traditions, religion, and clothing style specific to Romania. Migrating to a foreign country negatively presses the familiarity button, as there are very pronounced differences between Saudi Arabia and Romania, and Aman, to lessen the negative effects he feels, tries to surround himself exclusively with people from his country, migrants in Romania as well, or avoid knowing the Romanian traditions. Aman also considers that the position of migrant makes him inferior in the eyes of his colleagues or teachers because the status of migrant instils in him the tendency to internalise, but also the feeling of not belonging to the social group.

On the other hand, we can also talk about the barriers that the citizens of the host country impose on the migrant. Man is a socio-cultural product, so he cannot remain indifferent to the changes that take place in his living environment. It is all the more important to understand that the needs for certainty and familiarity are jeopardized when influences from different cultures manifest themselves in the immediate living environment of the subject. These obstacles are caused by the same buttons that, when pressed negatively, influence Aman's behaviour. Thus, people tend to protect their national identity, so if foreign nationals come to their territory, the familiarity is endangered, there is a tendency to reject the foreign citizen and to preserve a group composed exclusively of Romanian citizens. In addition, Romanians may try to protect their status by completely rejecting any form of migrant culture because they believe they are threatened by them.

## CULTURAL ASPECTS OF INTEGRATION

Culture is the identity of a nation and provides the necessary background to understand the way its citizens live and interpret the world. Cultural differences also exist in different regions of the same country, so there will be cultural differences between different countries. However, there are ways to facilitate the adaptation and integration of migrants into society. To solve this problem of adaptation and harmonious coexistence, both migrants and the inhabitants of Romania must be aware that the differences between people make strong connections and enrich the horizon of culture and cognition. Returning to the example, in the case of Aman, one way in which these obstacles could be removed is to organize, within the faculty, activities that support and encourage cultural diversity in which both Romanian and foreign citizens participate and in which each nationality presents customs, traditions specific to its national culture, and to carry out the most interesting ones physically. Thus, students will have the chance to interact with their colleagues, but also with the cultural baggage that each one brings in their relationship. Another activity that could help to adapt migrants is a meeting at which each participating student expresses in a civilized and polite manner, in a psychologist-supervised setting, his or her feelings about the admission process, migrants in a group or in the process of adapting to a new country. When confronted with the feelings of their colleagues, they will be able to be aware of and empathize with each other's situation, understanding that the rejection they sometimes show towards each other is not necessarily caused by people themselves but by their feelings about the situation itself.

Cultural barriers can be removed if we realize that the many contrasts between cultures do not prevent a harmonious relationship but rather enrich and fruit it. The differences between people bring a note of added value to society because learning about traditions, customs, new religions intellectualises the members of the community and opens new visions of interpretation of the world.

## ROMANIAN POLICIES ON INTEGRATION. IS ROMANIA READY TO "ADOPT"?

In recent years, Romania has received more and more migrants. The facilities they have if they choose to move here are very attractive. Romanian policies offer them almost the same rights as Romanian citizens, except the political ones. Thus, the migrants who acquire international protection in Romania have access to the following rights: the right to work, the right to education, the right to housing, the right to social and medical assistance, and the right to participate in specific linguistic and cultural accommodation activities.

The process of integration is carried out according to the Integration Program offered by The General Inspectorate for Integration, in which migrants can benefit from:

1. Accommodation, on request, in IGI centres for the period in which they are enrolled in the program (up to 12 months). For this service, people have to pay the costs of utilities except for vulnerable persons.

2. In exceptional cases, the integration officers can consider extending the program by a further six months

3. Romanian language courses, organised with the support of school inspectorates

4. Cultural accommodation courses supported by IGI or partner NGOs

5. Material aid for three months in an amount equal to that of asylum seekers

6. Social counselling that includes ensuring access to the rights they have in Romania

7. Counselling and psychological support

8. Non-reimbursable material aid in the amount of 540 Ron/person

9. After completing the program, it is possible to request financial support for the payment of accommodation outside the centre

Despite these benefits of the program, migrants still face certain problems related to the new lifestyle they have to adopt if they want to have a normal life. One of the biggest struggles they may have is finding a job to support their families. In the last years, the demographic decline has dramatically affected Romania. According to statistics, Romania has a practical deficit in terms of workforce. Therefore, only 15% of migrants have found a job, and only 5% have managed to grow small businesses. Also, Romania offers very low wages in areas of the labour market where migrants without higher qualifications are usually engaged: basic services, agriculture, and textiles.

Regarding the migrants' access to education, things are so much better. The number of students who choose to study in Romania keeps growing annually. A big part of them is motivated to attend the courses of Romanian universities by scholarships granted to encourage migrants. So, even though a migrant's family can't handle the study costs, scholarships can be a crucial financial support.

The biggest question is: "Is Romania ready to adopt migrants? ". Actually, the answer is that Romania is not quite prepared for migrants' adoption in the long term because the current policies can't allow them to stay for very long periods without ensuring the necessary conditions for decent living after finishing the Integration Program. The solution for that situation is still to be found, as work is still underway to add new policies to make it so much easier for migrants to adapt to society. In the end, they may be the ones who will lead Romania to economic growth.

## CONCLUSION

Migration is a contemporary, complex phenomenon in which the main intention is betterment or escaping from the non-favourable factors. Due to the insecurity feelings and non-availability of their own community members, the distress would turn into mental health consequences or other forms of health complications. Making the services inclusive, culture-specific and culture-free, providing necessary training for the personnel, making use of culture brokers and trained interpreters should happen at all levels. Providing the information about migration, preparing the migrants, ensuring the necessary health and public services will help prevent expected psychological distress and promote mental health well-being among migrants.

# REFERENCES


Adami Hervé, 2012, « La formation linguistique des migrants adultes », Savoirs, 2, (n° 29), p. 9-44

Adami Hervé, 2007, « Le niveau de scolarisation des migrants : un facteur déterminant dans le processus d'intégration », in Archibald James and Chiss Jean-louis (/dir.), 2007, La langue et l'intégration des immigrants. Sociolinguistique, politiques linguistiques, didactique, Paris, L'Harmattan, pp. 71-84.

Alastair Ager, Alison Strang, Indicators of Integration, Queen Margaret University College, Edinburgh, 2004.

Alastair Ager, Alison Strang, The experience of integration: a qualitative study of refugee

integration in the local communities of Pollokshaws and Islington, Queen Margaret University College, Edinburgh, 2004.

Archibald James and Chiss Jean-louis (/dir.), 2007, La langue et l'intégration des immigrants. Sociolinguistique, politiques linguistiques, didactique, Paris, L'Harmattan.

Boswell Christina, Addressing the causes of migratory and refugee movements: the role of the European Union – December 2002.

Braunmüller Kurt and Ferraresi Gisella (eds), 2003, Aspects of Multilingualism in European Language History, Hamburg, HSM.

Compendium – Transnational actions for the exchange of information and good practice – Call for proposals – July 2002.

Conseil de l'Europe. 2005. Le Cadre européen commun de référence pour les langues, Paris: Didier

Cummins, J. (2001) Language, Power and Pedgogy: Bilingual Children in the Crossfire. Clevedon: Multilingual Matters.

Esser Hartmut, 2006, « Migration, language and integration » Arbeitsstelle Interkulturelle Konflikte und gesellschaftliche Integration (AKI) Wissenschaftszentrum Berlin für Sozialforschung (WZB) Programme on I

Juaristi Patxi, Timothy Reagan and Humphrey Tonkin, 2008, "Linguistic diversity in the European Union: An overview". In Respecting Linguistic Diversity in the European Union, Arzoz, Xabier (ed.), 47-72

Mahshie, Shawn Neal. 1995. Educating Deaf children bilingually: With insights and applications from Sweden and Denmark. Washington DC: Gallaudet University Press.

Portas Miguel, 2005, Report on integrating immigrants in Europe through schools and multilingual education (2267(INI)), Committee on Culture and Education

## WEBOGRAPHY

https://www.ncbi.nlm.nih.gov/pmc/articles/ PMC4121889/  https://www.washingtonpost.com/news/ worldviews/wp/2015/09/04/the-arab-worlds-wealthiest-nations-are-doing-next-to-nothing-for-syrias-refugees/

https://en.wikipedia.org/wiki/Immigration_to_Romania

https://www.cato.org/white-paper/12-new-immigration-ideas-21st-century

https://canadianimmigrant.ca/settlement/the-3-stages-of-re-settlement/

https://www.realinstitutoelcano.org/en/work-document/language-and-immigration-an-analysis-of-the-development-of-linguistic-requirements-in-immigration-policy-wp/